frank sidebottom
OUT OF HIS HEAD

THE AUTHORISED BIOGRAPHY OF CHRIS SIEVEY

MICK MIDDLES

EMPIRE PUBLICATIONS

First published in 2014

This book is copyright under the Berne Convention. All rights are reserved. Apart from any fair dealing for the purpose of private study, research, criticism or review, as permitted under the Copyright Act, 1956, no part of this publication may be reproduced, stored in a retrieval system, or transmitted, in any form or by any means, electronic, electrical, chemical, mechanical, optical, photocopying, recording or otherwise, without the prior permission of the copyright owner. Enquiries should be sent to the publishers at the undermentioned address:

EMPIRE PUBLICATIONS
1 Newton Street, Manchester M1 1HW
© Mick Middles 2014

ISBN: 9781909360242

Printed and bound by CPI Group (UK) Ltd, Croydon, CR0 4YY

CONTENTS

- FOREWORD 5
- OUT OF HIS HEAD 9
- INTRODUCTION 11
- THE LAST GIG 17
- GROWING UP 27
- GETTING NOTICED 37
- WHITE BICYCLES AND PAULA 52
- MANCHESTER 1978 61
- TRANSFORMER 74
- WHEN CHRIS MET TOSH 93
- PRESS? PASS. 103
- CHRIS SIEVEY 1980 110
- MEGASTORE MADNESS 130
- ENTER FRANK 153
- MANCHESTER DIVIDED 165
- A NIGHT TO REMEMBER 209
- FRANK IS DEAD 233
- ART AS TV 247
- FINAL REEL 263
- EPITAPH 280
- EPILOGUE 305
- INDEX 313

For Vicky

CAST (IN ORDER OF APPEARANCE)

Dennis and Lois	Joe Barratt	Steve Coogan
Mark Radcliffe	John Barratt	Sandy Gort
Paul Stevens	Rosemary Barratt	Chris Coupe
Paula Sievey	Bill Sykes	David Hepworth
Paul Molyneux	Brian Little	Stephen Doyle
Michelle Pouncey	Daniel Parrott	Jon Ronson
Paul Latham	Nick Fraser	Bob Dickinson
Dave Arnold	Ken Nolan	Peter Gilmore
Chris Ewen	David Nolan	David Dunne
Michelle Ewen	Steve Forster	Darren Poyzer
Gemma Woods	Steve Hopkins	Tony Michaelides
Tosh Ryan	Martin Ryan	Steve Sullivan
Mike Doherty	Daniel O'Sullivan	Paul Cookson
CP Lee	Stirling Sievey	Mark Alston
Martin Sievey	Mike Nicholls	Jeff Jolly
Dick Witts	Asher Sievey	Len Brown
Steve Forster	Harry Sievey	Alan Jackson
Barry Spencer	Chris Hewitt	Guy Lovelady
Rick Sarko	Lesley Lee	Neil Taylor
Patrick Gallagher	Tony Walsh	Sandra Taylor
Simon Heywood	Kevin Cummins	John Otway
Mark Revell	James Nice	Martin O'Neill
Arash Torabi	Paul Ripley	Heath Common
Johnny Clarke	Henry Normal	Jill Adam
Steve Toon	Phil Jones	Michael Gallagher

FOREWORD

CHRIS SIEVEY WAS A WONDERFUL MAN to know. Back before he created his indelible alter-ego Frank, he was making effortlessly great pop records with The Freshies. And he knew all about great pop music. A Beatles obsessive, in truth an obsessive in all ways, he and his brother Martin had once blagged their way into the Fab Four's Apple studios to record some demos.

Life, for Chris, was lived as an adventure. Undoubtedly this made him difficult to live with but his impulsiveness was part of what made him so special. He married Paula in his lunch hour from work. Their reception was a bag of chips in a shop doorway before they both went back to the office. This is revealing. Everyday living was as much a performance as anything he did on stage. The fun and games on gig days started the moment you were picked up from home.

A casual chat in the boozer about ways to alleviate road boredom led to the ideas of Travel Twister, which involved having coloured discs on your hands and feet and putting them anywhere and Travel Snooker. Everyone else would have forgotten all about those notions when they left the pub, but not Chris. Being picked up for the next show at my house in Cheadle Hulme I climbed into the mini-bus to find him in a waistcoat and bow-tie with the balls set up on a half-sized table placed over the backs of the seats.

'Alright Mark', he said through puffs of cigarette smoke, 'do you want to break or shall I?'

Inevitably there were flaws with this plan. Not only did the presence of the table make it more or less impossible for anyone to sit comfortably for the five hours it took to get to London, but the balls slewed over to one side every time we turned a corner. Chris had the answer to that. Velcro balls. Of course.

OUT OF HIS HEAD

I spent a lot of time with Chris. He and Mike Doherty came to my house one night to outline his idea for Radio Timperley which we went on to record at Piccadilly Radio. It remains utterly brilliant in its fully rounded construction. Frank's Timperley is as believably drawn as Ambridge, but with more laughs and for a fraction of the budget. He had created a whole world in his head. As Billy and Barry Belly we played stand-up comedy gigs with no material just for the visceral thrill of testing the patience of the audience. As his keyboard playing greengrocer Emerson Lake, Chris Lowe to his Neil Tennant, I sat behind the Casio crying with laughter as he went off piste again and again with scant regard to his own safety. And though he had no money, and everyone had come to see him not me, he always tried to split the fee equally. I wouldn't let him of course. I had a good job producing 'The Organist Entertains' at the BBC and wanted him to go home with some money to give Paula to pay the overdue gas bill.

Also, I think Chris's inventiveness and vision were unusually prescient. He was designing his own computer games when most other people thought they were going to be a flash in the pan. He was convinced that stop frame animation was going to have a big future when others had consigned it to the past. He knew comedy was going to be the new rock and roll before rock and roll had stopped being the new rock and roll. His big problem was that he wouldn't delegate and so took too much on himself. If an animation needed completing, he sat up all night and drew and coloured it all in himself. He knew what he wanted, and he knew only he could do it that way. His obsessive nature was never more self-evident. Well, except with his equally fervent devotion to... how shall I put it... imbibing.

I've thought a lot about Chris since he died and something occurred to me. Quite a few people, and we all know who we are, passed through Chris's orbit on their way to relative media success. And I think if you pinned them down, there wouldn't be one of them who would deny that Chris's unique world view had played a part in honing the distinctiveness of what they, we, all went on to do. He changed all of us forever. I know with absolute certainty that my approach across my entire career would have been very different if it hadn't been for Chris.

One night a few years back I was driving back from doing my

evening show on Radio 2 and passed a pub called The Salutation, behind the Royal Northern College of Music. In the window a scruffy poster proclaimed: 'Tonight - Frank Sidebottom. Free admission'. I parked my car and wandered in to an unruly gaggle of students young enough to be my children. An enquiry led me upstairs to a shabby bedroom where Chris, cheery but wearied, was sitting on a candlewick bedspread with Little Frank and his other props strewn around the room. I hadn't seen him for a while. We talked for a long time and laughed and shared memories of Travel Snooker, Billy and Barry and the radio goings-on down Timperley way. Then it was time for his second set and so I got myself a pint of Black Sheep and stood at the back of the rabble to watch Frank enthrall as he had always done.

"Guess who's been on Match of the Day?" he crowed.

And though the punters seemed so young, they evidently knew what was expected of them.

"You have, in your big shorts," they chorused.

I smiled, drained and raised my glass, though he couldn't see me from inside the head and under the modest stage lighting, said goodnight to him and headed home with a broad grin on my face. He still had it. He was one of the very few people I've ever known personally who I would call a genius. Really.

The next time I was that close to him again was when his coffin slipped behind the curtain at Altrincham crematorium.

This then is his story. And Chris, I just want to say thanks for everything you showed me and the period we spent together. It was the best of times.

You know it was, it really was.

Thank you.

Emerson Lake (always with one 'M')
at Mark Radcliffe's house.
September 2014

OUT OF HIS HEAD

A WORLD IN A SHED; a shed in Timperley, albeit a Timperley of the mind. It is a lost space, a sacred place. A space of memory; a comfort, warmth, a place to rest awhile.

Surely an escape, an existential dream, bordered by timbered walls adorned with posters of varying juvenilia.

This is Frank's world. A place of pre-sex glory. Of an innocence that lay before emotional entanglements; before the myriad complexities of adulthood; before betrayal, hurt, loss, death, fear... tax! Before the pangs of realism, depression. Before the horrors of history and war and poverty.

This haven of simplicity is a place where, if only fleetingly, we all desired. Other than a lambasting from the unseen force of motherhood, or the belligerence of Frank's cantankerous side-kick, Little Frank, everything remains within control. If wars rage, they remain within the childish surrounds of Thunderbirds or Space 1999. Such things are, in Frank's World, in Frank's word, 'fantastic'.

Frank gave this world back to us. He lived it, we tasted it. It was fun. It was ancient. It had roots. Some got it. Some didn't.

It was Frank's World.

INTRODUCTION

ALTHOUGH NO FAN OF AUTHORS who attempt to explain their books – I am hereby pressured into doing just that. For this is the strangest book I have ever written. Fittingly so, I believe, because its subject matter(s) is (are) the strangest subject matter(s) I have ever written about or, indeed, have ever read about. Or have ever seen. Or met. Or heard about.

For few similar stories crowd the area still inhabited by Chris Sievey and Frank Sidebottom. Distant comparisons contained within this book mention the likes of John Otway, George Formby, Charlie Chuck, Edward Barton and John Shuttleworth but, while obvious, they are lazy comparisons really and the differences become all the more obvious when one begins to scrutinise the man behind the public persona. The only person, I suggest, who hovers within genuine view is Chris's son, Harry, who flutters inspiringly at the end of this story. As I write, Harry has just performed in a one-man capacity at one of Manchester's most enterprising new venues – The Folk Cellar. I meet Harry in the text. He doesn't personally remind me of Chris Sievey at all. Although similar, I guess, in the physical sense, Harry's mannerisms did not send me hurling back through time to the days when I was, genuinely, I believe, a close friend of Chris through the late seventies and eighties. But the night before I met Harry, he had written and uploaded two songs, designed his own label to slap on promotional discs and apparently conversed with many who would hover about his presence on Facebook. How Chris, I suggested, would have relished the onset of the age of social media.

"Yes," agreed Harry, "but there are so many people doing it now. My dad might never have broken through… but he would have had a lot of fun, I am sure." It was difficult not to square the thoughts of

Harry's flamboyant application towards his own ambition with Chris' similar and much celebrated postal attack on record companies and fans alike, back in the days when he fronted one of the great lost bands of Manchester, The Freshies, at the close of the seventies.

This is a book about Chris Sievey and Frank Sidebottom. Two separate and much loved identities from within one frame; one brain.

It is a strange tale that becomes all the stranger when one extends the vision to include the aficionados of the latter persona. Frank's large and devoted unofficial fan club is a curious breed. To a man, or woman, they always, without exception, are lovely to meet and, believe me, I have met, and continue to meet, so many of them. I have been meeting them since Frank's emergence in the mid-1980s. I have met them at gigs, on trains, in taxis, in the workplace, in pubs, cafés, bars, cinemas, art centres and football matches. They have, it must be admitted, changed in shape (literally, as middle age has firmly set in) and personality. For a Frank Sidebottom fan in 1986 would mostly arrive in the form of a student lost in the dizzying inebriation of a Friday night. This student would cling ferociously to the Frank joke. Grasp it as his own (or 'her' own, although males have always swamped the number of females within this fluctuating membership). Of course, there are obvious reasons for this. The student would grow old and, generally speaking, become a quieter and less obviously inebriated species. Mostly. However, the obsession that began in those darkened cellars of studenthood had, to a man, developed into an obsession of such intensity that, again, it is difficult to offer comparables. And I speak as one who has suffered the slings and arrows of intense fandom having once penned a book on The Fall's Mark E. Smith, himself a distant Sidebottom admirer. Fall fans are notoriously precious towards *their* band, even if they know little of the man himself. Anyway, I survived intact. I am not so sure I will emerge so cleanly this time around... for the almost religious like devotion to Frank is, at times, beyond belief.

This is a book that will, I hope, provide them with a rather different insight into Frank and, indeed, Chris. What it will not do is provided a solidly linear, blow-by-blow biography which believes, as they say, that the devil lies in the details. While I have no problems at all with the kind of person who designs the inside of his front-room to resemble Frank

MICK MIDDLES

Sidebottom's infamous Timperley shed, I am not interested in adding further train-spotter details. There is really no point, anyway, as such an approach already governs Steve Sullivan's exceptional documentary 'Being Chris Sievey'. Indeed, the making of that film surfaces regularly in this text as much of the filming, some of which I was involved in, took a place in parallel to my research.

As such, I became far more interested in the filming and, indeed, showing a snippet of the people behind the film and their obsessions, than merely providing a text heavy companion. That said, the idea is that people who ingest Steve's fine film may be surprised and delighted to discover a different kind of illumination.

I make no excuses for the personal nature of the text at all. It is not a book about myself but it is a book that builds from the base of an unusual friendship. It has to be that way as I simply cannot think of any other way of doing it. Further thoughts on this matter can be found on the encounter between myself and Chris Sievey that took place in the café of Altrincham Sainsbury's in March 1996. There are many similar encounters herein.

The book is structured strangely, I admit. It is, like its subjects, a little bit mad. A little non-linear. To write about Chris and Frank in any length is to meet an extraordinary array of highly talented and utterly fascinating individuals. Indeed, this aspect took me completely by surprise and I realise that Chris and Frank existed as magnets to those of an intelligently deranged nature. Some of them have attained considerable fame and status, although that seems fairly irrelevant. They all fascinate me which is why I have included italicised descriptions of the lead up to their interviews in the text. (Well, it was fun). We have even held 'Freshies' evenings at our old house in Ashton-on-Mersey. The memory, for instance, of ex-Freshies musicians Barry Spencer and Rick Sarko engaging in northern soul dancing while simultaneously chatting up pretend women on our rear lawn will remain with me forever.

While admitting a personal aspect here, and after a multitude of interviews, I have still allowed room for the people close to Chris Sievey, family, friends, band members and managers, to tell the tale in their own voice. Indeed, many quotes lie untouched. There is one main reason for this and this is the darkness that lies under the surface. It is, after all, the story of a man the local papers love to call the 'Timperley funny man' and, while I loathe that insulting description, it remains true that most 'funny men' hide a dark flipside. Chris Sievey, if not Frank Sidebottom - the two continually blur – was unquestionably something of a hedonist. The Chris I knew so well was a lovely and inspiring person – and in the years since his untimely demise in 2010, it has become abundantly clear that a huge amount of love and affection continues to bubble for both Chris and Frank. If anything, this has intensified during this period. A situation no doubt fuelled by the two films and the eventual erection of Frank's statue in Timperley in October 2013. That event at least seemed to provide a convenient full-stop and I initially thought that the tale that extraordinary day would be the end of it. Not quite.

However, the hedonistic undertone cannot be denied. It arrives here from the mouths of others simply because, while I have enjoyed a fair number of pints with Mr Sievey since our initial meeting in 1978, I had no idea of the full extent of his imbibing and indulgence. This book is not really about that side, but obviously it must be acknowledged. I am reminded of the great line that sparkles from the beginning of Michael Winterbottom's '24 Hour Party People', "This is not a film about sex and drugs and rock'n'roll… although those things are all in it."

One thing I attempt to make clear, however, is that a heavy cloud of unhappiness existed on the flipside of what is otherwise a delightful and inspiring story.

Freshies guitarist Barry Spencer tells the tale of his fortieth birthday bash at a pub in Sale was sullied slightly by the unsettling and untypical sullen nature of a dour-faced Sievey. "I was annoyed partly because it was my party but also because I knew that Chris simply wasn't like that," said. Barry.

The most obvious reason for all this, one might be forgiven for concluding, was the lack of mainstream success that Frank enjoyed in comparison to so many of his peers. Many stories will back this theory but I feel it is rather more complex that that.

That is another intriguing aspect of this book; how it fell together. Although, for many years, I had wanted to write a book about Chris, I simply couldn't see any way it could be published. No London based publisher could surely understand the weight of a subject that existed so intensely in the north of England. Although I had been writing about Chris for thirty-five years, I simply put the idea to one side and concentrated on more obviously viable projects.

Then the situation changed... and how. Steve Sullivan's aforementioned documentary was bizarrely accompanied by the emergence of the Jon Ronson penned film, 'Frank', loosely based on Sidebottom and starring Michael Fassbender. (...and, indeed, an accompanying explanatory book), this extraordinary news certainly provided a new if sadly posthumous spotlight on the subject. The unlikely activity was accompanied by the ongoing cause to build and erect a statue of Sidebottom to be unveiled in his beloved Timperley, initially in April 2013. The unfolding behind-the-scenes saga extended the build up of this unique event – which flickered continuously in the local media throughout the summer of 2013, before an eventual unveiling in October.

All of which made the prospect of a book on this subject considerably more appealing to vulturous London publishers. As such I am delighted to see it emerge under the guidance of Manchester's perceptive Empire Publications, who warmed to the idea in an unprecedented flash of enthusiasm. I have seen their sterling work on the Manchester guide books of Phil Gatenby, a plethora of football tomes which I had feverously devoured plus Bill Sykes' superb and highly unlikely study of Manchester (Liverpool and Oxford) music legend, Roger Eagle. Eagle himself was a Frank devotee, albeit in a somewhat guarded manner. For Frank albums didn't sit too easily within Eagle's vast collection of blues and beyond. Nevertheless, Roger Eagle loved Frank and promoted him on many occasions and in many venues. Most famously perhaps, he loved attaching Frank to an eclectic bill at Manchester's evocative International Club, often adding a bombastic sting to the foot of the bill.

Those gigs, the unlikely and uncomfortable ones, were always Chris's favourites. Frank as catalyst of anarchy and disbelief, pushing the boundaries, warping the reality.

MICK MIDDLES

THE LAST GIG

Warrington Parr Hall, June 2010

NATURALLY, THERE WAS THE SHED. It was placed on the right, to the rear. It seemed to hold a commanding omnipresence. Scattered around the stage were sundry items of post-gig debris. A keyboard on spindly legs, an abandoned cardboard body of Little Frank, a football, discarded sheets of paper, items of amplification.

I felt slightly awkward, standing on that darkened stage. I turned to see an audience politely filing out of the small, stark, contemporary arena. Faces gliding past through the gloom. Half smiling, though lost in strange reverie. There prevailed an eerie silence one would not normally associate with the aftermath of a Frank Sidebottom performance.

Standing there, my mind flashed back to the same scene in the same venue – Warrington's Pyramid Arts Centre - three years earlier, after witnessing Frank Sidebottom at his most hilariously bombastic. Indeed, back then I had found myself lost to the pain of frenetic runaway laughter. Not since the first showing of Monty Python's 'Life of Brian' back in 1982 had I experienced such stomach tightening frenzy.

Michelle Pouncey, Chris Sievey's partner and driver on that first gig, noted: "I remember the Parr Hall gig very well. Chris was at the very top of his game. He had stopped drinking and poured all his energy into Frank. It was a happy time and that reflected in his performance."

But not on *this* occasion. Something had changed. The gig had had its moments... a rather lovely rendition of The Ting Ting's 'That's Not My Name' had seen Frank, at once, unwittingly and mercilessly parodying the duo's finest moment. Likewise, his medley of Manchester hits – "Tony Wilson wrote *all* the songs for Manchester bands" – had seen Frank lumbering with disarming charm through the familiar angles of Mancunian pop anthems.

Nevertheless, it wasn't quite the same. Everything within and around the world of Frank Sidebottom and his illustrious creator, Chris Sievey, had changed... and famously so. Two months had passed since Frank's iconic image had graced the front page of the *Manchester Evening News*. Alas, this was no PR coup, no latent celebration of the artist's unique talent. It carried the numbing truth that Sievey − or, indeed, 'Frank' − had been diagnosed with throat cancer. While the article carried little in the way of illuminating further information, the fact seemed immediately shocking. Not Chris, surely? Not Frank!

"Frank has left the building," a character joked, after noticing my unease. Neither he, nor I, could possibly grasp the unintended poignancy of that statement. Not even amid the strangeness that prevailed as the gig settled into memory.

We weren't there to see Frank, anyway. I waited patiently to be guided backstage to meet his creator, Chris Sievey, who I had known since 1978 and with whom I had enjoyed my share of adventures. Again, my mind flashed back to that gig, three years ago, trundling to the same backstage area, to be greeted by Sievey who remained buoyant despite an onstage accident when Frank, in a fit of jubilant pique, had smashed a microphone into his gaping mouth, thereby dislodging one of Chris' teeth.

"Bloody Frank," said Chris. "He has done that before, he pisses me off, sometimes."

But it was Chris, not Frank, who came to the fore, that night, swapping man-hugs and amiably recognising my colleague, Chris Ewen, who had accompanied Frank on a daytime trip to Alderley Edge − of which more later − for a glossy magazine article. Back then, Chris had been as warm and eloquent as ever, his showbiz affectations all stripping away the moment he took the Frank head and nose peg off. Always a welcome moment, that. Back to Chris... Frank has left the building.

In 2010, things seemed different. The darkened backstage seemed oddly foreboding. We had been warned.

"Chris is feeling a bit fragile - be careful," came the voice of tour manager, Dave Arnold.

MICK MIDDLES

"You just pushed past me, told me to fuck off," Arnold will later tell me in this book.

I don't recall such rudeness. I guess I ushered passed with a blunt air. I knew Chris wouldn't mind. Dave did seem slightly abashed. His defensive stance completely understandable but nobody else, I noted, had hung around. They had swiftly filtered to the cellar bar, or out to the car park. A deadening calm prevailed.

I couldn't see him at first. Had to squint. I shuffled up the stairs, into the murk. Then, to the right, a silhouette lurked by the open window, smoking a cigarette – illicit, of course, in 2010 – gazing out into the Warrington night, soaking in the myriad sounds: sirens, screams, shouts, coughs, grunts, streams of expletives – before turning slowly to greet me.

"I know I am a bit thin… it's not the illness, really. I can't eat… not been able to eat properly for ages. It's not the illness… it's not…"

There was a clear paradox here. Chris seemed aloof from the vibrant bubble of precocity that he had always been; that lovely tumble of ideas and application which seemed all the more apparent now it was so noticeably lacking. This time he appeared cloudy-eyed, no longer completely sure what it was he really did. Or why. Chris's brilliant character creation, Frank, now diluted to self-imitation, a vague evocation of better times, better days when anything seemed possible and most things seemed probable. It might be taken as a classic 'tears of a clown' scenario; it might be more than that. The Chris I had known, back in the seventies and eighties, had always seemed fully formed and bustling with hope although, even then, I knew that he often sheltered within the warming complimentary hazes of alcohol and cocaine. For many years, it had seemed under control, vital even, less the creative juices should suddenly fade. For Chris loved life; quite often he loved it a little too much.

A slight awkwardness descended, rather like the elastic time that prevails on hospital visits. I complimented him on the evening's performance, of course, although Chris looked perplexed, as if unable to believe me. I felt a bit guilty at that point. I could hardly say, 'Wasn't quite the same as last time, Chris," could I? Although we all knew the truth.

What I didn't know, however, *couldn't* have known, as the talk fluttered around the highlights of the evening, was that I had just witnessed the final full performance of Frank Sidebottom and, perhaps more poignantly, of Chris Sievey. That truth escaped us.

However, as I filed out into Warrington's anarchic streets and settled with a bottle of wine in the Cultural Quarter's welcoming Lounge Bar. Again, a curious silence prevailed. I knew we had reached the end… of something.

A last full set it may have been, although the near future would contain one more outing for Frank Sidebottom. This would be a comparatively low-budget affair at Manchester's atmospheric Salutation pub. By chance, this was witnessed by Chris's long time friend, radio star, author and one-time member of Frank's Oh Blimey Big Band, Mark Radcliffe.

Mark, it seems, witnessed a similarly affecting vision, on that night. "When I last saw him, it was clear that something had changed. Although it was funny because he was being run around and looked after and taken to his gigs by a guy called Simon Taylor, who I knew. I bumped into Simon and he said that Chris was playing at The Salutation, just behind the Royal Northern College of Music. I had an evening show on Radio Two then. So I thought I would drive back and stop and see him. I went in and Simon said that Chris was upstairs.

"Gemma (Woods, Chris' girlfriend) was doing the merchandise downstairs. I didn't know Gemma. It was after my time when she started seeing Chris. I think I nodded to her and went upstairs. I found him sitting there, quietly. On his own and with Frank's head. I talked to him for quite a while about the old times. It was a good heart-to-heart. We had a few laughs, how could you *not* laugh. But he was more thoughtful than I had ever known him. For the first time ever he didn't seem to be full of that great Chris energy. He was more reflective, slightly distant. It was a strange experience. I drove home in silence, thinking about Chris."

The gig marked the launch of Frank's World Cup single, 'Three Shirts on the Line'.

Paul Stevens was another who attended that very last gig, "It was about a week before he died. Not many there, maybe a dozen. My friend Jenx, who had introduced me to Frank and had Little Denise's body in his bedroom, had come up to watch some big bollox band – Oasis, one presumes – at Heaton Park and didn't go. He came to see Frank instead. Frank looked quite thin but put on a hell of a show for the few that were there. There was supposed to be a Subbuteo contest but I don't think he was well enough and left after his set. His memorial at Castlefield basin was a bit of a do. I wish my last memory of him performing had been before that kind of crowd."

"I promoted Chris's last few shows and managed to capture a hilarious moment with Chris and John Cooper Clarke backstage doing an impromptu 'Walk Like an Egyptian' routine together. I loved the way that Chris would often, whilst selling his own merchandise anonymously, respond to requests for autographs by pretending to nip back-stage to get stuff signed by Frank."

DANIEL O'SULLIVAN

DENNIS AND LOIS

An image of Frank Sidebottom spits from the heart of Elbow's video for their 2014 single, 'New York Morning'. Initially, the inclusion seems incongruous, shocking even. But the single details the life and times of New York 'uber music fans, Dennis and Lois'. The lovely and eccentric couple are featured both in the visuals and, more so, within Guy Garvey's wry lyric. It isn't the first — or last, one presumes — time the couple have featured in a Manchester lyric. For they were more ambiguously depicted in Happy Mondays' paean to Manhattan life, rather naturally titled 'Dennis and Lois' (on 'Pills 'n' Thrills and Bellyaches, sandwiched between 'Loose Fit' and 'Bob's Yer Uncle').

The have accidentally — for they are no self-publicists — created their own cult following after 40 years spent as inspirational company to rock stars since the era of Andy Warhol. The connection with Manchester also runs deep. For the creation of The Hacienda was styled on New York's elegantly industrial 'Paradise Garage' and it is no coincidence that much of the music that excited the rather more danceable New York club-goers filtered into The Hacienda via the mixing desk of DJs such as Mike Pickering and within the core of the music of New Order and Pickering's own Quando Quango. The Manchester/New York connection deepens further when the Irish equation is brought into view: Smiths, Oasis, et al.

Indeed. It is difficult to find a travelled Manchester rock star who has not encountered these charming people.

However, it is slightly more difficult to imagine Chris Sievey, let alone Frank Sidebottom, managing to scale that Atlantic divide. But scale it he certainly did. Dennis and Lois gave house room to Chris Sievey on a number of occasions after initially befriending him on a trip to Manchester. I had seen them described many times as 'superfans' although I felt unhappy with this lazy description, I asked Lois how they would like to be introduced.

"Crazy, but not dangerous, and very lucky," says Lois, "music is our life's blood and we like to get to know those that have touched us with their gift."

It was BBC 6 Music presenter and ex-Fall bassist Marc Riley who initially introduced the pair to Sievey. As bizarre as it may seem, the couple had become fans of Frank Sidebottom after catching him on videos gifted them by visiting rock stars. This was the first indication that the unique elements that compose Frank's persona might travel beyond the heavily patrolled boundaries of northern cult comedians. Riley – who had met the pair back in The Fall days – picked them up as they arrived in Manchester and whisked them to catch Frank live at an impromptu gig at a Manchester 'Berni Inn'. There are several obvious reasons why this might be a somewhat disorientating experience

"We were *very* jet-lagged," states Lois, "It was like living in some surreal dream but we understood Frank immediately. He was everything we knew he would be. Very sophisticated humour. It was perhaps a perfect introduction."

Subsequently, the couple proved instrumental in re-introducing Frank Sidebottom to his unlikely niche following in New York. As stated, it remains difficult to see how, even in this most European of American cities, Frank could cross the cultural divide. Although, as I write, Jon Ronson's film seems set to prove otherwise, the assumption had always been that Frank is a distinctly 'English' phenomenon if not a distinctly 'northern' one. Two facts, however, that might themselves have opened the eyes of the Big Apple's multitudinous Anglophiles. That, it seems, really was the case.

"We called Chris one day and he asked why we hadn't been over for a while," says Denis, "he then decided, as my birthday was approaching, to fly over for one day and we asked our friends at Death By Audio if he could be squeezed in on a gig by one of the Black Lips – it was one day, two gigs, a TV spot and a radio spot. There was no difficulty with translation. Everybody seemed to love him. And he absolutely loved NYC. He wanted to keep coming back. We would get him some gigs and he would also get himself some gigs. Todd at the new Max's Kansas City was very supportive, even letting him headline there on his second time over."

The very notion of Frank at Max's seems incongruous, to say the least. Although several venues changes had occurred over the years, the brand name of Max's echoes back to days of Warhollian celebrity excess and much of the most inspiring live music ever created. For Dennis and Lois, the gig only helped deepen the friendship.

"Chris came and stayed with us a total of four times I think. On the last occasion he brought Gemma," confirms Lois, "our strangest memory was Chris 'becoming' Frank in the back of our van," she continues.

"Then there was his singing and Casio playing as a soundtrack to our travels. It was always great fun. We would speak on the phone often and every time we were in Manchester, which was a lot, we would go to his house, have a curry at the Timperley Hilal, and usually drive him to Liverpool. We came over dozens of times and stayed in at least three different houses."

However, the current unexpected resurgence of interest in Frank does seem to trouble them slightly. Two posthumous films, a statue and a book might appear a neat reward to this unique artist. But is it too late?

"We have mixed reactions towards the current Frank industry. He deserved it when he was alive. Also he was *very* insistent on keeping Frank and Chris separate. He even asked me to remove a photo of Chris from a group of Frank shots I posted on Facebook. We feel he will be better known, more respected but he was too original for the masses. If he does it won't be the real him that people latch onto."

AN INCIDENT IN TIMPERLEY

It was an elegant, silent salon; Just two ladies, heads tilted backwards over their respective sinks. Two female hairdressers were in attendance - both chatty and trendily attired. Beyond this scene, adjacent to the doorway leading to the Timperley street, there was something of a kerfuffle. The face of the bewildered receptionist edged towards panic. A man in a grey suit wearing a papier-mâché head, complete with gargantuan eyes, had entered her domain and was whirling his arms around in a state of bizarre gesticulation. One felt for her. It was 1986 and Frank Sidebottom hadn't yet stepped beyond a cult appeal within the inebriated world of studentdom. Clearly the receptionist, by now visibly shaking, had not previously encountered this local phenomenon and had set off for work two hours earlier, not expecting such a surreal encounter. Ten minutes later Frank, having pushed beyond her border guard surveillance, was sitting in one of the salon chairs, leaning backwards, hand on hips and engaged in a five way conversation that included the two clients, the hairdressers and the salon owner.

While the receptionist remained aggrieved, Frank had made the breakthrough. Many times after this brusk intervention, he would visit the same salon, settling in with alarming regularity. Within three weeks he would be greeted with "Oh hello Frank' from staff and clientele alike. He had achieved acceptance and familiarity. Quite how this extraordinary activity managed to assist his career remains the point. Why did he do this? What did it achieve? This is the crucial divide that separates the artist from the entertainer. Chris was living it. Chris was 'for real'.

Mark Radcliffe: "The thing I loved about Chris was that he always took the joke too far. When I was playing the role of Mr Emerson-Lake the greengrocer within Frank's 'Oh Blimey Big Band', there were so many instances of complete and natural madness. Like the times when Chris had this idea to create Travel Snooker and play it in the van going down to a gig in London. The gigs was at The Canal Café Theatre at Maida Vale. Chris Evans was driving the van. Jon Ronson was playing as well but I think we met him in London, probably Rick Sarko on bass. So we went round to pick Chris up in the van and Chris came out lugging a half-sized snooker table which he proceeded to put in the back of the van which had the seats up. Obviously, whenever you went round a corner the balls would all fly off one side and, of course, there was nowhere for any of us to sit. We went all the way to London squeezed against the windows. That night at Canalside Theatre, Chris Evans lost the keys to the van. So we finished up sleeping in the van and took turns sleeping on the snooker table. So it turned out alright, really.

"Chris Sievey did say afterwards that Chris Evans had actually found the keys but Sievey thought it better to pretend they were lost. What kind of perverse logic is that? Chris Evans used to be called Nobby at

Piccadilly Radio. He was always a nutter. I think he was Timmy Mallet's fall guy at that point. These were crazy days. I will never forget them."

GROWING UP

CHRISTOPHER MARK SIEVEY was born on August 25, 1955 at Sale Memorial Hospital on Charlton Drive, Sale in the Trafford area of Greater Manchester. His father, Victor Charles Sievey, worked as a travelling salesman for a local raincoat manufacturer. A natural salesman, he held an air of exuberance and used his powerful and pleasing personality to charm his customers and, indeed, his wife – Betty.

The family would soon include Chris' sister, Vicky, 17 months his junior and already included his elder brother, Martin. His grandparents also shared a house at 8, Cedar Road in nearby Ashton-on Mersey, a surprisingly pleasant village tucked between less salubrious Sale, Urmston and Stretford. Although pleasant, it was – and remains – rather mundane although it's pretty Norman-style church, St Martin's is often used as a location for Coronation Street burial scenes. The village lies on the Mersey bank which extends through Chorlton to Didsbury, as featured in The Stone Roses song, 'Mersey Paradise'.

It is a location that has thrown up few notables. However, the poet Lascelles Abercrombie was born there, as unlikely as that might seem. Less surreal, perhaps, would be the local births of Smiths' bassist, Andy Rourke and the television personality Karl Pilkington, most famously noted for 'An Idiot Abroad'. In many ways, Pilkington's television persona mirrors the unfortunate generalisation of 'Sale man'. It is, after all, a fairly non- descript area, containing little of the urban spice of nearby Stretford and Old Trafford, nor the Bohemian flash of Chorlton-Cum-Hardy nor the plush Cheshire vibe of Altrincham and Hale.

Cedar Road is a sleepy cul-de-sac lined with comfortable semi-detached houses. It isn't difficult to imagine a very young Chris – the family left for Park Avenue, Sale when he was three – being wheeled to the rather vibrant row of local shops in the village.

Paula Sievey, Chris's wife, remembers, "He got run over in Cedar Road when he was two. He was just playing football on his own in the road... which apparently was the norm at the time and this guy knocked him over. It broke his leg... all quite serious. He was lucky to be alive. But this guy in the car felt really guilty and, for years, kept bringing him loads of stuff. He would constantly ask if there was anything he could get and Chris played up to it, saying 'Yeah, actually, I want a football kit'. I think he screwed him for everything he could get for years afterwards, I believe."

As stated, Chris was three when the family moved to Park Avenue in Sale. This was a rather different prospect and one that hints at a continuing success in the raincoat business. Furnished with lovely rows of large Victorian semi-detached houses hidden behind luscious, mature trees, Victoria Avenue stretches from the frenetic rush of Sale's Washway Road and extends to an unexpected leafiness. It has the feel of a plush London suburb and it is easy to imagine how pleasant it must have been for Chris to wander round the corner to the large Park Road Primary School.

Although borderline, he failed his 11 plus and attended Ashton-on-Mersey High School, situated on leafy Cecil Avenue. It was, by all accounts, a pleasant although ultimately undistinguished schooling. As Chris explained, "I always wanted to be famous but my mum had other ideas. She wanted me to go and work in one of the bookstore chains, sweeping the floors and slowly working my way up to the top.

"My brother and sister were both quite brainy, so she would always say what they were doing when people asked. With me... well, she would pretend I didn't exist. I don't think anyone expected me to amount to anything."

Chris later stated, "School was a bit of a blur for me. I recall doing a lot of art stuff, messing around with anything I could lay my hands on although I don't think the teachers were particularly impressed. We played football... and that was about it."

When I contacted the school in regard to Chris's time there, the staff seemed slightly alarmed that Frank Sidebottom – whose mythical status was exploding all over the local press in the summer of 2013 –

had attended their school. However, they could find no trace of Chris Sievey nor, indeed, any older member of staff who could recall him.

PAUL MOLYNEUX

Paul Molyneux, who remained Chris' friend from the age of 13 until his death, still resides in the prevailing leafiness of Ashton-on-Mersey. Having worked in the international travel industry all his life, his current abode is a sumptuous house adorned with the 'wow factor' of a kitchen extension. When I met Paul, in October 2013, he was suffering from a serious throat condition that possibly required surgery. Despite the fact that he could barely eat, let alone speak with any resonance, he kindly agreed to be interviewed. As I sat at his kitchen table, I scanned the room. A profound love of The Beatles, a devotion he shared with Chris, was manifest with magazines, artefacts, his black T-shirt adorned with the ever familiar Beatles logo and a copy of Mark Lewisham's gargantuan tome, 'The Beatles; All These Years Volume One, Tune In', sitting on the table edge. At 940 pages – and still only edging to 1962, with a 'writer's edit' due a month later, it is the most comprehensive Beatles tome to date and one that dispels a fare few heady myths.

"Chris would have devoured it," said Paul, "he probably could have written something like that himself... or maybe half of it before getting bored and moving on to another project."

"It looks a little daunting," I noted, not being a fan of vast rock tomes.

"Oh I had to slow myself down. I just didn't want it to end... I have been off work... had a lot of time on my hands."

It was impossible not to warm to Paul. His affection for Chris spicing his every sentence and his parallel love of The Beatles seemed eerily reminiscent of Fab's related tales that Chris had once told me. Although I grew up with The Beatles hanging omnipresent in the air, once again I bowed to greater knowledge. It was inspiring to connect with such unbridled and honest enthusiasm.

"Chris was slightly more laid back than I was because his dad was like that. His dad was very arty, which is where Chris got it from. His mum was more relaxed. They were really chilled people. Lovely people, his parents. They weren't hippies or anything but certainly liberal. They treated me as a son, really. They used to buy us Snowballs (the drink) at Christmas because we liked them. That was our first taste of alcohol. But it was great being around his parents. Nothing would ever upset them at all so they made everyone feel relaxed. I mean, Chris could get a bit mad, especially with his art. While they were out, he could paint rainbows on the walls and murals on his bedroom wall. You never knew what he would get up to and they just kind of accepted it. It was part of what he was, even then. His parents were away on holiday once. I guess Chris would have been about 14 and he painted this big rainbow on the living room wall. He just finished it off when the door opened and his dad walked in. Most parents would get really annoyed about that but not Chris's dad. He just shrugged and accepted it. I remember being amazed. But Chris knew he wouldn't be in trouble. Later in life, I often felt that, with Frank, he occasionally went a step further than anybody else. I never knew if that was rooted in those early days… whether Chris even knew he was pushing the limits. It just came naturally to him."

Chris' parents created a music room downstairs with a stereo. Naturally this would be the room most occupied by Chris and Paul. They would often sit around and maybe listen to David Bowie or Mott the Hoople…the stuff of the day, really. His parents seemed to like the same kind of music.

"Perhaps we needed to rebel a bit. We started to search for music that was increasingly eclectic."

One of the most intriguing aspects of this story is the emergence of Chris as a serious artist. To many, even Frank's devotees, this remained clouded in the background of the Frank persona. But Chris was always far more than a mere prop-maker for Frank's myriad eccentricities. It was a situation that would cause Chris varying degrees of frustration. It was rooted, too, within his time at High School.

"I went to the same high school as Chris at Ashton-on-Mersey, Cecil Road. That's when we started hanging round together. I guess we must have been about 14. It was the second year. We hit it off straight away because we just seemed to have the same things in common. We were in the same house at school. We didn't support the same football team, though I am an Evertonian and Chris, of course, Man City. The interest was just in music, really. We were both completely mad on The Beatles."

Which may have seemed slightly incongruous, in truth. The early seventies saw The Fabs still somewhat clouded by their unholy collapse. Vast swathes of 'other music' had shifted into place and, it seemed, none would mix too freely. The extremes of progressive rock and glam, chart pop and Northern Soul, 'Philly' and the sexual stir of contemporary funk. So much to explore. Were The Beatles not clicked into a fading decade?

"From The Beatles aspect, I would go round to his parent's house on Saturday mornings. We would listen to albums. The Beatles came first and that might have been slightly unusual. But it was not *just* The Beatles but all kinds of stuff. Some albums that Martin, his brother, would bring as well. We were never into the run of the mill stuff. None of us. Some progressive like King Crimson, which was a big one at the time, '20th Century Schizoid Man'. We were definitely interested in looking beyond 'Top of the Pops'."

Nor was this mutual interest confined to music. From an early age Chris would be fascinated with ignoring the rules of Waddingtons and challenging them, changing them and eventually inventing his own.

"On Saturday mornings we would play games. But, yes, Chris would make his own games. There was one called 'Big Bluff' which we also called 'Big Bastard'. We played 'Chartbuster', too (a now collectable vintage board game featuring Radio One's Tony Blackburn). The thing about 'Chartbuster' was that it was just the British charts but Chris added an extra board with the American singles on it. He doubled the size of the game with a few crayons. Chris would never just play games straight. He would always do something extra. He would always work out how to improve them.

"So we had USA Chartbuster, which was unique to us. We invented this other game, 'Big Bluff', can't remember much about it but it went on for months. Saturday mornings would always be games time. There was one called 'Gogglebubbleland' (which Chris would later use for the basis of a song)."

Sometimes, the Saturday mornings would see the numbers of attendees extending considerably. Indeed, if only within the leafy edge of Sale and Ashton-on-Mersey and confined to an age group of early to mid teens, a certain mythical status was granted to Chris's excitable, precocious muse.

"We would play Subbuteo in the garage. It was never just a case of playing the game on some table. We would get all the lads round. We would have people standing around, chanting for the teams. We would have people selling tickets for the games. We would even make our own programmes and sell them. Anything that happened at a real football game, we would do. Chris was great at going that one step further than anybody else. It was usually Aston Villa versus Wolves. At half time Chris would wander about shout orders at his players… we would drink tea. The thing was to make it as real as it could be. We didn't have floodlights or anything. Today Subutteo is rubber figures that don't break. But back then you would always be leaning on the men and snapping them, so you would have to glue them together and they would be really short, so we would stick them on the wing. We would have little league tables and read out the results, as on the telly."

The extent of Sievey's immersion within these games undoubtedly reflects the completeness of the creation of Frank – who would often hold impromptu Subbuteo matches - which, likewise, would extend way beyond anything even the most thorough artist might consider necessary. Frank's world would expand, often with no noticeable gain in sight for Chris or, indeed, any real point beyond apparent self-amusement. If nothing else, Chris was early to recognise the truism that an artist or performer must never reveal *everything*. Something must be kept in reserve. In Chris' case, that element of reserve would be vast, bewildering and never fully discovered until the months following his death, when Steve Sullivan and Martin Sievey started seriously filtering through the extensive mass of Frank ephemera.

"And then Chris started getting into the music stuff. He started playing the guitar a lot. It kind of took over from the games for a while because he could be extremely obsessive. Musically, in Ashton-on-Mersey, we would go round to Robert Cook's house, because he had a drum kit. And Craig Clarke would come round and bring a guitar. Robert had a big house in Ashton-on-Mersey with an outhouse type of thing and would set the drums up in there. I didn't play anything but I would go and watch. They didn't gig anywhere but the performances did start to develop. I used to take a PartyFour can and drink that. This was just before they started to call themselves The Bees Knees… that is who they became. That was the earliest stage of the music side that I can remember. I can't recall Chris showing an interest in playing music before that although no doubt he was practicing at home. It came as a surprise to me that he was so adept."

The friendship was enduring and continued via the fringes of early seventies fashion, where juvenilia fizzed with a naïve mix of glam, streetware and fading traces of the sixties.

"We didn't quite know what we should be wearing and I don't think we looked like the other kids in the area. We would wear flares and tank tops, as a lot of people did but these were in really garish colours. I have a photo of us in the Isle of Man with the tank tops on. We would wear them all the time; longish hair, that kind of thing. He came with my mum and dad and me for a holiday on the Isle of Man. That was the first time the Isle of Man connection was made. We went to Port Erin. We would get up late, watch 'Deputy Dawg' on the telly. We loved it there. It seemed fresh and clean."

The connection with the Isle of Man and the North West of England hit a boom during the late fifties and sixties, when the gloriously named Isle of Man Steam Packet Company would run evocative car ferries from Liverpool with names like 'Manx Maid', 'Mona's Isle', 'Ben-me-cree' and 'The Manxman'. I remember Chris talking enthusiastically about the island. The colours, the small white cottages, pin neat buses, glorious glens and the small fishing ports of Peel and Ramsey. While I cannot recall his exact words – they were not taped for interview – it was clear that we had both experienced the same feelings on the island in the late sixties.

Chris's inspiration turned more into his art. Hardly an unusual situation for a burgeoning artist… a holiday to an island or area where the light seemed to hold a surreal and vivid spectrum. All the more obvious, perhaps, when holidaying from the still soot-blackened cities of the North West. Another obvious inspiration was the aforementioned omnipresence of The Beatles music that would seem to permeate every moment of every day, from 'Can't Buy Me Love' – forever associated with Kirk Michael for me, to the later waxings of 'Come Together' and 'The Ballad of John and Yoko'. It was simply a case of timing. The island's boom almost perfectly synchronised the sheer blinding brilliance of The Beatles heyday.

Paula Sievey: "Chris went to Ashton-on-Mersey High on Cedar Road. He went there with Paul Molyneux. No, I don't think he got any qualifications. Oddly enough we never really talked about that. He wasn't really into academic stuff, he was into his own stuff. And also, he was always stoned because he started smoking dope when he was 12. He would do his paper round stoned out of his mind. It was one guy – not mentioned in this book - who got him started on drugs and stuff. I think he had taken LSD by the time he was 14. Crazy man making him do stuff. I don't think Chris was completely all there when he was at school. There are some people who don't quite fit into the education system. A bit like his son, Harry."

One strongly senses that Chris Sievey was simultaneously just too bright and far too creative to be constrained by the dark borders of school curriculum of the early seventies. Emerging simultaneously with Morrissey, just two miles away in Stretford, his talents would fail to penetrate the formalised artistic blindness of the teachers. That stated and, unlike Morrissey who would unleash his loathing of Manchester schooling in 'The Headmaster Ritual' and more recently his autobiography, Chris didn't seem to leave in a daze of cynicism and hurt. Nevertheless, it was life outside the classroom that excited him the most.

Paul Molyneux: "We never really went to clubs and stuff, in town. We would go to music shops on Saturdays, sometimes. Flip through the new releases, look at the covers, maybe get the guys in the little Virgin store on Lever Street to play them for us. It was all extremely exciting and we seemed to understand that it was a great period in music. We went to a few gigs… though not that many. I think the first must have been Bowie, just before he did Ziggy Stardust, at the Free Trade Hall.

We were at the front, to the right. And after a number, Bowie held his guitar over the crown and Chris reached up and got it. He had a big smile on his face… it had Bowie's set-list on the back and he clung to it. About half an hour later, Bowie's manager (Kenneth Pitt, presumably?) came over and took it off him. We then went round the back of the Free Trade Hall to get to the dressing room. We got in and there was Bowie, Mick Ronson and Trevor Boulder. We told Bowie about the guitar and Bowie said 'next time, I will sort a guitar out for you'. Chris never forgot that. He would go on and on about how Bowie owed him a guitar. We saw Bowie at The Hardrock in Stretford doing Ziggy later. With some sixties rock'n'roll band supporting. No guitar that night. We saw Paul McCartney at The Hardrock too. It was just down the road from us so it was our local venue."

The building remains in place although its rocking days are well and truly over. It is now the Stretford B&Q, albeit one of the strangest B&Qs I have ever visited. The concrete tower to the front remains rather pointlessly in place while the garden area extends to touch Old Trafford Cricket Ground… ever so slightly surreal.

Another friend, Paul Latham – same network of teenage streets, different school – who now works as a managerial consultant in Kidderminster, recalls scurrying around the streets of Sale and Ashton alongside the cherubic Sievey.

"We were just learning about fashion and girls and all the usual stuff," he recalls, "but although Ashton was quite plush, Sale could be really rough. I think Chris had a Crombie and was really proud of it. I had brogue shoes 'Royals' and two tone trousers. We weren't that smart but we would wander across Washway Road into the town centre and almost always get chased back. We had a knack of getting out of scrapes as soon as they flared up. I was into soul but Chris wasn't really interested. I went back to his house a number of times. He seemed to like writing and drawing stuff but, mostly, we would talk about local girls of particular note."

This somewhat mundane description of a post-soul teenage existence is gifted an added grit some twenty years down the line. As Paul explained, "I left Sale when I was 18 and never really took any interest in music. As such, I never heard of The Freshies or knew anything about Chris or Frank. Then one day, when I was working in Burslem, Stoke-on-Trent we had an office staff party. It turned out that Frank was the hired act. I had no idea who he was or what he did until he wandered around the room asking people what their jobs were and generally taking the piss. To my embarrassment, he came to me and started asking who my favourite Fireball XL5 characters were. It was both funny and embarrassing. I became a bit of a Frank fan at that point although only from a distance. It was only after Chris had died and I read about it all in – I think – *The Mirror*, that the penny dropped and I realised that Frank Sidebottom was my childhood mate, Chris Sievey. I was staggered. We weren't friends for very long in truth but we did enjoy some wild times, usually running around under the orange street lights."

It is a little story that typifies the unique approach of Frank's one-time manager, Mike Doherty. What on Earth was Frank doing performing at a low key works 'do' in Burslem in 1987?

Strangely, Paul Molyneux and Paul Latham were not aware of the existence of one another. I thought this most odd, at first. But, time and time again a similar scenario would emerge. From an early age, it appears, Chris would stream his friends and acquaintances. While I can only presume this to be a result of his varying and simultaneous activities, it was a continuing situation that twisted into a lively absurdity at the conclusion of this book and the unveiling of the Frank Sidebottom statue, an illuminating and unique event where many lifelong friends of Chris Sievey would meet many other of his lifelong friends, and mostly for the first time.

★

> *"I remember Chris turning up at the Wigan gig, just after he had brought Frank out of retirement. (1995) He was so drunk that his flies were open and everything. Completely and utterly wasted. He did improve as Frank started to work, but I have never seen anyone so drunk."*
>
> **DAVE ARNOLD**

GETTING NOTICED

UNFASHIONABLY FIRED by his unabashed love of all things Beatles and harbouring a burning desire to create pop songs of perfect simplicity, Chris's work carried a powerful sense of innocence, that would have seemed wholly innocuous during the punk phase. Back at the turn of 1970, such a pop sensibility would have appeared unfashionable for a variety of reasons, not least the prevailing snobbery of loon-panted proggers shuffling to and fro between Yes and Emerson, Lake and Palmer gigs at the Free Trade Hall. But Sievey spent time in a variety of school bands that seemed happy to surf his unusual pop vision. Time spent chopping through chords in the village halls of Sale, Broadheath and Altrincham appeared to produce little more than an enchanting, though largely unsaleable, bonhomie. It seemed a long, long way from such deserted outings to the crass and garish glory of Top of the Pops. Sievey's habit of deluging record labels, potential managers, promoters and journalists began during this spell, when raw demo tapes languished in a state of existential aloofness on the desks (or in the bins) of Radio One DJs more interested in feeding their gargantuan egos than discovering some new school pop band. It seems likely that a tape also landed in the office of John Peel's 'Perfumed Garden' although one struggles to see how it would fit in among such lofty company.

Leaving school saw a change in the Sievey attack. Temporarily at least, the idea of playing in a band was dismissed and Sievey concentrated more fully on song-writing, aided and abetted by his older brother, Martin.

Tosh Ryan, owner of Manchester's Rabid Records, promoted and managed The Freshies and noted of the partnership: "Chris and Martin made a great double act, really. They were very funny together and would compete against each other with levels of daftness."

Mike Doherty, Freshies drummer and Frank Sidebottom manager, agreed: "Yes, they were brilliant together. For a time inseparable. I thought they might branch off into some kind of double-act at one stage. They certainly seemed to share the same kind of vision. Anyone who thinks that Chris' vision was unique should look at Martin too. It was the way they approached life. Full on but without causing offence. They weren't particularly competitive, but they were driven. Perhaps they got away with it because they were always very funny… dreaming up scams and stuff like that."

A scam would appear to provide some kind of answer. Bored and (as) yet undefeated by the flood of deadening rejection slips that bounced back from major record labels, Chris and Martin decided to combine their love of The Beatles with their desire to make some kind of headway by embarking on a precocious little sojourn to London, departing from Manchester Piccadilly with the aim of locating a genuine Beatle in the nation's capital. Not an easy task at the best of times, let alone in 1970, a time of famously fractious Beatle activity.

Nevertheless, Chris and Martin stubbornly parked themselves in the shambolic reception at Apple Records, happily deflecting the unsympathetic glances from the girls on reception and ignoring derogative remarks from famous and semi-famous faces who drifted by. Not that the Sievey's fully understood who they were dealing with.

"We just bedded in really," Chris would later admit, "looking back, it was probably highly embarrassing but we just said, 'We are not moving until we see a Beatle.' People just looked blankly at us. They told us that no Beatles were there and they hardly ever saw them anyway. That seemed kind of strange to me but we just stated that we wanted to record something. How naïve was that? However, eventually we were sent up to office of Tony King who was the head of A'n'R. Embarrassing again, but we sang a song together and he seemed to like it… or at least he liked our sense of resolve. We must have achieved our aim because we found ourselves booked into the studio because of Tony King who was head of A'n'R. He seemed to like us. I thought we were going to be instant stars. It was to prove a learning curve, that's for sure."

The Sievey's recorded 'Watercolour View' and, apparently, George Harrison really took to it but confessed that he was far too busy to be able to spend time in a studio with them. The name Tony Visconti was also mentioned, which freaked Chris and Martin out somewhat but, for a short while, it really did seem as if this would happen. Visconti, however, was locked in with the release of T-Rex's 'Ride a White Swan', the eventually success of which carried Visconti clean away on a wave of unprecedented success. Somehow, amid the glam and glitter, the possibility of working with two naïve northern lads became lost in the background.

'WATERCOLOUR VIEW'

A slight song – literally at just 1 minute 15 seconds long – that naturally leaned heavily on the brothers' Beatles fixation. Well, that and more. Listening to the poorly reproduced version that appeared as an extra track on Cherry Red's 1996 compilation 'The Very Very Best of The Freshies, some long and short titles', it also conjures up an atmosphere of 1967 British pyschedelia. Spooky Tooth, perhaps or mid-period Moody Blues. It is a lilting, misty piece of whimsy. One can imagine Chris and Martin, perhaps fazed by the studio environment, strumming through this simplistic ditty which, in their heads at least, carried all their hopes and musical desires. More than that, they no doubt harboured unrealistic expectations, believing, as embryonic musicians always do, that the song is far greater than latter-day listening suggests.

Inevitably, despite showing early promise, Apple soon quietened on the deal. Undeterred, Chris used the Apple demo again in 1972 – after the band formed around himself and he and Martin had drifted apart – to approach Apple (again, with the same demo), CBS and Polydor. Retreating to his bedroom, he emerged 12 months later with renewed vigour, only to be turned down flat by Elton John's Rocket Records – to which he had included a painstakingly written account of his life thus far, personally addressed to the superstar himself – CBS, Harvest, EMI, Polydor, Stax – a wild card, that one – and, ahem, Apple. One can only conclude that, while the other labels were duly swamped with thousands of such tapes and, therefore, Sievey's myth remained unknown, Apple might well have started to tire of him.

As Chris told me in 1985, "I found it hilarious when, years later, record company A'n'R men always referred to this kind of blanket demo sending as 'the idiot tapes'. Hardly any of those tapes are ever listened to. Of course I never realised that and took it all very personally. When I sent a demo tape, which was often, I envisaged an entire boardroom of executives all listening to it at once and mulling it over during lunch. It did start to dawn on me that this wasn't quite the case when I started to send the same tape a few times and nobody appeared to notice. But I like the idea that I was a dealer in 'idiot tapes' for… well, for six years or so."

STRAWBERRY STUDIOS

BY THEN, SIEVEY had also approached a famous Stockport studio. For local artists in an around Manchester in the early seventies, mainstream chart success was, to say the least, a distant goal. Chris had long since despaired of any remote chance of creating any kind of local scene that might intensify to the extent that London-based record companies would show any kind of serious interest. Not since the mid-sixties had this really been the case. Yet, as Chris knew, a heady collection of in-house talent had assembled their own studios – Strawberry – within the unfashionable centre of Stockport during this period. It was a curious mix of musicians, initially born out of the crumbling Wayne Fontana and the Mindbenders (Eric Stewart), various unsuccessful Manchester bands such as The Mockingbirds and The Whirlwinds – Lol Crème and Kevin Godley – and hit songwriter Graham Gouldman. The ethos of Strawberry was to negate the necessity for northern bands to be forced to make the trip to London based recording studios. It made commercial sense to create a world class studio in Stockport.

What Chris Sievey couldn't have known, of course, is that this in-house musical foursome would soon evolve into 10CC, an unlikely band who might have been expected to churn out double album chunks of prog. However, and probably because of their initial signing to Jonathon King, who, having secured a hit under the name Hotlegs 'Neanderthal Man' – changed their moniker to the whimsical 10CC. Their initial hit, 'Donna', had been little more than a swiftly churned out pastiche of Neil Sedaka who had just recorded at Strawberry. Perhaps by chance, this set them on course for a run of extraordinary chart success in which they would buck the prog trend and establish the possibilities and power of the 'intelligent light pop single'. 10CC were a heady mix of song-writing skill, technological innovation, solid musicality and overriding mischief. All these components came together for what would arguably become their finest moment, 'I'm Not In Love', which, given its innovative use of multi-tracking, virtually changed the course of pop recording history.

Again, Chris couldn't have know any of this as he relentlessly bombarded Strawberry with sundry lo-fi demos and a succession of artistically colourful demands for recording attention. This he never achieved, although examples of his endeavours languished dustily within the Strawberry cupboards fifteen years later.

Only later would the irony of this rejection seem so poignant. Chris would become a huge fan of 10CC… not so much their music; he was rather more drawn to the juvenile precocity of their approach to making the pop single. He also hugely admired the aforementioned 'I'm Not In Love', interrogating this writer about the moment when the band and manager Rick Dixon and two studio engineers stood around the mixing desk holding screwdrivers around which travelled the master tape. The fact that the band had had to add such a cumbersome extension to the technology available in their own studio, utterly captivated Sievey.

And why not? The irony here is that Sievey's mischievous muse would have been so perfectly at home within the cycle of creativity that Strawberry became. Not to mention Jonathan King, another precocious pop phenomenon admired by Sievey, who would surely have warmed to his unorthodox approach and talents.

It wasn't to be. What's more, no one would ever know if anyone seriously listened to any of Sievey's demos at Strawberry. Nobody I approached could recall actually listening to any music, although the bombardment; had been registered. However, he would eventually manage to record at the famous studio...

★

The T-Rex connection may have softened the blow, for soon Chris would be an avid follower of Bolan, who fired up Sievey's pop sensibilities. The glorious contained power of the seven inch single… in the case of Bolan, edging towards a singular perfection, with T-Rex managing to court the rampaging young female market and, although unhip to older eyes at the time, still cementing themselves fully within pop's mystical framework. Forty years later the girls may well have moved on but, strangely, men still look back with a fondness they couldn't feel at the time.

More intriguingly still, Chris once confessed an unlikely love for the dumb-ass glam excess of Sweet, a fine rock band, initially simplified to the commercial tweeness of the Chinn and Chapman song writing team, before fattening to a rush of admittedly excellent glam outbursts as 'Blockbuster', 'Teenage Rampage', 'Ballroom Blitz' and 'The Sixteens'. Again, many of the loon panted fraternity scorned at such obvious lightweight antics but Sievey could see the value.

I discovered this minor obsession by accident. Back in 1993, I had visited Sweet's sadly fading singer Brian Connolly in his stripped out house in Denham Village, Uxbridge. He cut a sad figure on that day as I interviewed him for a glossy magazine. Chris was truly amazed by this little story, his eyes clearly welling with incredulity when I spoke of the glam rocker's untimely demise.

"How could that happen?" he asked before drifting into a trail of thought. (Oddly enough, on the occasion of the Connolly interview I was accompanied by photographer Martin O'Neill, later to take infamous and highly original shots of Chris and The Freshies scampering down the spiralling car ramp at Sale Tesco.)

His glam leanings were probably best realised within his band, the aforementioned Bees Knees, formed in 1974. Within this rather loose unit, Chris managed to instigate a DIY postal link with local followers.

The 'Bees Knees' name came from his maternal grandmother, who used to say to Chris: 'You lot think you're the bees knees.' As it was the time of glam rock and fan clubs were *de rigueur;* he roped his sister, Vicky, into helping run a little fan club. Together they printed membership cards with stencils and started to establish a low key information service. As small as it was, it was also rather satisfying, even if gig attendances failed to swell.

'THE NAME OF THIS BAND IS THE BEES KNEES'

'EMBRYONIC' IS THE KINDEST word to describe the fluctuating unit known, if it was known at all, as 'The Bees Knees'. As stated, they did perform infrequently and, whether as a unit or merely as Chris, they produced 18 recordings – including two live tracks, which now gather largely unheard in Chris' archive which, having passed through his brother, Martin, now sits in the abode of 'Being Chris Sievey' DVD director, Steve Sullivan.

While Sievey sent many of these recordings to record companies, there doesn't appear to be any indication that they filtered strongly into mail-outs for The Bees Knees miniscule fan club. However, knowing his love of all things postal, one can be pretty certain he managed to fire off garishly coloured cassettes to occasional fans in Hartlepool.

There does exist a Chris stencilled design for a tape entitled 'Nogodemos', although I would suggest this is little more than his own personal archive.

The surviving track-listing for the 18 song set is as follows:

'Hey Marj'; 'Last'; 'Slump'; 'Slump'/'Last'; 'Frapper Dehours'; 'Washed Up'; 'The World Song'; 'The Martins Leave'; 'Chat… well a Little'; 'What's This Feeling?'; 'She Seeing Me'; 'Frapper Dehours 2'; 'Hey Marj' (Live); 'Falling Apart'; 'Love Me Through'; 'So Down'; 'Get Together'; 'Feeling'.

For the most part, the music here does indeed sound as if it was recorded in a canal or, at least, on some bedroom Dansette. Aspiring musicians of the seventies will harbour fond memories of creating a sound of similar spindly structure. Nevertheless, through the murk it is possible to glimpse a few rare shards of a bright future.

'HEY MARJ?'

A stalwart of the live set and, indeed, a live version is included later in the tape. Those expecting the glam-racket that The Bees Knees are slightly known for would find this to be the most surprising song of all.

The intro sees a sliding piano clump into a stomp pulled from Sievey's fixation with 'Lady Madonna'. More surprising is the fact that the song grasps the same Fats Domino/Humphrey Littleton ('Bad Penny Blues') base that McCartney had used on 'Lady Madonna'. The link soon fades, however, as the entire thing sinks into an unlikely sax break (at least, I think it is a sax…difficult to hear, through the murk). Given that this became 'The Bees Knees' signature song for a while, it strongly hints that Sievey intended to extend his musical vision beyond his beloved three-minute pop song. That he didn't quite have the chops to manage this, is typical of many of the demos of the day where embryonic bands attempt to emulate the complexities of what would one day be termed 'prog'. Mostly, these demos crash horribly to the floor. 'Hey Marj?' - great title too - shows promise and ambition, if little else. One imagines the record company A & R Man giving this a swift listen and not getting beyond the Beatles-esque intro.

'LAST'

Taking time's arrow, perhaps, it is intriguing to track back down the years of an artist, cut through all the triumphs and flops and land somewhere near the beginning. Given the huge benefit of hindsight, one can easily identify the origins of identifiable sounds. This is a classic example. For the song that would later surface on a Razz double A side under the guidance of producer Martin Hannett, 'Last', would become a favourite with Sievey's small circle of devotees. However it began life as a Bees Knees song and how intriguing to hear the gorgeously simplistic melody slipping beneath rather lumpen guitar breaks typical of the mid-seventies. Sievey himself couldn't have known any better, for that is what you did. Here the song is given an uneven boost and ends up sounding like an off-take from a Heavy Metal Kids album, rather than the lilting beauty it would one day become. For Sievey, 'Last' would survive as a constant reminder that there could be an artistic life beyond his band, whether The Bees Knees or The Freshies. It is a song that would sit flatly in the undertone of his oncoming work with The Freshies offering a lovely low level melody that could only emerge as a Sievey 'alternative'. It would grow in a strange way, gaining a meditative quality as the years would pass and, on one latter-day demo, would nod sagely to Nick Drake. It contains none of the hooks and quips that Sievey would become famous for but would drift in a determinedly serious manner.

As such, it would always be something of a delightful oddity. However, even if it would never manage to take its rightful place within the rich tapestry of Manchester music, it would still serve him well. It would become the song that would hook and land Rabid Records impresario, Tosh Ryan and his talented and legendary producer Martin Hannett.

'SLUMP'

When played to Barry Spencer in 2013 – the first time he had heard the song – he acknowledged its inherent promise.

"Well, we could have made something out of that," he replied, strongly suggesting that the song is rather like a ball of clay, created by Sievey and passed across for aural sculpting. It seems unlikely that such an experiment could take place at this late stage.

Most intriguing of all, perhaps, is that 'Slump' appears to contain a number of 'Frankisms', which certainly suggests that a Sidebottom type character was bubbling around Sievey's head as far back as the mid-seventies. As Sullivan noted, "It could even be a prototype Frank song."

Included is this fascinating lyric-line.

> "When you get to Timperley, you start to feel fine
> and you'll want to be in Timperley all the time."

The line must have been formed as part of a creation of a character. One presumes that the song was recorded in the bedroom at the flat at 3, Moorside House, Oakleigh Court, Timperley. It was the first time that Chris had any known association with Timperley, although it lies just three miles from the heart of Sale. He certainly enjoyed the leafy terrain.

Nice guitar intro though, spiralling away before a feisty little pop song kicks into action. Like a chugging traction engine boosted by Mick Ronson-style guitar breaks. Perhaps this is one song that fits the fading notion we all had of that lost band called The Bees Knees; where pop hits glam and aims for Radio One omnipresence. Oddly reminiscent of Manchester's The Drones in their pre-punk vehicle Rockslide who would have been performing heavily in and around Manchester at the time.

'SLUMP'/'LAST'

The odd, clumsy chunk of 'Slump', presumably from an earlier recording. The guitars hit a repetitive pseudo-funk that hints at a slight musical ineptitude. One senses that the guitarist would have loved to have broken from that ungainly chug. Nevertheless, Sievey's voice seems to have gained its melodic grace on this. However, without the benefit of the aforementioned hindsight, the multitude of record company A and R men – if, indeed, they ever really listened, would have – at best – filed under 'interesting'.

'FRAPPER DEHOURS'

Military style drum intro leads to revolving guitar break and a lively number ensues. 'Frapper Dehours', another stalwart of The Bees Knees live and practice sets, actually contains Sievey's finest twisting pop-tones of the period; a lovely dipping vocal line which contrasts sharply with the buzzing backbeat. It does, indeed, sound like The Freshies and hints at an unfolding confidence within the ranks. I would have loved to have heard latter-day Freshies, Barry Spencer and Rick Sarko add their dynamics to this. As it stands, the music fades disappointingly towards the conclusion. What might have been.

'WASHED UP'

Again, armed with knowledge of Chris Sievey's later musical exploits, it is easy to sense the infancy of a distinctive sound here. Again we discover Sievey vocal marred by somewhat clumsy musicianship. There is also a sense of distance here... something that, in pre-punk Britain, was undeniably prevalent within anything that laboured under the derogatory tag 'local'. Obviously part of the reason for the punk explosion came from this very situation... the naïve sense that pop and rock stars exist on some higher level, a level that would always be beyond the bands that crowd the local halls and venues. Events such as the five-day Led Zeppelin gigs at Earls Court only served to exaggerate this suppressive gigantism. And, frankly, that is how the big bands wanted it to stay. Nevertheless, a pressure cooker situation would soon prevail... born of frustration, perhaps? As the title strongly suggests, The Bees Knees felt 'Washed Up' on some island of profound obscurity; a lost, existential place from which no ambition could ever be fulfilled. Are there, therefore, traces of punk within this – surely – four track demo. Faint, perhaps, although this remains the sound of a band attempting to emulate their heroes. Ironically, this conundrum had already been answered by Sievey's wired and driven DIY approach. Therein lay not the problem but the eventual cure. Too late however, for The Bees Knees.

'THE WORLD SONG'

Musically speaking, this is a rather more ambitious affair which begins with a solemn block chord and soon trips along to the kind of simplistic drumming that wouldn't have taxed a formative version of Ringo. This is a dirge that tugs along and gains impact only as it reaches its fourth minute. Too late for any A'n'R man, I fear. Intriguingly camp spoken vocals appear – perhaps he had been listening to Jobriath? The song is delightfully rescued, however by a surging and simplistic guitar solo which more than hints at greater moments to come. While the song never quite manages to arrive at its own true destination, it achieves one thing, the very point of a demo recording is to lay out the possibilities. A pity this wasn't allowed to further evolve.

'THE MARTINS LEAVE'

The oddest dirge of the demo, sliding from what appears to be a euphonium intro – probably a regular keyboard disguised by electronic fuzz – into an off-beat avant-garde attack which marries stodgy spoken vocals with a chugging prog back-beat. It is hard to sense any direction, or indeed much in the way of melody, although the entire bizarre affair lifts shortly before the end as a spiky guitar cuts into the groove and takes up the central position.

'CHAT... WELL. A LITTLE.'

It does what it says on the lid. 37 seconds of practice room banter, left in the mix for reasons not apparent to this writer.

'WHAT'S THIS FEELING?'

Sievey toyed with the pun, 'What is this Feeling Called, Love?' for a while and allowed it to settle down to this more sober run–through. Curious pre-echoes of 'Bouncing Babies' which fall into typical over-ambition. Yet again, there is a sense that the song-writing was moving apace towards the Freshies pop beast, even if the surrounding musicality tended to peel away. The basics were clearly in place.

★

MICK MIDDLES

Although Sievey's DIY approach to musical promotion can be said to have been rooted in 1971 – a full five years before Buzzcocks claimed to have cemented the DIY punk ethos – it was 1974 before this became manifest in an actual release, rather than demo. That said, and given the fact that Sievey would always like to decorate every release with highly personalised daubing, the distinction between 'demo' and 'release' is a matter of some debate. Nevertheless, in 1974 he did manage to record a cassette only album, largely on his own, containing five tracks. Despite bringing the mail order pretensions of early Virgin Records on board, he would historically challenge Mike Oldfield in terms of sales, if not artistic content. Nevertheless he felt reasonably content with his five genuine sales, even if at least three of them were seemingly purchased within the spirit of submission following Sievey's postal bombardment. Sales were sales after all.

Following his decision to discontinue the postal actions of The Bees Knees, thereby closing the embryonic 'label' of the same name, he once again approached record companies in a spirited if more traditional manner. This time his rejection slips arrived from EMI, RCA, CBS, RAK, Polydor, Rocket, Redifusion and Harvest (for whom he made promises of a band expansion into full blown prog). While this might appear rather against his love of simplistic pop, ventures into more complex areas of orchestration and concepts were never far from his wandering mind. It was a contradiction that proved too much for Bees Knees, who duly split due to an unfolding musical indifference.

1975's approach, despite pre-echoes of punk arriving from New York, proved little different in terms of Sievey's attack and the record company reaction. This time around, the well used welcome mat in the Sievey household gathered rejection slips from RAK, Bell, CBS, Island – well that was worth a try (he scribbled the words, 'I really really like reggae' on his open letter to Island Records boss Chris Blackwell) RCA, EMI, Polydor, Harvest, Charisma, Decca and A & M.

Lost in blanket rejection, he transformed mass negatives into singular positives by forming the rather loose 'Hey Boss Box' record label – set for Virgin territory, he hoped – and set about recording a cassette-only album. Released at the turn of 1976, and containing several nods to the pre-punk ideals of London pub rock, he formed a new band and promptly sent demos to Virgin, Bell, RAK, CBS, A & M, EMI, Island, MAM, GULL, WEA, Polydor, Swan, RCA, PYE, Rocket, RSO, Jet and Decca. Said band left Chris following blanket rejection. It was, of course, the same story one year later when, in the full flush of punk, he retained true to his course, having his 1977 demos rejected by Bell, Gull, Cube, MAM, WEA, RAK, Polydor, Phonogram, Swan, Atlantic, Chrysalis, Warner Bros, Manticore, Virgin, Island, EMI, RCA, CBS, Rocket, Charisma, Decca, Stiff, A & M, Arista, DJM, Music for Pleasure, Pye, Spark, RSO, United Artists, Magnet, Jet, Chiswick, GTO, Creole and Anchor. The band, such as they were, drifted away due to lack of interest. Chris was intrigued. He had steadfastly kept every rejection letter and now had hundreds, bulging from a Dunlop Green Flash tennis shoe box stuffed under his bed. By night he would unearth this treasure, marvelling at the sheer scope and hopelessness of his quest. He did notice, even then, that several streams of identical phrasing had been used by almost all of them. However, as stated, it didn't dawn on him that hardly any of his mail-outs had met the ears of any of the receiving A & R men or even the junior talent scouts.

Music historian, Alberto Y Lost Trios Paranoias leader, professor of pop at Salford University, Salford Sheiks singer, puppeteer extraodinaire and ebullient raconteur, CP Lee, noted: "It's funny, looking back at Chris Sievey and Frank because, although everyone else seems to have hundreds of stories, for once, I haven't. And yet there are many links between The Freshies and The Berts. (As proven by the Pete Frame style Albertos Family Tree that adorns the Lee's dining room wall). It was only recently that I remembered that Chris had published his book of rejection slips, in a modest kind of way and I had reviewed it for the *NME*."

MICK MIDDLES

DISCOVERY?

THERE WAS A PARADOX at the heart of Sievey's love of simplistic pop which, one strongly senses, emerged from his constant flirtations with the world of juvenile sci-fi. I recall him – must have been in '78 or '79 – talking enthusiastically of a vision of the future in which people remain in their bedrooms and have 'entertainment and information' pumped directly to them by a controlling force. While I couldn't quite grasp this at the time it now seems rather obvious to note the similarity between this vision and the Internet. However, he hadn't picked this up from some Phillip K. Dick novel. It was, he stated, based on something that Pete Townsend had said in an interview. It was only while working on this book that I realised exactly what this was. Back in the early seventies, The Who were a band torn between the gargantuan faux mod anthems of the sixties and the – I thought – rather pompous notions of rock opera established by the hugely overrated 'Tommy'. Townsend's initial idea to follow 'Tommy' was an embryonic notion called 'Lifehouse', the basic concept of which was exactly the same as Sievey's vision. 'Lifehouse' incidentally died a death after partial recording as Townsend hit the Remy Martin and failed to convince his band mates of the validity of his vision. The band soon retreated to their trademark simplicity and produced the mighty 'Who's Next'. The paradox is that it was Townsend's concept that most appealed to Chris and this little story reminds me of Chris's idea to add concept to the pop simplicity of The Freshies (see 'Red Indian Music', 'The Johnny Radar Story').

Mind you, as punk grumbled and buzzed from across the Atlantic, Chris's thoughts and feelings started to wander elsewhere.

He fell in love.

WHITE BICYCLES... AND PAULA

I WAS HESITANT, during the writing of this book, to visit Paula. We had communicated through 2013, though only by email and Facebook. I sensed a reticence and I could understand why. She must be regarded as the person closest to Chris and, as such, had been through an awful lot. Her marriage and continuing relationship with Chris had been both beautiful and tumultuous; indeed, at times, nothing short of harrowing.

I hadn't seen her since one day in the mid-eighties when we attended the 'Seaside comes to town' event-day at The Pelican Inn in Sale. Her life had changed immeasurably since. She had moved into a new era, a new phase... hopefully a place of light and clarity. I was concerned about dragging back a few black clouds. Also, I knew that Steve Sullivan and Dave Arnold had been filming heavily with the family. I had more time. Mine was a different angle and I wanted to allow that moment to pass. It isn't a competition.

However, two thirds of the way through, I realised that I had to go and see her, if only to reassure her that I wasn't adding extra spice to a story that already popped and bubbled furiously in the pan. I was just reaching for the phone when a message came in. She had apparently reached the same conclusion. A time was quickly set for mid-day, Friday. We agreed this at 9.30pm on the Thursday. It happened in a flash and, yet again, one couldn't help wondering about some kind of other worldly intervention.

For some reason, that Friday morning, I decided to walk the three miles from our house in Ashton-on-Mersey, to Paula's current abode, deep in the heart of – where else? – Timperley. Why I chose to walk, I can't be sure, for the sky was leaden and full of Autumnal menace. The beautiful summer of 2013 had finally been defeated. So I wandered through Sale centre and, with plenty of time to spare, decided to drift along the canal towpath. Naturally perhaps, my head was lost to Chris that morning. It had been on many such occasions, although this time it seemed on a different level. I felt light footed... floaty even and my head swirled like some monstrous psychedelic bubble. Full of colour and sharp flashes of light. I hadn't taken any acid and had barely kissed a dubious mushroom since my mid-twenties. I couldn't imagine what it was. However, I arrived at Timperley early and, as the heavens opened, dived into the café that adorns the Metro stop. Settling with a coffee, I glanced down to see a copy of the *Sale and Altrincham Messenger* – I swear – lying open at a page depicting the forthcoming Frank Sidebottom statue. Well, that could be a coincidence, I know. It is a story that carried a large amount of interest in the immediate vicinity, although the newspaper was six weeks old.

Twenty minutes later, I carefully opened Paula's garden gate and strode to the front door. She immediately diffused my nerves and ushered me into the airy and pristine lounge, complete with a highly attentive Labradoodle named Kooky which, apparently, had been Chris' pet name for her.

"I perhaps shouldn't have called him that," she laughed, "couldn't help it, though."

If Chris were a dog, I thought, somewhat absurdly, he would probably be a Labradoodle!

"I never really believed in that stuff but sometimes I think I am going a bit mad, because things keep happening. Chris always said, 'If there is anyway I could come back, I would do it and drive everybody round the bend.' I said 'Don't ever do it to me... don't come back to me because it would freak me out.' And things keep happening. I bought this house a couple of years ago... I had a big house and I sold that and downsized. Chris died and Gemma, his girlfriend, decided that she didn't want to keep living in that house at Hawthorn Road. We had originally moved in there and then I eventually left him but there was a lot of my furniture in there that I had bought with Chris and I couldn't be bothered taking it. And there was this big old dresser that Chris and I had loved and it was full of his old stuff. We had bought it years ago in Levenshulme. He always said, 'You're not having that... that's mine.'

I couldn't be bothered carrying it out of the house, anyway. When she said she was moving out, she asked if I wanted anything. I said I would have that dresser. We arranged for a guy to pick it up.

"She had completely emptied it out. Cleaned it and everything. There was nothing in it at all. So the removal guys came and brought the dresser in. Put it in my new house. But I looked at it and thought, 'I can't have it here', it just brought back too many memories. It had all his cig marks on it but he always said, years before that when he died, he would do the John Lennon thing; where John said to Yoko that he would make a feather fly past her and that would prove there was something there. Anyway, I opened the draw and a brown feather flew out. I thought, 'oh my god, where did that come from?' I just got a really funny feeling.

"Loads of other things have happened. I went to the pub with a friend to a clairvoyant evening - just for a laugh. I never said a word to this woman. When she asked how I liked it, I told her I was a bit disappointed that my ex-husband hadn't made contact. She said, 'Oh he is here, he just can't get through. He is talking to your mum.' I thought, what a load of shit. At that second my phone rang and it was this guy called Stephen. He rang out of the blue and told me that he had just opened his desk drawer and found this letter that Chris had sent him telling him how you and Chris were getting back together and how you really loved each other after all that had happened. That did seem a bit freaky."

PAULA DEAN WAS LIVING in the leaf strewn suburb of Brooklands when she initially encountered Chris. They were both seventeen and Paula was taking the short daily commute to Sale where she worked in the post room in a local factory.

Intelligent, attractive, well presented and effortlessly likeable, it was no surprise, perhaps, when she gained Chris's attention. Well, he certainly made an impact on her on the day he wandered into the factory to attend an interview for a position in the same post room.

"As he walked in I burst out laughing", Paula recalls, "he was wearing knee-high red leather boots, a green suede jacket and had this unruly long, wild hair. And this was for a job interview! He had clearly made no effort whatsoever to present himself properly for the interview. However, somehow he managed to convince them to take him on. He must have used his charm to full effect."

Not that it immediately worked on Paula.

"He really wasn't my type at all, I didn't fancy him initially. Didn't think of him in that way and, anyway, we're poles apart. He was into glam-rock and all kinds of weird stuff. I was all Northern Soul, Tamla Motown. He told me later he only took the job coz he spotted me and was gonna try his luck. We worked together in the post room.

"We became great friends instantly because he made me laugh so much. I thought he was completely crazy. One lunch-time he took my bike home and when he returned he had painted the whole bike white, including chain tyres... everything! It looked extraordinary but I couldn't understand why anyone would do such a thing. He was obviously different to anyone else I had ever known. He had a determination about him and seemed to see things differently to anyone else. Of course, I was intrigued. Who wouldn't be?"

Chris was basking in a modest wave of local notoriety, partly because of his position in the ever-crumbling Bees Knees. Not that they had gained any genuine following... but just to be in a band in pre-punk Britain seemed extraordinary enough. For rock musicians were not allowed any degree of normality. They were untouchable superstars from some wild celebrity planet. This very distance would soon help to accelerate the dark local thud of pub rock and punk, both profoundly in the capital in the early years. But Chris clearly milked the local attention. He was, if only in his mind, truly on his way... somewhere! To encourage this... to encourage the notion that he was 'different' or 'special', his behaviour became increasingly outlandish.

"Later on things like that never surprised me, in fact I became used to them... I expected them. I remember him meeting me in Sale one afternoon with his face painted bright blue. I don't think I gave it a second look. It wasn't that I became blasé... I loved the eccentricities. They brought us closer."

It is not easy to wander through Sale, of all towns, with a face painted bright blue, even in the centre of the glam bubble. In many ways, especially in the twist of the mid-seventies, it was a time of rampant and uncontrollable homophobia. The garish excess of Top of the Pops, Cabaret and Clockwork Orange did not translate easily onto the stark working class streets of the north-west. As if lying in wait for the enemy of punk, a brisk Woodbines'n'bitter conservatism flooded the towns of parochial Britannia. Mindless and linked with the thuggish idiocy of right wing elements of the skinheads – and, even more absurdly, the unholy rebirth of the Teds, not to mention the outsider twisting of Northern Soul... all in all, armies of people lay in wait to attack anything that railed against their version of the norm. This was a serious matter in 1976. Shallow aspects of fashion were seen as a serious threat and, seen as some kind of insult to our supposedly glorious nation. This conservative slap against any form of subversion would soon ironically fuel the fires of punk. Before that, one would become a viable target simply by wearing straight leg jeans, let alone walking along heady Washway Road with a face painted blue. Either Chris didn't recognise this very real threat or his outsider artist mindset, embryonic as it was, allowed him to take such risks.

Paula remains unsure: "It is a good question and I don't think I recognised that at the time... that Chris would be making himself a target. Sale could be a bit rough. I think I was just too swept along with it all to notice.

"I do remember the day I realised I had fallen for him," she continued. "We were walking down by the canal and he pushed me in. Completely, just shoved me in, ruining all my clothes. I was mad as hell but walking home, drenched to the bone, shivering...I thought 'I can't live without this stupid man'. So I became as stupid as him and we were soon inseparable. It was a madness shared. Anything seemed possible. He brought me out of my shell, really. It was very liberating."

It was as their relationship gathered momentum that, to simultaneous effect, his hold on Bees Knees started to fade. Local notoriety was clearly overrated. There was the usual tumble of consternation as rehearsals were missed and Chris, clearly, had started to revise his chosen route to stardom. As stated, the band, a fluctuating beast at the best of times, were simply no longer connecting.

"Bees Knees were on the way out when we met, to be honest. I think he tried to use them to impress me and it probably did. But his enthusiasm for it was on the wane. Soon he stopped playing with the band and started to play talent shows for a while. Terrible places like bad pubs and working men's clubs. He drafted me in... it was part of his focus on me. I started to play keyboards but, in truth, I was worse than Linda McCartney. I think he might have liked that comparison."

As ever with Chris, things remained complicated. "On our lunch hour, one Monday after seeing each other for about six weeks (in secret, because he had a girlfriend at the time living in his mum's house), we went and got married at Sale Town Hall. Nobody knew and we walked back in to work with a bottle of Martini and Chris had a cigar. Nobody believed us. We had to get two strangers off the street to be our witnesses."

The shocking sentence there lies in brackets. Chris had a girlfriend living in his mum's house. Not for the last time in this story, a life changing moment appears in almost run-of-the-mill fashion. Chris, perhaps, not sensing the true gravity of his actions.

Paula agrees... "It seems crazy in retrospect. But we were on this rollercoaster. It just wasn't going to stop."

The newlyweds decamped for the harsh realities of Manchester's funky and downbeat Moss Side for a while, living with Chris's brother. The domestic bliss of this slightly cramped situation crumbling when Chris and Paula chose to cook themselves a hot-dog tea within a seriously 'veggie' kitchen.

"We then moved in with my mum for a while and Chris brought loads of recording stuff into the house. He had it all in the bedroom. But my dad was dead tight and used to creep in and unplug everything. Chris would be there, with headphones on and it would all go quiet."

They also lived for a short while in the more Bohemian climes of Chorlton-cum-Hardy before settling at their flat on Brooklands roundabout... "Yes, our first real family home was at the flat at the roundabout in Timperley, where you came and we had two kids there, Asher and Stirling. They were happy times and it was a very happy place. Everything felt right... I think you picked up on that. We suddenly became a perfect little family. It didn't seem so absurd and we fell into a reasonable state of normality. It wouldn't last.

"He went to art college in Northwich. I think he only did about a week but left because they wouldn't let him draw. It was all about registration. He didn't last. They wouldn't let him do art. But he was a brilliant artist. People might know him for being Frank but that was nothing compared to the other stuff he was doing. He used to amaze me because he could just draw anything straight out of his head. Before I met him I used to sit and draw for hours. I thought I was really good. Then when I met him I thought 'why am I bothering?' He was just great."

"Art was always his forte... at home or at school. He was such an obviously creative boy, he would just explode with ideas and was always into something. I don't know why he didn't do well at school, really. I can't understand why the school didn't recognise such obvious talents. In fairness, he always seemed to have other things on his mind. He always had a plan. So I guess he never fitted in with the curriculum average. He was ok at football. He would enjoy that. Not one of the main footballers at school, but pretty good."

PAUL MOLYNEUX

MICK MIDDLES

DARKEST LINCOLNSHIRE, 1993
NOT MABLETHORPE BUT OF THAT ILK...

REGIMENTED LINES OF CARAVANS... standing like perfect teeth, lining the coast-line and extending deep into the sandy green dunes. A whiff of the fifties. Fading pastel signs carry the promise of ice creams, racks of plastic windmills, beach balls, yellowing paperbacks. The aroma of frying chips hang in the air. Big beery men in singlets... flags of St George, wafts of blue smoke. The shrill of so many children, circulating parents stretched on beach towels. It was in a gargantuan bar, amid this ancient holiday haven, that a bristle-chinned Chris Sievey sat within a circle that included two local party entertainers with, I sensed, comic ambitions of a stand-up nature. This would be proven, deeper into the evening, although I would estimate their chances of success dubious, to say the least. Holidaying thirty-somethings surrounded them, unaware - I think - that they would be providing the 'entertainment' that particular evening.

Chris seemed unusually chipper, talking about the lost career of Stoke-on-Trent comedian Ted Chippington. It had been Chippington's brand of non-comedy... the complete and stubborn refusal to deliver anything resembling a punch line or observe the rules of comic timing, that had made him such a hit, at least within circles of student inebriation, in the mid to late eighties. There he would be safe. Especially when supporting The Membranes or The Three Johns. Those – at Manchester's Boardwalk perhaps? – were the places on one side of the divide. When the joke had been accepted and grasped. Other gigs, in less youthful and Bohemian areas, would prove bombastic. Chris, it transpired, adored Chippington. Not so much the comfy championing of studenthood, but the anarchic 'other' side, close to an area where the Chris Sievey and Mark Radcliffe double act, Billy and Barry Belly, would dare to tread. But Chippington had made his lowly mark, before suddenly disappearing. He would return, albeit briefly, twenty years later. Chris admired this trick of disappearance and, again on this afternoon of solid inebriation, he professed the need to make Frank suddenly disappear but Frank was rather different than Ted. Frank had a silent but obsessive fan base to consider. Ted, on the other hand, would be little more than a warming memory. A smile. A lovely flash of intelligence and courage. Chris knew that Frank had edged deeper into the collective psyche of his fans. And in the true sense of the word, they remained 'fans'.

Yet Frank would leave. He would go and subsequently release Chris into some kind of freedom. Release the hidden artist. Whether Chris still craved fame or not at this point, I am really not sure. He had certainly been 'burned' by living with Frank. I know he desperately craved artistic freedom. I also believe he craved normality.

That night, in the east of England, he was jeered offstage. I don't think he cared, remotely. I am not sure he cared about Frank at this stage. I think he enjoyed the frisson.

"I interviewed him at The Reading Festival for a listings magazine around 1993. I asked who I would be interviewing, Frank or Chris. But when I got to his allotted caravan, Frank opened the door and answered as Frank... funny, crazy answers which I played along with. He then got out Little Frank and started to have an argument with him. This became quite violent. I sat there – the sole audience – watching a man in a papier-mâché head arguing with a doll. He got out of it by blaming Little Frank and getting him to apologise. It was very funny and equally unsettling for their audience of one."

DICK WITTS
PERCUSSIONIST, AUTHOR, ACADEMIC

MANCHESTER 1978

ALTHOUGH NUMEROUS LATTER-DAY texts have decreed otherwise, post-punk Manchester was not a veritable hot-bed of explosive innovative talent, all crashing and colliding as the city readied itself for its greatest musical age. In truth, the still soot-blackened city centre was often lifeless, sometimes patrolled by knots of white shirted oiks *en route* to some chrome disco, a gallon of ale and the expected aggravation on the dreaded late night bus home.

True enough, on May 19 1978, the good folks about to invent a mythical beast called Factory Records managed to commandeer the Public Service Vehicle Club, deep within the foreboding shadows of the Hulme estates and – on Friday nights at least – Manchester enjoyed a gloriously downbeat venue that played host to travelling rain-coated bands of an industrial and/or funk ilk. It was a welcome release, of course, and one of my favourite venues of all time, although it did help to create a false vision of a city on fire; a scene that could effectively compete with the vast networks of our dear capital.

Glancing through the Factory club gig list between May 1978 and its eventual closure in June 1980, it is true that many Manchester bands flickered optimistically there, although often the less fashionable would be shunted to the comparative ghostliness of the more unfashionable Thursday nights. Nevertheless, if only for one night and in front of three punks, two Rastas and a fanzine editor from Nottingham, they had technically played The Factory… they could be said to have played a small part in some kind of scene.

But beyond The Factory Club and its fading cousin, Rafters – later to be re-invented as the incongruous Jilly's Rockworld, the Mancunian gig scene was sparse and scattered wide and far. One could grasp this by scanning the gig-listings in the earnest fortnightly 'what's on' guide, *New*

Manchester Review which, in and among much political mischief-making, provided a much-needed platform for bands attempting to shake off the banner 'local'. These gig listings may have included the classic nights at The Factory Club, Rafters and the crumbling Mayflower in Gorton… they were indeed there. But they also told of a different Manchester. A different, disparate desert of a place with pubs and parochial clubs scattered far and wide, from Rochdale taprooms to vast brick super-pubs in Swinton, from backrooms in Warrington to blue-lit discos in Hazel Grove. Nobody could really call it a 'circuit' for there was little to bond these venues or, indeed, the bands that performed in them, together.

Ah yes… the loose outsider bands of post-punk Manchester. Some had been thrashing ineffectively since the golden years of Merseybeat and the mid-sixties, latterly taking to the wearing of thin leather ties and skinny jeans in a rather desperate effort to gain a foothold in the power-pop shading of post-punk. While none of these bands would surface in Simon Reynold's mighty post-punk bible, 'Rip It Up and Start Again', published in 2005, many of them added a fringe frisson to the disparate circuit. The aforementioned 'What's On' guide would repeatedly throw up intriguing names – Bicycle Thieves, Giro, Salford Jets, Gamma, Distractions, Spherical Objects, Private Sector, Two Tone Punks, IQ Zero and, perhaps most intriguing of all, The Freshies.

For myself, this aloof little circuit held an existential charm. It was also, in the eyes of a provincial music writer working the sticks for national magazine, *Sounds*, a circuit that offered boundless possibilities. For nobody else, not in *Sounds*, *NME*, *Melody Maker* or *Record Mirror* would ever be so game as to plough this lost furrow, giving unexpected instant credibility to this lost generation. Nobody, for example, would expect to gain national press attention by performing on a damp Tuesday evening at a pub called The Boundary, vaguely in the vicinity of Oldham.

Nevertheless, this is exactly what happened. After spotting the name 'Freshies', several times in the *New Manchester Review*, I decided to travel blindly – and alone, for who would go with me? – in my decaying Ford Escort, from my home in Disley to the dank blankness of outer Oldham, pausing only to breath nervously as The Boundary slipped with intimidating intent, fully into view. Courageously, I felt, I pulled into the car park and wandered towards a deadening rectangular watering hole. Once inside, it was essential to melt instantly into the background. Not an easy feat when one was wearing a yellow leather biker's jacket and red corduroy trousers. A garb that seemed all the more ostentatious considering the average age of the audience (slouched around the semi-circle of tables that fronted a tiny stage) seemed to be pushing sixty. And on that stage, a modest array of performance equipment all of which had been mysteriously painted pink.

I realised that, within the confines of a *Sounds* live review, I would probably have to dress this up a little. The scattering before me didn't exactly spit the kind of urgency required in post-punk England. To be honest, it was the kind of audience who might harbour the Dire Straits or Sad Café album in the rack that sat next to their living room Dansette. I was more into The Pop Group and Throbbing Gristle and frankly, to my somewhat closed sensibility, I really didn't think this was going to work.

On the stroke of 10 pm the unlikely assemblage of normality who had governed the corner of the bar decided to wander onstage and announce their arrival. Four lads of disarmingly agreeable disposition grasped their guitars. One of them, dark haired, good looking to the point of smiley, took control of introductory duties. They weren't quite of the challenging quality one had been enjoying in Fall shows.

"Hello we are The Fall and we are standing in front of typical student idiocy…"

No. By contrast, this was conciliatory in the extreme.

"Good evening. Thanks for coming along tonight. We are called The Freshies and we really hope you like us."

Huh? What was this?

The band fell amiably into a set that quietly defied the newly formed conventions of the day. It threw me, for a while. These were not standard pop songs. They did not relate to anything that bounced around the Top of the Pops studio wearing thin leather ties and tight white jeans. Not since I had stumbled upon XTC – who had topped a bill featuring Manchester's Drones at the London Roxy – had I witnessed something so startlingly unique. These songs fell into no noticeable camps.

Intriguingly – and all the more so in hindsight – a curious innocence flowed from the stage. Slightly warped love songs – "I must be dreaming of ballrooms and moon," sang the singer, before an audience who barely even attempted to look at the stage.

What is this? A *love* song?

Another song... 'Two of the Same Girl' flicked by with unassuming ease. I understood the crowd's confusion, if not their downright apathy, for it was difficult to pigeonhole. The melodies a mite obvious – crafted, one sensed, and correctly, by a devotee of all matters Beatle – well, I would have incorrectly guessed it to flow from the McCartney side of the spectrum although the creator of these strange songs, Chris Sievey, was more inclined to Lennonisms – and, to some extent, listening to The Freshies was a pre-punk experience.

But there was something else. A charm? An innocence? It was something so distanced, so dislodged, so aloof, so stubbornly alone it seemed mildly subversive. I tried and tried but couldn't quite place it. The songs held a curious allure. A warmth. But they also lacked the edge of the era and seemed curiously sexless. They exuded an innocence not heard since days of pre-rock'n'roll dreaming. This itself carried a faint sense of magic.

I tried to gauge the 'look'. The distinct lack of image. They could have been plumbers and, despite the singer's film-star looks – and none of the band were exactly grisly – the band seemed locked in some desire to melt into something one might equate with a particularly precocious thirteen year-old.

As the set stumbled to a close, the singer smiled and offered the words, "Thank you... you have been so kind" without, I swear, a trace of irony.

As they shuffled their pink amps off the stage, I approached them with a tentative air. I needn't have worried. They seemed delighted that I had attended, although somewhat dubious whether such a low-key affair could possible furnish a review in a national music paper. The question that lurked in the back of my mind – just what *is* it that is different here? – was not answered as I shared a post-gig pint with them, allowing myself to wallow in their rather affecting camaraderie.

The singer, the one they called Chris, seemed particularly amiable

Chris and Paul Molyneux in 70s Isle of Man.

Chris taking in the sun at Sale Water Park in 1976...

...as moody mid-70s T-Rex fan...

...and relaxing in bed.

Chris and Paula make a fashion statement - as tramps.

The Bees Knees

The Bees Knees finest moment.

The Early Recordings 1975

Chris and Paula in photobooth gurnfest.

act between Razz
...ds and Rabid signed
...ris Sievey, Tosh
...and witnessed
...wrence Beedle of
.../Absurd Records.

Original Razz label work by Chris Sievey from 'Banana Island'.

...rtefacts courtesy of ...s Hewitt Music Archive

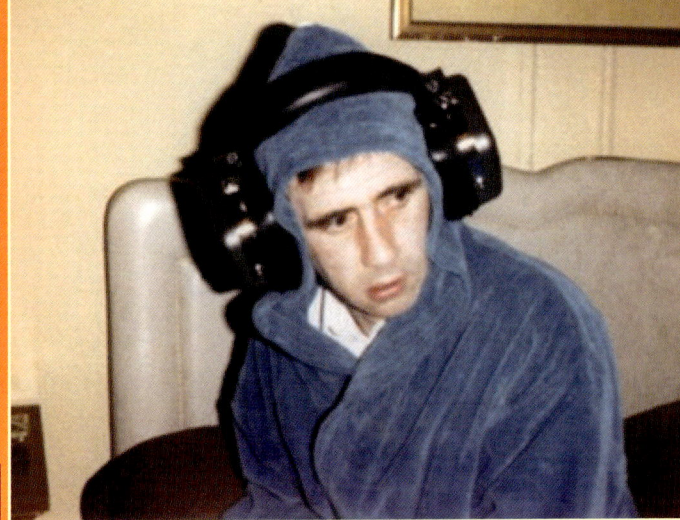

Tosh Ryan modelling state of the art aural wear; A selection of The Freshies output; Phil Jones' Carnival Poster - alas neither Hawkwind nor Ronnie Laine appeared on the day.

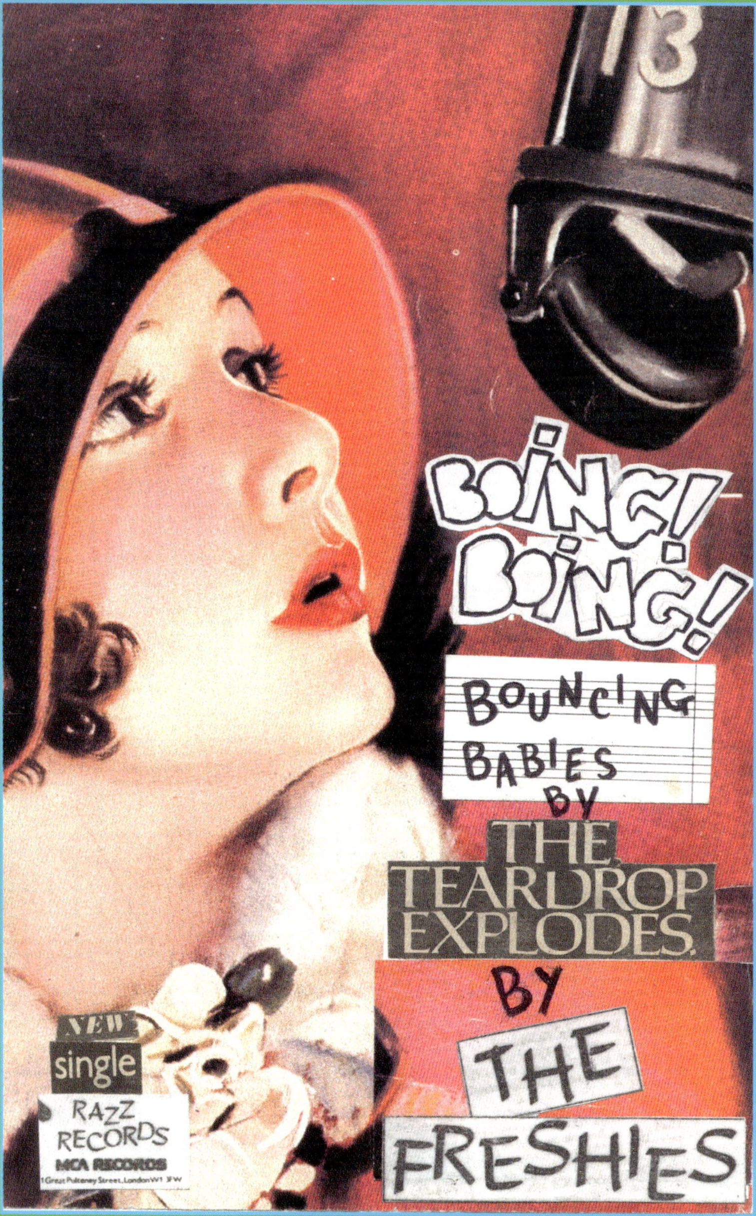

Original Chris Sievey artwork for a 'Bouncing Babies' promotional poster.

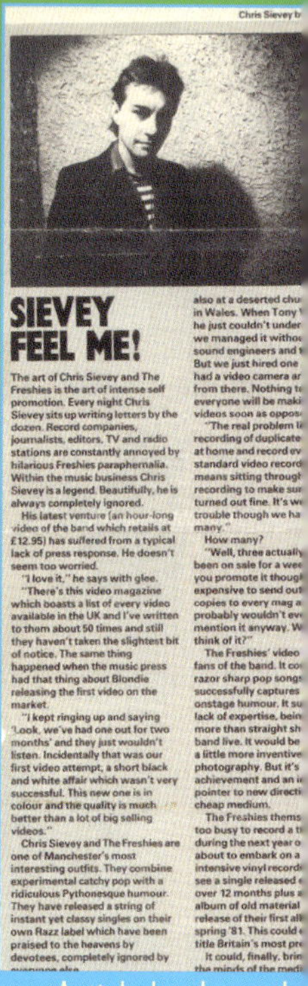

Cour[tesy]
Chris Hewitt Music A[rchive]

Article by the auth[or]
for 'The Face' in 19[__]

The author and his wife recreating the original Freshies photo shoot on the ramp at Sale Tesco's car[park]
Both pics by Martin O'Neill

A selection of Freshies reviews from a Chris Sievey designed promo sheet

Record Mirror's staff top singles of '78?

1. FOLLOW ME, Amanda Lear — Ariola
2. HANGING ON THE TELEPHONE, Blondie — Chrysalis
3. NEVER LET HER SLIP AWAY, Andrew Gold — Asylum
4. I LIKE TO BE CLEAN, Mumps — Bomp
5. ARIEL, Dean Friedman — Lifesong
6. TWO OF THE SAME GIRL, Chris Sievey and the Freshies — CV
7. EVER FALLEN IN LOVE, Buzzcocks — United Artists
8. SURRENDER, Cheap Trick — Epic
9. MILLION DOLLAR HERO, Radiators — Chiswick
10. MR BLUE SKY, ELO — Jet

JAMES PARADE

FRESHIES: 'All Sleeps Secrets' (RAZZ CS

DIFFICULT to know to say once you find word that you like, a more difficult when its simplest, st form — recorded inadequate four-tape - machine for

It may be good for your average of - the - mill punk — or any old new k hippie co-op from effield way but it in't good enough for reshies.

is Sievey is the man and in front of the les. He is one of the op and shakey pop-osers of the eighties. Nickel Lowdean, not Frog, only he is the Gilbert McCartney. He has more melody index finger than the human mekal gang he Freshies first n is in cassette form use it was cheaper nem to make it that That, in itself is tunate because all special effects and action techniques ssary to give these with everything extra something possible with a four - track rder (unless you en to be George in). Mr Sievey has very well though. is an album of rious lullabies. Put it seconds before an day into the land of and those infectious tunes will keep you for the duration.

re are two hit singles The No 1 sound is minute epic 'Two Of Same Girl' (this 's melody?), and the sound is 'Baiser' ich is to be re-recorded nk God) and will be as a single from Man-ter's own Rabid rds very soon. Other lassables are the shetish 'Ballrooms Moon' and that ty little popsicle ly Bars'.

only one pound and pence from Razz Records, 3 Moorside e, Oakleigh Court, sport Road, Tim-s, Cheshire. (Thanks having such a short ess, Freshies.) + + + + ES PARADE

THE FRESHIES: Straight In At Number 2 (Razz)

To redress the balance a little — The Freshies bound through in a most welcome way. They sound alert and alive and deserving of some higher form of indulgence. However, the pressing here for review jumps all over the shop in spite of the collection of world coinage I've assembled on the stylus. Anyway, from Manchester, the Freshies join the Zips on the ever-growing list of talent in need of some megabuck made-it to pump moolah into the tune of three quarters of a million pounds. (Ah, Moriarty, they don't write tunes like that anymore . . .)

CHRIS SIEVEY AND THE FRESHIES will support John Cooper Clarke on tour which begins this week.

RAZZ EP 1 "CHRIS SIEVEY-THE FRESHIES" SOLD OUT
RAZZ EP 2 "STRAIGHT IN AT NUMBER 2" 80p / £1 PH
RAZZ EP 3 "PET UNTITLED" — OUT SEPT/OCTOBER 79
RAZZ CS 1 "ALL SLEEPS SECRETS" £1.50 (CASSETTE)
RAZZ CS 2 "MANCHESTER PLAYS" £2.00 (CASSETTE)
RAZZ CS 3 — OUT OCTOBER 79

THE FRESHIES, Bowdon Social Club

IF YOU'VE the slightest bit of interest in the rock 'n' roll world, you're likely to have heard of The Freshies. If you live in Manchester it's a foregone conclusion.

Spearheaded by the irrepressible Chris Sievey, their publicity campaign over the past 18 months has verged on the legendary: afternoon roof-top gigs; missives to department stores warning about imminent take-over of the premises and Freshies TV week, a masterplan whereby the intention was for a member of the band to get on every programme going out. Mention that name at Granada Television or Piccadilly Radio and normally arrogant broadcasters flop into a quivering mass as harassed secretaries reach for the valium.

'Have you got our latest record yet?' asks Chris. 'No? Well, if you twist my arm I might just let you have the last one. Er, what I really mean is there'll be one in the post tomorrow.'

In fact The Freshies have unleashed several records on an un-suspecting public, the best being their cassette-only 'All Sleep's Secrets', on Razz Records, the independent label run from Chris's bedroom, which, like the rest of his parents' house, was painted pink while they were on holiday. Some of the band's equipment is similarly splashed and, yes, they're all nuts. Bonkers. They make Jonathan Richman look positively taciturn.

Live, The Freshies are unable to capture the same magic, but their instrumental flair and general exuberance makes for a grand night out.

They unashamably draw from a number of influences, although their overall humour and creativity set them apart as being very much in-dividuals. 'All Sleep's Secrets', for example, is about a dream sequence while elsewhere their musical patterns explore forms as disparate as the Flamin' Groovies and Hawkwind.

The Freshies open with a grotesquely tuneless parody of Holst's 'Planets' before belting through a series of 60s-style beat tunes. 'It's So Easy', 'Ballrooms And Moon' and 'Oh Girl' crank up the pace before the band drifts into the ex-perimental suite of 'Johnny Radar' / 'U-Boat' / 'Skid Room'. It climaxes with some astonishing guitar in-terplay, the figures building up to a Motors-style work-out.

In terms of rhythmic prowess The Freshies could be placed alongside modern pop - rock bands like The Skids or Un-dertones, except their sound is more substantial and their ideas more fully realised. They might not take themselves very seriously but I've a feeling that before long the dotted line brigade will.

MIKE NICHOLLS

THE FACTORY
At The Russell Club
Royce Road, Moss Side
Strange sounds, new music,
psychedelica etc
TONIGHT
THE PASSAGE
plus
THE FRESHIES
Friday night is Factory Night

Rabid have a Chris Sievey retread of 'Baiser' coupled with 'Last', which previously appeared on the Debut Freshies EP, that most of us don't want to remember. The Rabid version features The Invisible Girls, also known as Martin Hannett and the regulars

All images on this page courtesy of Chris Hewitt Music Archive

CHRIS SIEVEY AND THE FRESHIES

CHRIS SIEVEY AND THE FRESHIES, who have a new EP called 'Straight In At No 2' released by Razz Records, will be supporting John Cooper Clarke at Bradford University June 8, Middlesbrough Rock Garden 9, Liverpool Erics 15, Birmingham Barbarellas 16, Nottingham Tiffany's 18, Manchester Free Trade Hall 25.

RABID RECORDS announce that they have returned from hibernation and will be releasing singles from Chris Sievey - 'Baiser', Tim Green - 'Who Can Tell', Gordon The Moron - 'Fit For Nothing' and Jilted John - 'Mrs Pickering'

THE FRESHIES fir release their second from on their own Razz available for 80p from House, Oakleigh Co Road, Timperley, Ch

WEDNESDAY 13 SE
* The Freshies Birt

reshies "In at Number (EP) (Razz Records). The produced record here with the Razz record and labels/sleeves. That erm is still there though the world's most enter-gly ramshackel band.
Steve Forster

The multi-track from 'Oh Girl'.

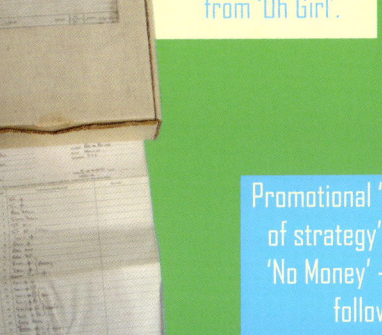

Promotional 'plan of strategy' for 'No Money' - the follow-up to 'Megastore'.

```
                              RAZZ RECORDS
                              3 MOORSIDE HOUSE
                              OAKLEIGH COURT
                              TIMPERLEY
                              WA15 6UG.
                              061 - 445 - 2661

PLAN OF STRATEGY

For THE FRESHIES forthcoming release 4th JULY.

"OH GIRL"/..."NO MONEY". Double A side single.

1000 promotional copies pressed (RAZZ 7).

To be distributed as follows:-

Date to post.   To whom.                                             No. of records.

Mon, 9th June.   John Peel: Select national Fanzines                      27
Tes, 10th June.  Rock DJs on IBA Local stations.                          25
Wed, 11th June.  Rock DJs on local BBC radio stations.                    13
Thu, 12th June.  Select Producers of independant TV shows.                 6
Fri, 13th June.  Rock DJs on Pirate Irish radio stations.                 15
Mon, 16th June.  Phil Sayer!                                               1
Tue, 17th June.  Select oversea's DJs and press/fanzines.                 18
Wed, 18th June.  Review copies for Music Week, Record Biz.                 4
Thu, 19th June.  Review copies for local Fanzines                         19
Fri, 20th June.  Review copies for NME MM BM Sounds MO plus staff         43
Sat, 21st June.  Copies to major label A & R depts                        12
Sun, 22nd June.  Copies to directors of major record companies.           24
Mon, 23rd June.  Copies to all Piccadilly radio DJs.                      11
Tue, 24th June.  London gig venue's DJ copies.                            15
Wed, 25th June.  Northern newspapers with bios, photo's etc.              18
                 Select DJs at venues around the UK                       48
Fri, 27th June.  Copies (without centre's) for local juke box's           15
Sat, 28th June.  Copies (without centre's) for national juke box's        36
Sun, 29th June.  Programme controlers on Independant Irish radios         15
Mon, 30th June.  Heads of BBC radio, plus daytime Irish radio stations    39
Tue, 1st July.   Programme controlers on all IBA radio stations           41
Wed, 2nd July.   ALL IBA DJs, Radio 1 producers, Local BBC directors.    322
Thu, 3rd July.   ALL Radio DJs                                            15
Fri, 4th July.   (RELEASE DATE) "Oh Girl" comences week on Tip Sheet       1
Sat, 5th July.   Producers/Directors BBC/ITV Pop, music shows etc         47
Sun, 6th July.   Odd Radio 2 DJs. 25 copies to ATV Music                  30
Mon, 7th July.   All local BBC radio libraries (2 copies each)            46
Tue, 8th July.   Daily papers, odd music publishers                       13
Wed, 9th July.   Heads of BBC radio's 1 2 3 & 4, & libraries              24
Thu, 10th July.  All IBA Radio libraries (3 each)                         69
Fri, 11th July.  "NO MONEY" on Tip Sheet for following week                1
Sat, 12th July.  Copies to record distributors.                           18
                                                          Total          937

Remaining copies to be used for any forgotten.
```

Chris announces new direction in a fanzine from his new label 'Random Records'

RANDOM RECORDS PRESENT
A WORLD FIRST FROM CHRIS SIEVEY

FROM THE MAN WHO BROUGHT YOU SUCH CLASSICS AS "I CAN'T GET BOUNCING BABIES" AND "I'M IN LOVE WITH THE GIRL ON THE MANCHESTER VIRGIN MEGASTORE CHECK-OUT DESK";.....FROM THE SAME MAN WHO PIONEERED THE INDIE BOOM IN 1976;....THE SAME MAN WHO PUT OUT THE FIRST PURPOSE MADE POP VIDEO AHEAD OF 'EAT TO THE BEAT".THE VERY SAME MAN WHO MADE INDIE-AUDIO CASSETTES ACCEPTABLE AS FAR BACK AS 1974;.....THE VERY SAME WHO WENT ON TO PUBLICLY DISPLAY 3DTV FOR THE FIRST TIME IN THE UK;.....CHRIS SIEVEY DOES IT AGAIN..!

THE WORLD'S 1ST COMPUTER POP PROMO

FOR HIDDEN IN THE GROOVE'S OF CHRIS SIEVEY'S NEW SINGLE "CAMOUFLAGE" IS A COMPUTER PROGRAM, WHICH WHEN LOADED INTO YOUR ZX81 HOME COMPUTER WIL[L]... 'CAMOUFLAGE' ALONG WITH [...] THE 'B' SIDE ALSO CONTAIN[S...] WRITTEN BY CHRIS SIEVEY, [...] YOU 2 VARIATIONS OF AN [...] CALLED "FLYING TRAIN" [...] THE IDEAL GAME FOR THOSE WHO ARE [...] BE AN ENGINE DRIVER OR AN ASTR[O...] THE SINGLE COMES IN A PICTURE S[...] USUAL SINGLE PRICE... ON "RA[...]

THIS SINGLE WILL RUN AND RUN......

FLYING TRAIN
BY CHRIS SIEVEY
RANDOM RECORDS

```
"THE BIZ" STATUS IN WEEK 2 1999
ARTIST         = the recital
FROM A SUBURB IN LONDON
RECORD LABEL   =
CURRENT SINGLE =
MUSICAL DIRECTION = ROCK'N'ROLL
RECORDS IN STOCK  = 0
THIS WEEKS SALES  = 0
TOTAL SALES.....  = 0
WEEKS IN CHART..  = 0       *MANAGER
HIGHEST POSITION  = 0       @£24&11?

BAND TIGHTNESS  =  1 %
STAGE PRESENCE  =  2 %
VISUAL IMPACT   =  0 %
SONG QUALITY    =  3 %
FAN FOLLOWING   =  0 %
DRIVE/AMBITION  = 82 %
OVERALL 'STAR' RATING = 5 %
WEEKLY TAKING'S  = £  123
MONEY IN THE BANK = £ 2123
PRESS 'X' TO CONTINUE 'THE BIZ
```

Chris became a master of the Sinclair ZX Spectrum in all its incarnations during the early 80s. In 'The Biz' users could become fully fledged record company moguls.

FRESHIES VIDEO RUINED

ON SUNDAY 19TH DECEMBER 1982, THE GALLERY CLUB IN M/CR WAS OPENED ESPECIALLY TO RECORD THE FRESHIES LIVE IN CONCERT FOR THE FINALE OF THEIR LAST VIDEO RELEASE BEFORE CHRIS WENT SOLO. ALL WAS GOING WELL UNTIL AN OVER ZELOUS FAN NAMED FRANK ARRIVED AND BROKE ONE OF THE CAMERAS. UNFORTUNATLEY THIS RUINED THE LAST FEW MINUTES OF WHAT OTHERWISE IS A GREAT ONE HOUR EPITHET TO THE FRESHIES. THE VIDEO WILL STILL BE RELEASED BY RAZZ AT A SPECIAL NEW LOW PRICE OF £9.99p, UNDER THE TITLE OF "CHRIS SIEVEY AND THE FRESHIES — BEING FRANK". AVAILABLE ON VHS OR BETA, IT INCLUDE 'CHRIS AND BARBARA' SINGING "SEAT-BELTS", THE UNSEEN "BOUNCING BABIES" VIDEO PLUS THE FRESHIES BEING INTERVIEWED, THE LINE UP FOR THE LIVE SECTION IS AS FOLLOWS........ CHRIS SIEVEY-GUITAR; BARRY SPENCER-GUITAR; RICK SARKO-BASS; PETE JAMES-DRUMS; PLUS A GUEST APPERRENCE BY THE LOVELY YVONNE ON KEYBOARDS. THERE IS ALSO SOME MORE 3DTV FROM CHRIS PLUS A SHORT ZX81 PROGRAM (ANOTHER FIRST!) AND ALL FOR LESS THAN THE PRICE OF A NEW FORD CAPRI. (SEE RAZZ MAIL ORDER FOR DETAILS.)

All images on this page courtesy of Chris Hewitt Music Archive

The first mention of a Freshies 'superfan' known only as 'Frank'

A never before seen 1982 Frank outing with 'Roger the boy next door' played by Chris's son Stirling aged 8.

Courtesy of Karen Middlehurst

A publicity shot from Piccadilly Radio, 1985. Frank with friends including Bob Dickinson, Caroline Auty and Kevin Cummins - for Tony Michaelides' 'Last Radio Show'.

Frank's page in Oink inspired by 'Frank's firm page' in Muze magazine

Frank became a success on the burgeoning Manchester music scene of the 1980s, helped by regular appearances in Oink!, a magazine edited by Patrick Gallagher (below), who would later become house roommate to Chris S...

and genuinely intrigued to discover the reason I had ventured out on such a wild night to watch such an unknown quantity. He held about him a gentle, enquiring air and an ability to put the other person perfectly at ease. I felt that I could talk with him for hours and felt faintly aggrieved when the drummer – Bob Dixon, I believe – pulled him from the heart of the conversation. For once, it felt as if I had been the interviewee. After inviting me to see the band at work in an Altrincham studio, he politely offered an apologetic shrug before shuffling backstage.

'That was different,' I mused, 'to meeting Gus Gangrene'. How strange they seemed, in their blanket normality.

How strange.

As I drove home, winding through yellow-lit murk towards Disley, I still felt affected by… something. The feeling reminded me of that unearthly state one gains after seeing a particularly evocative film and, while walking away from the cinema through some godforsaken northern town, still feeling lost in some cinematic unreality. So it was with The Freshies.

I wasn't sure where the band were going but I did start to wonder how they had arrived at this lonely point.

THE FRESHIES - OLDHAM

> "...they took to the stage looking perversely ordinary and to little applause. I was preparing myself for a dreary evening before suddenly noticing the unlikely melodic strength of the opening number. It bore faint resemblance to the heavier side of Wings ('Rock Show', 'Medicine Jar') but with greater element of experimental endeavour... as well as 'Ballrooms and Moon', which attained classic status within my mind after twenty seconds, other stand out songs were 'Last' and 'Oh Girl', both songs stacked high with intrigue...and intrigued I duly was..."
>
> MICK MIDDLES, *Sounds*

If my feeble and immature journalese might seem somewhat forced, I soon discovered back-up in the form of an even more over-the-top appraisal in the German magazine, *Gorilla Beat*.

> "At last, here they are. THE NEW BEATLES. Consider them simply indescribable. They have got the humour of The Bonzo Dogs, the song-writing ability of The Beatles plus the style of themselves."

'Blimey', as the hero of the latter half of this book might have noted. I hadn't realised they were *that good*.

MICK MIDDLES

FAB CAFÉ 1997

VISITING MANCHESTER'S FAB CAFÉ is rather like scurrying around the inside of Frank's head. Everywhere, a hint of sixties juvenilia. A Thunderbird model here, a Dalek there, a Tardis by the pinball machine. Screens displaying images of Anderson, of the Man From Uncle, of James Bond and The Saint. The vivid aromatic allure of frying fish fingers. It was a fun time for middle-aged imbibers, weary of the flash of discos or, indeed, the discomforts of traditional gig going. You couldn't go wrong here. Take a new girlfriend and use the multitudinous telly props to encourage entertaining banter.

Frank had performed on several occasions. Happier than a pig in shit. A perfect fit. This night would be rather different. Enticed down to the venue by the effervescent John Barratt, who had coaxed Frank though the video for an edgy danceable outpouring based on 'The Sweeney' from the Pete Waterman stable, Chris made a bar-side deal. He would agree to be introduced to the crowd as 'the man who is Frank Sidebottom'. The payment for this was simple – a freebie bar tab. And it was a tab of seemingly bottomless proportions. A tab hit hard and heavy. Chris wasn't happy that night. He held an air of dissolve, of collapse even. I had never seen him looking so bereft of ideas and excitable banter. He shrugged and walked greyly into the spotlight after his introduction.

"Thanks," he muttered to sporadic applause, before walking straight back to the bar.

"Glad I am not performing tonight," he muttered, staring into the ether. I believed him and thought it wrong to pass judgement. He was seeking some kind of oblivion. He deserved to find it, I thought. I secretly hoped it was nothing more than the exhaustion of performance, of carrying two people into too many gigs.

"Why not have a holiday?" I offered. He smiled, as if the thought had never crossed his mind.

STEVE FORSTER

In his dual capacity as writer for New Manchester Review *and sound engineer at the city's leading small venue, Band on the Wall, Steve Forster was often viewed as first port of call for aspiring young bands. Especially so as Forster often presided over the Manchester Musicians Collective gatherings on Monday evenings. Few people can lay claim to providing a more solid grassroots base during the post-punk period. The Freshies were clearly aware of this and wasted no time in approaching him. Forster would later work as agent, PR and manager, at one point helping to guide The Distractions smoothly through their transition from Factory to Island. In later years, while living in London, he became particularly close to Chris Sievey, sharing many musical and, apparently, footballing adventures. When I caught up with Forster, in Summer 2013, he was living in Norwich and working solidly as a theatrical PR. In particular, he was gearing up for that year's Edinburgh Festival. He seemed particularly saddened to note that Frank Sidebottom had never had a serious 'crack' at that all important annual event.*

Steve Forster: "In 1978, the *New Manchester Review* was just about the only outlet for new local bands in the Manchester area. Well, the only one that was easily accessible. I know Morley and you and Ian Wood were writing for the nationals, but we were in reach. This could be a problem as we became flooded with demo tapes from bands who sounded very interesting. Then, more often than not you would listen and go …hmm, maybe not. But we were always a helpful platform.

"The Freshies actually sent me a demo cassette that was wrapped in a £10 note. That was a hell of a lot of money in those days. There was a scribbled note from Chris Sievey pleading with me to give it a listen. But I didn't feel comfortable about that at all and duly sent the money back. I can't remember what was on that first demo but another one arrived a few days later wrapped in Monopoly money. That was more like it. I could tell they had a sense of humour… itself a rare thing in Manchester in 1978."

Three days after the *Sounds* review appeared, a package arrived at the front door of the house I shared with my parents. The package was to provide a further hint that something rather unusual was happening within the dynamic of The Freshies. It was a simple square box, though rather large, I felt. Across the front, my address glowed with childlike multi-coloured writing. I had no idea who had sent this or what treasures lay within. Impatiently I ripped the brown tape from the package, roughly yanking the cardboard leaves apart. To my amazement and, to parental dismay that would echo down the years, thousand of tiny polystyrene balls exploded into the air, eventually settling far and wide across the newly refurbished living room. (The packaging balls would still be surfacing in nooks and crannies of that room five years later). I don't know if I found this trick amusing or not, although I did admire the sheer audacity of it. Whoever sent this was capable of carrying a joke way beyond the limits of accepted normality. Deep within the giant box, a cassette tape was discovered. It was a self-release from the singer with that band… The Freshies. A self-produced and, obviously, bizarrely promoted EP entitled 'All Sleep's Secrets' by the one named Chris Sievey. My parents might not have been impressed but I sensed that I had chanced upon a most affecting, unique and special kind of madness.

WYTHENSHAWE

It can be argued that The Freshies are as grounded in neighbouring Wythenshawe – gargantuan overspill estate - as much as in Altrincham, which can be seen as its antithesis. Needless to say, Wythenshawe's music legacy seems vast and extends to sixties beat bands through punk to this very day. (Toggery Five, Sad Café's Paul Young, Durutti Column's Vini Reilly, Ed Banger, Slaughter and the Dogs and The Cult's Billy Duffy seem particularly relevant here).

From The Freshies point of view it might be noted that guitarist Barry Spencer hailed from the Baguley area of Wythenshawe and the estate also saw Freshies bassist Rick Sarko growing up there before relocating to Sale in 1977. The connection between the estate and The Freshies continues as Billy Duffy briefly flitted in and out of Sievey's charges.

Prior to joining The Freshies, Sarko was working with Muffet on, in Sarko's words, 'heavy music', which was unusual if not unique in post-punk Manchester. Leaving this liaison to join The Freshies 'around the same time as Mike Doherty it has been noted (by Barry Spencer and Mike Doherty) that Sarko's musicality was more embryonic than the rest of the band although he improved steadily through their career, surfacing later as a member of Frank's 'Oh Blimey Big Band'.

Rick Sarko: "My first impressions of Chris were that he spoke nicely, was charismatic with a great sense of humour and very easy going. Yeah, we seemed to get it together very quickly and I felt quite at home within the band dynamic. I certainly stayed for about three years solid and then played with the band for odd gigs afterwards."

Guitarist Barry Spencer seemed to perfectly embody the spirit and verve of this young band. Amiable, likeable, endlessly talkative, thoughtful and talented, he seemed capable of taking Chris's basic songs and stretching them to a whole new level. Not merely filling with handy guitar solos, his work helped add light and shade to Chris's stark melodies.

Incredible as it seemed, a 35-year gap bridges the days when I would swig pints with The Freshies and re-meeting them during the research for this book. This time around, we hooked up within the rather brash juvenilia of a canalside pub in Sale. It seemed odd too that Barry, Rick and myself had seemingly gravitated to this unassuming town. The years melted, however, as I joined them at the bar before drifting to an outside table. Nothing, it seemed, had changed. Barry; still boyish, precocious, pleasantly cheeky. Rick; slightly quieter, though equally willing to help - thoughtful and full of intriguing memories. They hadn't changed at all. Still a gang. Still a band.

MICK MIDDLES

Barry, a successful salesman – though without the smugness that often arrives with that package – was a noted local actor. Rick, more obviously Bohemian, musicianly and faintly camp. Both had served time, not just with The Freshies but with the hyper-eccentric Ed Bangor. During the lead in to this book, we met Barry and Rick several times. Even asking them around to our house for an evening of banter and beer. As an unofficial 'double-act' they remained priceless. In fact I have never seen such an easy flow of intelligent loonery. Not in evidence at all, the usual sting of bitterness that middle aged musicians generally carry on their shoulders. There was even a curious air of innocence that reminded me directly of the heady days of The Freshies. Both admitted to 'hardly having heard of The Fall'. When I handed Rick a bundle of Sievey related material – the actual folder from Tosh Ryan's Rabid office – he started flicking through it enthusiastically – "boy, Chris sure did a lot of stuff, didn't he?"- before seemingly welling up and handing it swiftly back.

This happened a great deal during the six months where this book came together. This curious balance between an obvious continuing and deepening affection and an overwhelming sense of complete exasperation. How could somebody who had so much, who *gave* so much, fall away in such spectacular fashion? It is the delicate subject that remains at the core of this book. It remains the question that sits on the lips of, it really does seem, everyone who knew Chris Sievey. Aware of Rick's fleeting discomfort, Spencer smiled, took a swig of Polish lager and abruptly changed the subject. Within ten seconds both ex-Freshies were displaying their comedic inept attempts to chat up girls while affecting a Northern Soul dance. By the end of the evening, they fell out, sans taxi, into the night and trundled gaily into the postulating black Sale night, happy to avoid sundry drunks and wayward lunatics.

Both, however, were more than happy to embrace the renewed interest in Chris and Frank and, obviously, The Freshies. How strange that, deep into middle age, their past would reach out and add colour once more. Indeed, more interview requests – this book, the 'Being Chris Sievey' DVD and, immediately prior to meeting, a session on Stephen Doyle's radio show (on Salford City Radio) - than seem to come their way during the band's actual lifespan.

It had been Barry who joined the band first. After a long gestation period which consisted of Chris attempting to find a suitable platform to follow Bees Knees, Barry slotted firmly in place from the first trickle of gigs.

Barry Spencer: "Before I joined The Freshies, I was immersed in music. I used to go and see loads of bands in my early teens. Used to love Rory Gallagher, Clapton and Ry Cooder. Used to love Dave Gilmour's guitar work with Pink Floyd. I suppose I used to like guitarists whose solos were different – melodic and thought provoking, the goose bump effect. Learning the guitar all came very naturally to me... I was quite good after one week. I was asked to join Cliff Richard's band when doing a gig at The Victoria in London but turned them down because I heard there was a drinking and women ban on tour. True that! Chris could strum a bit and Sarko was very raw but did improve."

The search for the 'goose bump effect' indicates a love of melodic simplicity. Ironic, as I would later moan about the overt dexterity of his solos. I wondered how he had filtered into the band. Had he known Sievey since childhood?

"No, I wasn't at school with Chris. I first met him at a party at a friend's house. I have two best mates who I went to school with. One of them is the brother of Paula Sievey, hence the connection. I of course thought Chris was odd, but very funny and likeable. I also immediately thought he was a bit different... *special* in a way. Paula said in jest, 'hey, Barry's a good guitarist,.. get him in your band!' The Freshies had already been through a number of members. He said, 'Do you want to join The Freshies?' I said 'yes' and that was it! Daft really.

"The main thing about The Freshies was having a bloody good laugh. That was it. Right from the very first time I rehearsed with Chris. I knew it would be a long term thing because we just got on so well. We genuinely got on really well. I have got to say, with The Freshies, I cannot remember one ill word in the entire lifespan of the band. I can't remember anyone arguing with anyone at all...ever."

Paula Sievey: "Yes they were happy times at the flat on Brooklands Roundabout. Well, mostly. And Chris was doing gigs and kept going off for a few days at a time. I was so naïve though because girls would often ring up and ask for him. He used to tell me that it was just fans. It wasn't. There was all sorts going on. I only found out about that later. I didn't think in a million years that he was up to anything… but apparently they were up to everything. I just thought that nobody else would love him or fancy him the way I did. Because, when I met him, he was not the type of person who had many girls. He was the freakiest boy I had ever seen and I didn't fancy him at all at first. But I fell in love with him because he made me laugh so much. And was so romantic it just never ever dawned on me that he would be interested in anyone else or that anyone else would be interested in him. The way I saw it was the absolute opposite of what was happening."

TRANSFORMER

FOLLOWING ON FROM the evening at Fab Café, I didn't think that I would meet Chris again. I had been living in Warrington and, despite being just a bus ride from Altrincham, I wasn't attracted by its bistros and wine bars. I had also mislaid my precious copy of The Freshies Greatest Hits… a fact which caused me considerable irritation. Indeed, my only vague connection with Chris was the fact that I remained in contact with Tosh Ryan, although his contact with Chris had similarly faded. Nevertheless, he had always been more than happy to keep distance between him and Frank, who he still regarded as the obnoxious antithesis of the Chris that he knew and loved. One more wedge supplied by the, at one time, omnipresent Sidebottom.

It was a normal day, I sense, down among the banter and push of a heavily loaded 'features' department in a Warrington newspaper 'hub'. The usual bundle of promotional packages ripped open by journalists numbed to the lure of the freebie; CDs, DVDs and books often languishing for weeks in unloved desktop piles. A few lines of championing reviews emerging in a variety of newspapers and magazines spread thinly across the North West. I was luckier than most. Indeed, I was able to combine the local torture of a subs job in a diminishing industry with strings of national freelancing. Nothing made me happier, however, than being allowed *carte blanche* to work on acres of stylised, if often rather bland, advertising heavy magazines of the *Cheshire Life* ilk. This, at least, was a colourful distraction.

Maybe it seemed so, as it flopped down on Chris Sievey's Altrincham doormat. Perhaps it was merely a case of Chris being Chris, in the old driven and industrious manner, never one to miss out on a little promotional mischief.

Whatever his motivation, he duly created a lovely and garishly scribbled package that once past the twenty layers of packaging that included a not-altogether-welcome return to the joke of the exploding polystyrene balls. They spread all over the office much to the angst of the editor. Revealed within this was a DVD containing an animated adventure entitled 'Frank's World'. This particularly surreal and hilarious affair would see Frank deceiving Little Frank and taking a borrowed canal boat down the River Mersey, through Carrington, Partington, past Fiddlers Ferry power station and, eventually out to the Liverpool waterfront. Needless to say, the animated Frank proved every bit as anarchic as the 'real thing'. The entire mad affair tumbling into a showcase for Frank appearing as Morrissey and Freddie Mercury. (The animated film was directed by Brian Little, formerly of Hot Animation. Of which more later).

The promotional aspect obviously worked, for the DVD kept the office entertained for a week before the editor asked me to take reporter Chris Ewen along to interview and photograph Frank for a magazine feature that would flood into Cheshire's 'golden triangle' of Alderley Edge, Wilmslow and Prestbury, an honour normally afforded to footballers' wives, fading soap starlets and dubious up-and-coming female singers with scrambled yellow hair and little identifiable talent. Frank would prove a most welcome insertion into the crass world of the WAG and I didn't think that he could resist such an unlikely promotion. I was also rather stunned to find that the entire editorial team were fully aware of the antics of Frank Sidebottom despite their state of fantastic and occasionally irritating youth. As Frank had lain dormant for five years at this point, I wondered how they had even known of Frank Sidebottom. The answer lay buried in their teenage years, as they succumbed to non-terrestrial television.

The idea – a good one, I think – was to pick Chris or Frank up from his Altrincham home and take him for a walk, initially along the mystical Alderley Edge and then through the main street of the village, hopefully attracting interest from the lavish range of shops and restaurants. The notion being that Frank has moved upmarket from his days trawling the streets of Timperley. An interview between the two Chris's would then take place over lunch in Prestbury's Admiral Rodney pub.

Putting this idea to Chris, as he hovered in the shadows of his

Altrincham home, proved slightly unsettling.

"Well, it's slightly embarrassing…" he mumbled sullenly. "The problem is that you will have to buy me lunch…"

No problem Chris.

"…and two pints of Coke… not drinking, you see."

No problem Chris.

"…and 20 fags. Haven't got any money, you see….and neither has Frank unless his mum has given him some spends. But that seems unlikely given that she doesn't actually exist."

Again, it was no problem. After all, a shop window for the re-emergence of Frank or not, we were borrowing both Chris and Frank for the best part of a day.

Chris seemed unusually silent at first but then soon softened to the flow of general banter. It seemed odd to find him living in a Victorian terrace on Hawthorn Road. It was a perfectly decent house but cluttered to the point of neglect and somewhat darker than my image of him had ever suggested. While he was upstairs, changing into his Frank suit, we glanced around nervously. From a bag on the kitchen table a round shape protruded eerily. It quickly dawned on us that this was Frank's head or one of them. Small photographs – Polaroids – were scattered across the kitchen wall. Chris and Frank. Chris and a girl (Michelle Pouncey). Shaky onstage shots, a stack of CDs and DVDs and, tellingly perhaps, stack of unopened bills, some with a rather threatening appearance. I knew how it was… I'd been there, to that place where you shudder with terror at the sound of the post-box. Although Chris, I guessed, would eternally be expecting some positive return to some new scam. He smiled warmly as he returned downstairs and soon the three of us, plus one extra head – were edging through Hale Barns and out to the plush climes of the Golden Triangle.

Frank anecdotes soon flowed thick and fast. "I forgot to take Little Frank to a London gig last week and the crowd were demanding to see him. I told him that I would make one and they all screamed… 'noooo…we need the *real* Little Frank'. Even I couldn't quite get my head around that one. He is made of bloody cardboard and I make him every week. So, anyway, I quickly made a joke of it and created a new Little Frank there and then. Not a very good head but, after about ten minutes, they all started cheering and egging Little Frank on. They were taking *his* side against Frank's, even though they had just seen him being made."

It was a relaxing drive, through the Cheshire sunshine, although Chris looked puzzlingly at my car – a green Astra, hardly flash but somewhat imposing – and seemed to make a mental note... something to be passed on as ammunition for Frank later in the afternoon. It was the only time I ever noticed a tangible connection between the mind of Chris and that of Frank. It was, however, a genuine 'handing over' from one entity to the other, a baton across the divide perhaps. Other than that, the relationship between Chris and Frank always seemed tenuous. This was highlighted by Chris's instructions that we must *not* make any mention of Chris and/or The Freshies within the boundaries of the article. I thought this a shame but understood that the element of mystique needed to be maintained even though, within Manchester music circles, it was the worst kept secret of all time.

There was something else that struck me about this. Having written several rock star biographies, I have often felt a cold shiver when softening the divide that always exists between the persona of the performer and the actual personality. Mostly, if not always, the personality will robustly defend the existence of this divide. None of them seem to enjoy 'real person' features; those that glimpse behind the myth and engage in the art of demystification. This is one reason why, in times where celebrity PR far overshadows real, probing journalism, pop and rock stars often appear curiously content. It's simple, it *suits* them. The journalist, by contrast, risks unsettling the star and, therefore, probably losing that vital connection – this is the main problem with modern rock journalism... it is built from the shallow foundations of sycophancy. From the reader's point of view, this is not a healthy situation. But that's how it is.

I must say, this never really occurred with either Chris or Frank in the singular. His problem only ever occurred when the two were presented as one. Bizarrely, the same might appear to apply to the barrier between Frank and Little Frank... and maybe Little Denise, before her head went missing and the lesser spotted Amoeba Frank, although, in truth, I would find it difficult to demystify a piece of cardboard.

OUT OF HIS HEAD

Chris Ewen: "I was completely stunned when Chris put that head on and, in a flash, he was gone. It was a transformation that seemed almost violent. The person I had just interviewed had completely gone. We had to introduce ourselves again, to Frank. I just couldn't sense that Chris was there at all.

"'Ooooh is this your car? It's a posh one, isn't it? Are you in showbiz. I am but don't tell my mum...' and so on and so forth."

And at Alderley Edge, deep within the mystical trees and evocative humps of sandstone, glancing across the Cheshire plain... right there, Chris transformed completely into Frank. Chris Ewen was suitably staggered as mild mannered Chris clicked-a-switch and emerged as Frank: bombastic, naïve, arrogant, hilarious, insane, sexless and somewhat dark. *He* had arrived, bouncing around the trees, playing with imaginary rocket ships and unleashing that lovely tumble of inquisition.

The day was a success. In Alderley Village, down among the flush WAGS and sundry office workers... and after five years away from any kind of spotlight, nobody could have known if instant recognition... time after time... could be the order of the day. But that is how it was. First floor office windows were flung open. Rows of them and 'Hi Frank' bellowed from above.

"Get back to work," countered Frank, clearly relishing his return.

MICK MIDDLES

THE FRESHIES AT SALE TOWN HALL, 1979

ON HALLOWED GROUND; a gorgeous gothic building sitting squat within the aromatic debris of a Saturday night in Sale. The very building that saw Paula marry Chris in secret. Not the same room, mind, but the larger seated concert lounge, complete with all the ambient allure of a Welsh chip shop. Sale Town Hall proved a convenient home gig and offered the chance for the comparatively long term local fans and mates and family to wander from home to venue without too much discomfort caused by marauding youth.

Nevertheless, it provided an unusual twist to a Friday night. I'm fairly sure I attended with a tentative air before moving on, afterwards, to the comparative comforts of The Mayflower. Sale was, at that time, unknown territory.

Yet it provided an opportunity to study the band in a comparatively sterile atmosphere and they appeared somewhat exposed. Naturally, this served only to amplify the band's discomforting edges although, given great heart and a courageous desire to blast through that deadening ambience, they emerged at the set's conclusion with their minuscule reputation intact.

Steve Forster: "The Freshies were always active and highly creative in the art of self-promotion. There was always something going on and it was obvious that Chris had a very lively mind. Always ready with a scam. I recall 'The Freshies for TV Week', which was something that Chris had dreamed up. The idea was to try and get The Freshies on every Granada programme for one week. Of course, Chris being Chris, this was an idea that was completely doomed from the start. They turned up at Granada and set up playing on Quay Street. I seem to recall them being swiftly moved on after a few numbers. They were always trying stuff like that. There was a rooftop gig near Oxford Road Station, I think. Obviously that came out of Chris's love for all things Beatles."

Oh to be a Freshie! While the quartet of Sievey, Spencer, Sarko and drummer Mike Doherty must be regarded as the classic line-up, if we widen the circle just a little then all manner of names hove into view. One of the most notable must be the esteemed Wythenshaweian guitarist Billy Duffy famously of The Cult and most infamously of The Nosebleeds with whom he has often been linked (in rehearsal if not live). Intriguing indeed, given the fact that both Sarko and Spencer had close musical links with The Nosebleeds, both performing stints within that most loose of units, neither of them have any recollections of this at all.

As Spencer notes: "I don't think that Billy Duffy or Johnny Marr or any of the other listed guitarists who were said to be in The Freshies, ever actually got to play. I know it is true that Marr turned up at Chris' house and asked to join when he was aged 14 and Chris just felt he was too young which, of course, he would have been. That wasn't surprising because The Freshies were a fairly well-known local band at the time and Marr simply wanted to get involved. But I am pretty sure it didn't get to the rehearsal or audition stage. Certainly not when I was there and I was in the band for the majority of the band's lifespan."

The Johnny Marr issue is one of those situations that would obviously never have arisen had the man himself not attained godlike status, arguably as the last great British axe man. Sievey himself referred briefly to the incident within the pages of John Robb's 'The North Will Rise Again' where he succinctly states: "The Freshies were looking for a guitarist and this lad came to my house but we said he was too young. He was 14 and he was Johnny Marr."

As Marr was born in October 1963, this must have been late 1977, unless the lad was lying about his age. It does tie in with the time immediately prior to Spencer joining when Sievey pinned a note to the notice board at the old Virgin Records on Lever Street asking for a guitarist. The young Marr, hungry for any kind of band action, could well have seen this and immediately taken a bus through Stretford to Sale, no great distance, seeking out said address.

Had Marr played a note, he could have taken his place alongside a wild and disparate membership that falls from the edges of 'the big four'. These, at various times, would include Rick Maunder on bass,

MICK MIDDLES

Neil Tomkinson on drums, Lyn Okey on guitar, Steve Hopkins – member of Hannett's Invisible Girls crew and son of famed nostalgia novelist, Billy Hopkins – on keyboards, Barbara O'Donovan on vocals – of whom more later – Lisa Stansfield, no less, on backing vocals on 'Will You Remember' recorded at Drone Studios where she would often be found, Paula Sievey, Jane McGlennon as well as his brother Martin. One other notable might be photographer Kevin Cummins who, in the absence of Rick Maunder, photographed himself as a member of the band for a *Sounds* article in 1978. A wide array indeed, in terms of style and standard of musicality.

At times it is better for a lower grade musician to be allowed to grow with the band, adding to the camaraderie and very soul of the band. Such was the case, it seems, with Rick Sarko, who admits: "I wasn't a great musician. Chris would say, 'just play the bass and make a noise'. Listening back to some of those records, we all felt that perhaps we should have done this or we should have done that but so what? They were what they were. I learned a hell of a lot, especially playing all those small gigs. There is no hiding place there. Much better than learning at home. I became a part of the band. Years later, when I could play, I still found those the most satisfying times. That said, a lot of the earlier stuff could have better production value. And that would have helped gain a bigger audience. Maybe. There are some things that make me cringe now."

MARTIN RYAN

Martin Ryan, Editor of Manchester's Ghast Up fanzine on which both myself and Paul Morley worked, recalls another intriguing encounter with Sievey. I contest that this was actually the third time I had seen the band and this time it was a gig at the legendary Manchester post apocalyptic punk venue, The Electric Circus.

For the record, my 'second' encounter happened on September 1 1978, at the aforementioned Factory Club. On that night, The Freshies were supporting The Passage. It was an ill-fitting and rather uncomfortable coupling. The Passage, led by ex-Halle Orchestra drummer Dick Witts, were an intellectual offshoot of The Fall. Not without appeal or talent, though quite the antithesis of the circle of boyish normality that called itself The Freshies. I left feeling more confused than ever.

Martin Ryan: "I can't remember the precise date, it was late 1978, probably September, on a Saturday night. The Freshies were supporting The Trend (whom I recall Chris later describing as the Sex Pistols crossed with the Boomtown Rats) and there was about 200 people there, including Kevin Cummins. After their set we met up with Chris who bought us a drink, or rather he asked what we wanted and then said that's 10p, and he took 10p off each of us and bought us a drink from the Circus bar. He also claimed to be avoiding a record company rep who he said was trying to sign The Freshies - he was avoiding him because he didn't think the band were good enough then to have a record deal. He must have been a convincing actor, because I remember us both being impressed with his artistic stance of being unwilling to just sign a deal, although when you recounted the story to Mark E. Smith and Kay Carroll, I recall they both said, "are you sure he didn't just want you to think that?"

Intriguing. I do not recall Chris 'poncing' 10p from us, although I do recall the conversation with Mark and Kay. Mark, I seem to remember, was particularly intrigued by Sievey. At the time, I couldn't understand why. They seemed quite the antithesis of one another in terms of personality, attitude, musicality and vision. Well, at least to my naïve eyes and ears at that time. Unbeknown to me, this exact moment was the source of a curious parallel between the two artists. Mark, it may be easily noted, was easily the more successful in terms of establishing a status that, although cult-oriented, would be regarded as 'world-wide' and The Fall slowly emerged as one of the great underground bands of the past three decades, whereas The Freshies flickered and failed to reach their true potential, turning a few heads but, I would concede, never managing to establish themselves as a genuine force. It is a subject to which we shall return, deeper into the book.

The Freshies had their detractors, though. An *NME* writer dragging his considerable – and deserved – reputation around, explained to me in no uncertain terms: "That band you wrote about. The Freshies. I saw them the other night at the Band on the Wall. Terrible. Fucking terrible. A band like that would never feature in the *NME*."

The comment irked me, somewhat. Partly because I felt I had seen something unique lurking within those songs, within that attitude… and I still feel that. But mostly because of the soaring arrogance of the writer in question who deemed a band not worthy of the *NME*, even though they had featured in the admittedly more streetwise pages of *Sounds*. That stated, as he had had seemingly no problems discovering artistic worth within the fun-but-juvenile posturing of the solidly unmusical 'The Worst', I found his attitude difficult to stomach. This feeling was only amplified when, six months down the line, said writer starred fleetingly in a pseudo-punk outfit with the intention only to cause mischief and ridicule.

I had been naïve with Mark Smith though. Despite his apparent interest, I failed to understand the common truth that no musician or artist likes to hear endless tales about the qualities and amiable madness of their competitors. It was a basic fact of life that took me years to fully comprehend.

ALTRINCHAM

THE FRESHIES SEEMED synonymous with Altrincham… always. Even ignoring the fact that Chris was from Ashton-on-Mersey and Sale, three miles down Washway Road in the general direction of Manchester *and* that guitarist Barry Spencer and Bassist Rick Sarko hailed from Wythenshawe, or thereabouts - there remained something intrinsically 'Alty' about them.

Although bordered by areas spiced by a noticeable edginess – the gargantuan sprawl of the Wythenshawe overspill estate which stretches towards Wilmslow… the downbeat wariness of Sale… the deadening new-town of Partington – Altrincham remains defiantly upbeat. Evocatively linked to the plush climes of Cheshire, it enjoys pockets of immense local wealth, in Bowdon, Hale Barns and Lymm. Flushed with this footballer economy, it bustles with restaurants, bistros, café bars, evocative pubs, venues and a splattering of upmarket retail establishments. Going to visit Chris and The Freshies in Altrincham proved quite the antithesis of, say, visiting Mark E Smith in Prestwich. There be a cold air; an unwelcoming gloom; a sense that you have to follow the star on the trip. Never so while visiting Chris in Altrincham.

Admittedly, in 1978 and thereafter, Chris wasn't a star in the same sense. Perhaps that was partly his problem. His welcoming air. His accommodating touch. The plain fact that he was *fun* to be around. Even if visiting him at the flat he shared with his wife Paula in Timperley – on the roundabout on the junction of Brooklands and Stockport Road. He barely knew me back then and, yes, there might have been an element of the musician/journalist dynamic (possibly, though it never felt remotely forced). The flat felt warm, too. A happy home. Filled with a notable sense of love and contentment. A round familial vision, in which Chris could indulge in his gloriously childlike artwork, painting a mural of The Beatles' 'Yellow Submarine' on the children's bedroom wall. Thunderbirds models sitting on the dining table. Garishly coloured marker pens scattered across a giant pad. Scribbles and ideas. Naturally, the significance of this vision was beyond me at that time. Aside, perhaps, from Chris's driven DIY sensibilities, his daubing and attractively low brow scribbling on promo cassettes, accompanying booklets and personal letters alike. I recall his map, explaining directions to his flat, sent to my Disley home. It arrived completed with complicated drawings of 'Kids playing football' and 'Mrs Davies walking to the doctors'.

Beatles memorabilia would also scream from the living room wall and, later, the cover of the Island Records album from Manchester's great lost pop band, The Distractions. I did see some significance in this. The Distractions, at that point, could be seen as true contemporaries of the Freshies, even if their soul vision wasn't particularly shared. For a competing musician who had rejection slips by the thousand bulging from his 'record company file', to actively celebrate a local band's major album release, did seem somewhat rare, to say the least. A suggestion that, however driven Chris might have been, his competitive edge did not darken in the usual way. Believe me, I cannot think of a single other musician within the Manchester scene of 1978 who would react in such a way.

In later years I wondered if the Beatles bedroom belonged to Stirling?

Stirling Sievey: "Yes, this was the bedroom that my sister Asher and I shared when we were very young, I also remember there being a Dalek in the mural. I have a picture we took when we cleared his house out, there were two shelves Harry – Chris and Paula's third child - had with his Star Wars toys on, he painted the walls behind the shelves with different backdrops. We also painted some John Lennon animals for his friend Paul's (Molyneux) nursery."

We spent two or three New Years Eves in Chris and Paula's flat. Gently listening to Chris's plans for The Freshies to rise to the next level but mostly, mostly, listening to his unbridled enthusiasm for all matters Gerry Anderson and similar television outings of a pre-sexual nature. Even then, it seemed curious, conjuring up memories of visits to old school pals bedrooms, playing Subutteo on a green baize stretched across the floor, sounds of prog filling the room, flicking through football programmes and annuals. Of course, this time around, it was accompanied by copious cans of beer and exposure to the elongated New Years Eve version of The Old Grey Whistle Test. Chris would watch with steely intent. Scrutinising every band, soaking in their visuals but mostly working out, in his head, the thrust and dynamics of each and every performance, be it new wave or loon panted and ageing, as was Whistle Test's uncomfortable balance at the time. I recall him openly asking, "Do you think The Freshies could fit in on this?"

It was a good question and one that was difficult to answer. For, in truth, I couldn't quite see The Freshies fitting in with anything. That, I told him, was both a good thing and a bad thing. For it offered an outsider individuality that, even then, seemed impressive and unlikely. It also created a barrier against those who saw music arriving in a templated genre – a horrible record company trait that was beginning, back then, and would echo down the years until the vacuous 'X Factor' ethos began to take hold.

On another occasion one recalls meeting at the flat on a Saturday morning before departing together to visit Mars Studios, Altrincham, where The Freshies would be lost to a day's inexpensive recording. The songs recorded would comprise The Freshies EP 'All Sleeps Secrets'.

The recording was unlike anything I had heard… and certain bore no relation to any contemporary sound. A winding alarm clock ushers a lilting tune into view. The backing somnolent and lovely. It transpires that a theme is in place with songs that drift through dream sequences, touching on nightmares and jolt, like sudden awakenings. Unusual indeed; almost pre-punk in inception. Only one thing started to concern me. Where would they find an audience for this? Who would write the press? The answer to that would, as ever, lie with the prodigious hands-on attack of Sievey who – in a neat parallel with the, as yet, unrecorded Stephen Patrick Morrissey five miles away in insalubrious Stretford – had already started a relationship with the world via the stack of envelopes in his bedroom and the local post office. As mentioned, he had been doing precisely this for at least five years, stretching back to the now forgotten Bees Knees. It was not so naïve either. Indeed, even in an era of huge mainstream record sales, the power of niche mailing was not to be under-estimated.

BOWDON VALE SOCIAL CLUB

THIS WAS ONE OF THE STRANGEST and most infamous gig venues on Manchester's post punk circuit. Once again it was often championed by the *New Manchester Review* and even commanded the odd flickering in the national music press (see below). Bowdon Vale was little more than a scout hut. What's more, it was snugly situated in the soft heart of leafy suburbia. Quite a change, indeed, for punk attendees more accustomed to the post-apocalyptic landscape of Collyhurst (Electric

Circus) or the crushing semi-romantic seedy vibes of Dale Street (The Ranch) or Swan Street (Band on the Wall). These were dangerously deserted, night-blackened areas, at all times evoking a palpable tension.

Unusual therefore for punks to travel down Washway Road, leaving the snarl of the city behind and a chance to dip their Doc Marten-ed toes in the fringe of Cheshire suburbia.

The venue was made famous via two appearances by Joy Division in 1978 and 1979. Appearances made famous by the bizarre flock wallpaper as featured in the stage side photographs of Martin O'Neill. Other bands to perform at the venue included The Distractions, Private Sector and, on home turf really, The Freshies.

Without worrying a jot about the demystification process that occurs when artists meet their ragged public in person *before* the gig, I recall Chris Sievey heavily bombarding the queuing post-punkers, shamelessly urging them to purchase the cassette of 'All Sleeps Secrets', many of which, perhaps in response, were stolen that evening. I often wondered what on earth the thief actually thought he/she could possibly do with them? They were not something one could sell down the pub. Perhaps he/she was hoping for oncoming mega stardom for the band concerned. It seemed a distant goal, to say the least.

Mike Nicholls, a sprightly young *Record Mirror* hack from that very parish, appeared to fully approve of proceedings. To Sievey's delight, he published this early review... and long did it languish in Sievey's fanzine-style promotional paraphernalia.

(Mike's first line always bothered me, hinting, as it so clearly does, of a disillusional take on the importance of the then miniscule Manchester scene).

THE FRESHIES - BOWDEN VALE SOCIAL CLUB

If you've the slightest interest in the rock'n'roll world, you are likely to have heard of The Freshies. If you live in Manchester, it is a forgone conclusion.

Spearheaded by the irrepressible Chris Sievey, their publicity campaign over the past eighteen months has verged on the legendary; afternoon rooftop gigs, missives to department stores warning about the imminent take-over of the premises and Freshies TV week, a master-plan whereby the intention was for a member of the band to get on every programme going out. Mention their name at Granada or Piccadilly Radio and normally arrogant broadcasters flop into a quivering mass as harassed secretaries reach for the valium.

"Have you got our latest record, yet?" asks Chris, "No? Well if you twist my arm I might just let you have the last one... I mean there will be one in the post."

In fact, The Freshies have unleashed several records on an unsuspecting public, the best being their cassette only, 'All Sleeps Secrets' on Razz Records, the independent label run from Chris's bedroom which, like the rest of his house, was painted pink while they were on holiday (not true, of course. Chris was living with Paula). Some of the band's equipment was similarly splashed and they are all nuts. Bonkers. They make Jonathan Richman look positively taciturn.

Live, The Freshies are unable to capture the same magic but their instrumental flair and general exuberance makes for a grand night out. They unashamedly draw from a number of influences although their overall humour and creativity sets them apart as being very much individuals. 'All Sleep's Secrets', for example, is about a dream sequence while elsewhere their musical patterns explore forms as disparate as The Flamin' Groovies and Hawkwind.

The Freshies open with a grotesquely tuneless parody of Holst's 'Planets Suite' before belting through a series of 60s style beat tunes, 'It's So Easy', 'Ballrooms and Moon' and 'Oh Girl' crank up the pace before the band drifts into the experimental suite of 'Johnny Radar'/'U-Boat'/'Skid Room'. It climaxes with astonishing guitar interplay, the figures building up to a Motors style work out.

In terms of Rhythmic prowess, The Freshies could be placed alongside modern pop – rock bands like The Skids or The Undertones except their sound is more substantial and their ideas more fully realised. They might not take themselves too seriously but I have a feeling that, before long, the dotted line brigade will.

MIKE NICHOLLS

A slightly confusing review that perhaps manages to place the band in the context of the age. The review certainly confused Chris Sievey, as he called me and asked how Mike Nicholls could drum up a comparison with... erm... Hawkwind. I had to admit, it was difficult to place a finger on that connection. I told him that Mike, being an Altrincham lad and fresh out of the rag trade, should perhaps not be taken too seriously. It wasn't a criticism of Nicholls, for he was a young writer exploding with energy and ambition.

MIKE DOHERTY

The last time I had seen Mike Doherty was back in the early 1990s. As manager of Frank Sidebottom at the time, he accompanied his charge on a journalist-filled charabanc sojourn to Alton Towers, arranged by sundry PR people and intended to provide a timely press push for the winter attractions – 'Snow White on Ice' and a full-on Christmas dinner, Frank's addition to the party perhaps adding a necessary focal point to a rather dull occasion. The fact that we had been provided with year long press tickets also meant that over-exposure to the myriad attractions, all of which I loathed, had dulled the experience even further. It was down to Frank, really, to inject a touch of spice.

He didn't disappoint, either, and it was Frank who accompanied us through the entire journey and, indeed, the entire day. I recall him greedily attacking the chocolate stacked 'tuck box' and attempting to blame Little Frank.

"I can't have eaten the chocolates because I am cardboard," was the basis of Little Frank's defence and most chose to believe him. Most impressive of all, however, was the manner in which Frank locked onto an unsuspecting and hapless Father Christmas, unleashing all manner of demands and refusing to let him off the leash for the entire day.

And there, tall in the shadows, was Mike Doherty, constantly bellowing into a mobile phone, lost in the curious and idiosyncratic world of stage managing Frank Sidebottom. Doherty proved a commanding character blessed with a variety of Chris-isms that would often evoke comparisons between the two.

On the occasion I interviewed him for this book, back in March 2013, times had changed although his endearing and artistic heart had, it seemed, not. Mike's story filters into the following text although I wanted to convey the warmth that flowed through the interview. Despite spending many years as a high level drummer, a stage and tour manager and jazz percussionist in Bangkok, he was seemingly reduced to life with an amiable cat, Bob, in Stockport's unfashionable Cheadle Heath.

He had moved into the flat five years earlier and, depressingly at the time, it seemed a dour, featureless collection of cubic rooms. As, in Mike's words, "A man with too much time on his hands" he set about armed with only a felt tip pen, to completely transform every room via a maze of intricate designs, mostly intended to celebrate his time in the Smirks, his time with Frank, Manchester music in general plus the odd nod to his beloved Manchester United. Stencilled with great wit, I couldn't help but find myself reminded of the time Chris created the 'Yellow Submarine' mural in his childrens' bedroom in Timperley. I like to think, rather than as an indication of a man with too much time on his hands, the flat is a true indication of a still active artistic mind... of no small talent.

Mike Doherty: "Initially I had been learning the guitar when I was a boy but, rather like Tony Iommi of Black Sabbath, an accident changed my musical career path, such as it was. I cut off the best part of my little finger and, though I tried, having four fingers wasn't really conducive to guitar playing. That is why I turned to the drums. I had a pretty good musical grounding and spent a long time learning the drumming basics. I was pretty focused and, foolishly I know now, I sought out a career in music. I played in Europe, mostly in cabaret clubs in Copenhagen in what was really a covers band. But we played for hours... on and on into the night so we would be free to experiment and play stuff like Frank Zappa. Amazingly they seemed to go down well with the drunken hoards of Denmark. I don't know why. We were playing a lot of the music of the day... Steely Dan and The Allman Brothers. But it really gave me a good musical knowledge. I had learned about the dynamics of a band, I could spot weaknesses and knew how to make the best out of a band, however bad they may be."

It was an enviable and unusual position for a young Mancunian musician to find himself in on the cusp of punk. While the musical ineptitude of the new and sudden spread of punk bands was often exaggerated –

with the noble exception of The Worst – Doherty was clearly head and shoulders above many of his spiked topped peers.

Mike Doherty: "Back in Manchester I was delighted when punk finally happened. Things had got fucking ridiculous with bands getting more and more pompous. I did like a tune, still do. So when punk happened and things started to simplify, I knew that it had become a good environment to play in. I don't like bands that start to show off onstage. Do that in rehearsals but not on stage. Always remain in your comfort zone. This would come in very handy when, later, I joined The Freshies.

"But before that I was in The Smirks. They were a really great band with decent songs. A good songwriter, a decent bassist and guitarist. I guess we did well in certain places. We got a following in Manchester… well, kind of and always went down well in Liverpool. We enjoyed some good press as well, although we were never considered hip in any way. I had a kind of showbiz attitude. I must admit, I couldn't see the worth in Joy Division because I knew they couldn't play. It totally escaped me that Ian Curtis might actually fucking mean all this stuff. It was a different attitude but there was room for both. It was also the time of power pop and new wave. We did fit into all that and really did think we would go places. We even learned to play reggae – which means unlearning just about everything – and fused this with rock. We didn't play it as well as the originators but, like The Clash, we did it in our own clumsy way. I kinda worked enough for us to eventually gain a record contract with Berserkly. We thought this would be the one, no doubt about that. But way down the line, the plug was pulled pulled on Berserkly which, in truth, had run its course. We were unceremoniously dropped. It was a big lesson for us all and, of course, crushing at the time. The Smirks fell apart really, partly surfacing later as (the Mog-led) Distant Cousins."

Doherty swiftly gravitated towards the Freshies drum stool via his association with Wythenshawe scenester, saxophonist and survivor, Anthony Ryan Carter, more infamously known as Tosh.

"I survived though. I did some fly-posting for Tosh Ryan – former co-owner of Music Force agency in Manchester – who had a really thriving business at that time. Those were the days when you could try your hand at all kinds of things and often they would work... also some of them could be very dubious indeed. I will gloss over that for the moment but, right up to and including the years I worked with Chris and Frank, there might be import and export ideas going on. They wouldn't last long, because dubious things never did, but there always seemed to be a way of making money. Most of the musicians in Manchester were a bit like that. You would find ways to survive in order to play music. This necessity did encourage people to try out all kinds of ideas and that could be said to be part of the motivation for Chris. Throughout his life he was a little on the edge, as it were and he always searched for a way out... a way to pay the VAT perhaps, though he was never motivated by money."

WHEN CHRIS MET TOSH

BEFORE CHRIS SIEVEY MET TOSH RYAN, he was looking for him. He didn't know it, but he was looking. He needed a Tosh and, although he denies it now – having poured approximately £30,000 into Sievey's dormant career, Tosh needed Chris. When they finally met and started to work together, something clicked. That this didn't twist into huge commercial success seems irrelevant. They were like two corresponding pieces of a bizarre jig-saw clicking into place. Both artistic demons, Chris filled an unfulfilled chasm within Tosh and vice versa. Wherever they went, be it London or Didsbury, they created a zone of chaos. Drink and drugs plunged this into absurdity but the raw materials were always there. Tosh 'n' Chris, punkish twosome, tearing up Manchester's music legacy. They should have been rich but, had that been the case, had they ended their days in some Malibu adobe, the story would have lessened in intensity. It wasn't meant to be. It *was* meant to be.

TOSH RYAN

Tosh Ryan (Anthony Ryan Carter) may baulk at the suggestion but he can be regarded as a hidden legend of Manchester music. Born and brought up in the sprawling Wythenshawe overspill estate that borders Altrincham, he earned his musical reputation as a saxophonist, initially performing with swing bands at Warrington's Burtonwood aerodrome where, it has been claimed, the concept of rock 'n' roll first seeped into an unsuspecting English nation. Well that's a lazy claim, really.

However Tosh's greater claims to fame came later, as he hovered as enigmatic impresario, as half of the mid-seventies Music Force promotions agency – alongside producer Martin Hannett, as fly-poster entrepreneur and as owner of punk label Rabid Records, who shunted out Hannett produced goods by Slaughter and the Dogs, Ed Banger and the Nosebleeds, Jilted John, Giro, John Cooper Clark and Chris Sievey and the Freshies. Interestingly, the severed half of Rabid – Hannett and Joy Division/New Order manager Rob Gretton, became intrinsic aspects of Factory Records. Tony Wilson, whether he chose to deny it or not, observed Rabid closely before utilising the same ethos to kick-start Factory.

For the research of this book, I visited Tosh in his home in the village of Menai Bridge, on the welcoming fringe of Anglesey. He was still performing as guiding saxophonist of the once-a-year disgracefully ageing collective known as The Orchestra of Fools. Soon he would decamp for the enveloping warmth of Crete. He wasn't particularly taken with the idea of being interviewed on the subject of Chris Sievey. I also had to beg him to speak with Steve Sullivan's film crew. He preferred aloofness and a shot of Cognac. I provided him with the latter.

However, his importance in the Chris Sievey story cannot be overstated. During The Freshies period it was Tosh Ryan, flushed by the success of that unholy poster business, who effectively bankrolled The Freshies, in management and record company capacity, for many years. Frank, it seems, provided the cut-off point. For Tosh could never stand Frank... and still can't. Nevertheless, his belief in the pop genius of Chris Sievey remains.

When I met him, in his be-suited and loafer clad seventies, he was an amiable old character in the Menai Bridge locale. During his 'Freshies' years, I met a younger, punkier character, who sat in his Rabid (and, later, Absurd Records) office on Cotton Lane Didsbury, who couldn't resist pushing his greatest discovery.

"Chris's stuff always blows me away," he said then, while wondering why no one else felt quite the same.

I did though. I did.

Tosh Ryan: "I can't remember when I first met Chris, to be honest. He would have sent me demos, I guess, when I was working at Rabid Records on Cotton Lane (Withington). But it was Martin Hannett, who was my producer at Rabid, who I think suggested that we work with Chris. He came to the office and I thought he was suitably insane so I thought it might be good to work with him. Well, first and foremost, we seemed to get on but I noticed a certain possessiveness within him. He told me about the way he had established a secret fan base with Razz Records. I really admired that. It made him an outsider and I was drawn to outsiders."

It might be noted that, while the pair bonded to an instant and enduring friendship, similarities between them were few. Outsider, Chris certainly was, he always carried an air of effortless amiability. Tosh, on the other hand, enjoyed that fierce reputation as hard-bitten Wythenshawe punkster. What's more Rabid was a 'company' fired by a punkish anger that, in a number of ways, seemed rather detrimental. Chris didn't suit that unholy ethos at all.

"He basically set up in our office. He was running Razz Records and, as I said, I had already built up a good mail order business with his small fan base. One thing about Chris, he was very fastidious. He always answered every letter fully and would spend hours colouring in and drawing. Some of it did seem just daft but I thought he was funny too. He was great in the office… just nice to be around. We really became friends and, somewhat stupidly, I decided to invest in him. One of the worst decisions of my life, really. I started to manage The Freshies and we put them on a wage. A small wage but they were always tapping me up for a bit more money. They would drift in the office and scrounge bits of money. This never stopped. It started with fish'n'chips and ended up with guitars and much more. I was lucky because I had money at that time from the postering. So I was glad to go along with it. It ended up costing me about £30,000 plus to fund The Freshies, Chris Sievey's solo stuff and his drug and drink habits… which were considerable."

There was always a noticeable difference between the camaraderie blast of noise that spiced The Freshies recordings and Sievey's comparatively wistful solo work, including the coy and cultish 'Baiser'.

"He came to us with the idea for 'Baiser', which I thought was great. Unfortunately, nobody else did. But we recorded that with Martin (Hannett) with, I think, 'Last' on the other side. I really can't remember whether we put it out on Rabid or whether he kept the Razz label at that point. It didn't really matter. I was just funding him, whatever."

Martin Hannett actually first heard The Freshies when their third EP was played on BBC Radio Manchester's late show on Saturday night, presented by Peter Sharratt and John Woodruff. It was pretty much the only local radio show that would play Manchester bands at the time and, although the Beeb always boasted high audience figures, the reality would be that, maybe 200 might tune it. It was excellent post-pub entertainment. Tune in and see if they play your mate's band. But something impressed Hannett and he managed to get in touch with Chris Sievey after a phone call to New Broadcasting House. It was Hannett who invited Sievey down to the Rabid office to meet Tosh.

The process was natural. Ryan had printing and posting machines within his office. Almost immediately, Sievey camped in the room, designing posters for Rabid acts such as John Cooper Clarke. This marked an identifiable improvement in Sievey's situation. Suddenly he wasn't just a bedroom self-promoter. He was actively 'working' for someone and utilising his artistic skills. Through the Rabid connection, The Freshies also expanded the scope of their live performances and they started opening shows for the top Manchester punk bands at the time... Slaughter and the Dogs, The Drones, Buzzcocks, The Fall and The Distractions.

If Tosh Ryan and Chris Sievey was a marriage made in some kind of hell then what on earth are we to make of the anarchic partnership Sievey briefly enjoyed with Hannett? Could there be two more wavering obsessives in the history of Manchester music? And was it one of Tosh's flashes of inspiration, mischievous meddling or plainly insane blackouts that triggered their in-studio collaborations.

Tosh carefully placed the couple in Drone Studios and patiently awaited the results. It had been Chris's gentle song, 'Baiser' that had initially alerted Tosh to Sievey's talents and he had been equally impressed by the song that would adorn the flip, 'Last'.

These were not Freshies songs. They lacked the simplistic power pop thrust of the full band and one would struggle to imagine them recreating then onstage.

"I really do believe that Chris will be a huge star," Ryan told me at the time. He was sitting in the Cotton Lane office that would see the influx of Razz as well as the slow metamorphosis of Rabid Records into the more eclectic – to say the least – Absurd Label. Once the notion of Absurd – being, let's say, a home for a darker kind of madness

– leaked out into the populace, largely via Paul Morley's hilarious punt in the *NME*, all manner of largely unlistenable dirges flooded into the office in the form of the 'hastily arranged hopeless cassette demo. Tosh and Chris enjoyed many an hour slapping these artless items into the office 'beat box' and, more often than not, whipping them out after three seconds of excruciating cacophony. Of the dirges that would eventually make it to vinyl would be a sprightly ditty called 'Gerry and the Holograms' which would enjoy a spell illuminating the more alternative dance floors of Manchester. This 1979 disc would seep into Manchester mythology as it clearly lays the template for New Order's gargantuan 1983 global smash, 'Blue Monday'. Neither Tosh, nor the musicians involved in the disc, John Scott and CP Lee, ever seriously attempted to force this issue through legal means. This ironic train crash of a song would have been worthy of Sievey himself who, no doubt, empathised about the pair's preposterous bad luck.

"Myself and Chris would have incredibly lengthy discussions about how we were going to shake up the music business. More often than not these would take place in pubs over endless drinks and other things. It wasn't a healthy relationship at all. We got on so well that I think we just wanted to keep talking and keep drinking. We did that for about six years, if I remember rightly. Non stop."

Ryan's immediate plans included a practical twist. As an accomplished musician, he wasn't keen on the prevailing trend of musical looseness that, in truth, had permeated the ranks of The Freshies. But he knew how to arrest this situation.

"Yes, it was me who got Mike Doherty in as The Freshies drummer. Mike was working for me on the fly posting thing and had left The Smirks. I knew he was an excellent drummer too and thought he would help pull the band together. They weren't a bad band. Barry Spencer was an excellent guitarist. He looked a bit like a plumber but was a really nice guy too. Rick Sarko wasn't great on the bass but I knew we could get him through. He had the perfect attitude and they were definitely a gang. One of the problems was Chris who never learned to sing. He really wasn't interested in that at all and just wouldn't get the phrasing right. He never ever learned to do this which I felt was stupid as a few lessons would have sorted it. But he was a brilliant lyricist, I always felt that. Stuff like 'Dancin' Doctors', I felt was extraordinary."

"We always tried to accommodate Chris's talent for PR at the New Manchester Review. He made things seem like fun and was a dream to work with. For the band's gig at The Sale Hotel, we ran a competition where we gave away 25 Freshies singles that had been placed in individually crafted sleeves. With Chris drawing spirals on the labels, like Vertigo. They were photocopied sleeves, individually glued together. I think this was the first time anyone had done anything like that in Manchester. It seems a bit simplistic now, but Chris was always thinking ahead of the game. Always looking for a new angle."

STEVE FORSTER

MICK MIDDLES

March 6th 2007

YOU DIDN'T HAVE TO BE IRISH to enjoy the crazed televisual comedy of the two puppets, Podge and Rog although, at times it helped. The puppets – Padraig Judas O'Leprosy and Rodraif Spartacus O'Leprosy - were created and performed by Cairan Morrison and Mick O'Hara and initially featured as the guiding characters in 'A Scare at Bedtime' which ran between 2000 and 2006. However it was the Podge and Rog Show, which aired between 2006 and 2010, which took the idea to a new level. The Podge and Rog Show became a phenomenally successful chat show, scooping a number of awards including – twice – Best Irish Entertainment Show. More importantly, 'Podge and Rog' were generally seen as the most effective way of breaking a new artist in Ireland. Particularly of note was the 'Sham Rock' section in which celebrity judges cast their votes after somewhat tentative performances from newcomers.

Frank being Frank, he used his numerous outings on Channel M – including a recording of 'The Test Card' – to force his way into the position of contestant. It was in this slightly bizarre parody of Britain's Got Talent that a quiffed and bespectacled Frank surged through an irrepressible medley of Smiths songs including, and most famously, 'There is a Light and it Never Goes Out' and 'Panic'. The judges, James Nesbitt and Glenda Gilson, were suitably impressed, giving him an unprecedented score of 22 points, the highest score of the entire series. Subsequently, demand for Frank related material in both Eire and Northern Ireland, hit a remarkable high.

"I don't think Frank has ever been so popular in any country," stated Chris in 2008, before mysteriously concluding, "Of course, he completely blew it."

OUT OF HIS HEAD

May 17ᵀʰ 1980

A SATURDAY NIGHT. Paula and Chris travelled into the dubious heart of Stockport to spend time at a downbeat discothèque-come-nightclub called The Blue Waterfall. They duly sat in a corner and, while deflecting amiable chit-chat with the assorted throng, felt slightly out of place. Well it was an odd gathering and a rather odd occasion. But what a disparate gaggle, sitting there, munching away at salmon en croute or whatever was the dish of the moment. Panning back, I must admit to doing a double-take. For there is a photograph that captures the moment; Chris and Paula, looking utterly the bright and cheerful suburban couple, Mark E. Smith of The Fall alongside his girlfriend and manager, Kay Carroll. The Manchester punk/glam band, V2 – or two members of – decked out in full garish regalia. Rob Gretton, the manager of Joy Division, at that precise moment the most respected band in Britain, Manchester music photographer Kevin Cummins and my Auntie Margaret and Uncle Phil who, to my knowledge, carried little musical weight in the Manchester scene.

They were in attendance because it was the occasion of my first wedding. I do not mention this in order to impart a particularly obvious multi-namedrop… well, not much but it seemed like an almost perfect snapshot of the sheer scope and diversity of the Manchester scene at that precise moment. It is especially poignant as Paula and Chris sit at the very edge of the table. They seem profoundly un-rock'n'roll. A fact born out by the wedding present they kindly brought to the party. Mark E.Smith's offering came in the form of a small tin-foil wrap, the contents of which I will not divulge although, at it turned out, it was perhaps not entirely suited to the spirit of honeymoon ("He seemed a nice young man," said my mother, "what was that present he gave you?"). Paula and Chris, meanwhile, brought a home made peg-bag. This was, I stress, gratefully received and supplied many years service, even extending into the 1990s.

"Oh I was so housewifely," Paula would state in 2010.

To the best of my knowledge, this was the first time that Chris Sievey had met Mark E. Smith and their unlikely friendship would flicker on down the decades. Mark always completely 'getting' Frank… at one point mentioning that Frank's version of 'Hit the North' was better than theirs. Not that I would necessarily concur with that, although Frank naturally brought an added frisson to the famous song.

The significance of the date cannot be overstressed, although it doesn't really add to the Chris Sievey story. That night, somewhere in the UK, a genuinely concerned Genesis P-Orridge was frantically attempting to contact Rob Gretton, among others. He was highly concerned about the mental state of his friend Ian Curtis who seemed to be suffering dangerously with depression. The call never managed to come through. Whether it would have made any difference is something we will never know. At the end of the evening, Kevin went back to Rob Gretton's house, no doubt for further beerage. History, alas, can be left to complete the tragic story of that night.

Ten days later, myself fresh from honeymoon, I met up with Chris Sievey again. This was at Manchester's suitably downbeat and Bohemian Beach Club, run by Buzzcocks manager Richard Boon and various ladies from the Factory side of the city. It was a curious club, set on three levels and the evenings included a film showing – A film about Lenny Bruce – and bands from the left field fringe. Oddly enough, Chris Sievey and the Freshies had been offered a date at the club at a later date* and Chris was simply checking out the scene, along with Barry, Rick and Tosh.

For reasons that I have never really understood, Chris and I had one thing in common that Wednesday night. We were the only two people

---

* *In James Nice's excellent Factory tome, 'Shadowplayers', The Freshies are listed as being the first band to play at The Beach Club, bizarrely in support of The Durutti Column. While that would have made a truly fascinating evening that just about spans the entire spectrum of modern music with just two acts, it can never have taken place. However it must have been mooted and listed at some point.*

James Nice noted: "Although I strived for accuracy all through that book, I wasn't in Manchester at the time. It must have been in the listings although, I do admit, it seems an odd pairing' who entered that club who did not know what had happened to Ian Curtis on that fateful night. I must stress, despite being the Manchester correspondent for *Sounds* magazine, I had the excuse that I had been lost in a honeymoon daze, somewhere in the Lake District. Quite what Chris had been doing, I am not sure. Also, quite why none of his Freshies colleagues had mentioned it seemed equally odd. When I broached this subject with Chris several years later he just shrugged and suggested that he "…probably went into one of his lonely work-at-home modes… you know, shutting off from everything."

PRESS? PASS.

'NECESSITY IS THE MOTHER OF INVENTION?' Could any phrase seem more perfectly suited to this story. Nevertheless, it is still a little crass. Being skint has never been a barrel of laughs and while it might well stir the aesthetic muse, turning ethereal, inventive thought into tangible action often requires a degree of investment. There must be a way. Some other way?

That was always Chris's battle and his lo-fi genius was arguably the perfect response. However, nestling within his artistic desires, throughout this story, would always be a – largely unfulfilled – desire to make films. A filmic brain denied full access to cinematic resource. It was something that always niggled… partially (and only partially) satisfied by The Freshies occasional ventures into video and, more successful, Frank's hogging of the omnipresent camera but it was far from being fully realised nonetheless.

This came as a surprise to me. It was an article that appeared in *The Face* magazine in 1980, itself a legendary and innovative organ. It surprised me because I had apparently written it, albeit under the moniker Middlehurst. It was uncovered as I visited the Northwich home of serial archivist and label owner Chris Hewitt in June 2013. The purpose of the visit was to unearth one of Tosh Ryan's legendary Chris Sievey files that had made their lonely way from Anglesey into The Chris Hewitt archive. I didn't mind this at all. Some Manchester music archivists – and exhibition curates – have displayed a level of ownership that borders on feverish greed. Not so with Chris. But as I sat in Hewitt's home, I couldn't help but enjoy the disparate nature of The Freshies press cuttings. Here are three sample, the first from *Record Mirror*.

OUT OF HIS HEAD

A Tosh Ryan period article with pre Tosh intro. Weird. Here goes.

> *As a swansong to one-man Razz, Sievey re-introduced public and press to 'All Sleeps Secrets', albeit on cassette only format. All 11 tracks, including the original 'Baiser' ('Taste of a Boy/Girl', 'Two of the Same Girl', 'Ballrooms and Moon', 'No I Fear', 'Bogey Man' and 'Lovely Bars') had been recorded or re-recorded... or patched up at Mars Studios under the guidance of Richard Sutton.*

Intended as both an introduction to the band and a pointer to their new Rabid finery, many of the band's loyal postal fans found a complimentary cassette dropping through the letter-box, delivered by way of thanks, and intended – no doubt – to deepen the loyalty. Certainly it served as a neat method of tidying up and, if nothing else, one could slap it in the car and drift awhile. It would also serve as a reminder that The Freshies were in dire need of more expensive studio production and Rabid, given their link to producer Martin Hannett, could possibly re-address that trying problem.

Despite its semi album status, 'All Sleeps Secrets' did pick up a small scattering of reviews. Most notably this one, written by Morrissey-mate James Parade which thoroughly emphasises that particular point. (Again, the irony being that many would look back most fondly to the lo-fi of the early years, rather like the eternal love that Buzzcocks devotees always feel for 'Spiral Scratch'). Catch 22, indeed.

AND THIS LITTLE BEAUTY
The Freshies - 'All Sleeps Secrets' (Razz)

> *It's difficult to know what to say once you find a record you like, a lot. More difficult when it is in its simplest, crudest form – recorded on an inadequate four-track machine for £150.*
>
> *That may be good enough for your average run-of-the-mill punk panic or any old/new music hippy co-op from up Sheffield way but it just isn't good enough for The Freshies.*
>
> *Chris Sievey is the man behind and in front of The Freshies. He is one of the real pop and shaky pop composers of the 80s. Not Nickel Lowdean,*

> not Elvis Frog, only he is the new Gilbert McCartney. Only he had more melody in his index finger than the whole human metal gang put together.
>
> The Freshies first album is in cassette form because it was cheaper for them to make it that way. That, in itself, is unfortunate because all the special effects and production techniques necessary to give these songs that extra something aren't possible with using a four-track (unless you happen to be George Martin). Mr Sievey has done very well, though. His is an album of luxurious lullabies. Put it on seconds before an away-day into the land of Nod and those infectious little tunes will keep you away for the duration.
>
> There are two hit singles here. The number one sound is the minute epic 'Two of the Same Girl' and the No 2 sound is 'Baiser' (which is to be re-recorded, thank God) and will be out as a single by Manchester's own Rabid Records very soon. Other unmissables are the Bernstein-ish 'Ballrooms and Moon' and that lovely little popsicle, 'Lovely Bars'.
>
> It's only one pound and fifty pence from...etc

Anyway, this following half page feature, topped by the obligatory moody Kevin Cummins snap I felt captured Chris at his most refreshingly optimistic. It also – and I had completely forgotten this – proves the innovative prowess of the young band as early as 1980. The Freshies, staggering into a lonely future, gaining little praise but pushing forth nonetheless.

SIEVEY FEEL ME
The Face, 1980

> The art of Chris Sievey and The Freshies is the art of intense self-promotion. Every night, Chris Sievey sits up writing letters by the dozen. Record companies, journalists, editors, TV and radio stations, are constantly bombarded by often hilarious Freshies paraphernalia. Within the music business... and very much within the business, Sievey has attained a near mythical status.
>
> Beautifully perhaps, he has always been completely ignored.
>
> His latest venture (an hour long video of the band which retails at £12.95) has suffered from a typical lack of response. He doesn't appear to be overly concerned.

"I love it," he exclaims. "There is this video magazine that boasts a list of 'every video available in the UK'. I have written to them about 50 times and still they haven't taken the slightest bit of notice, the same thing happened when the music press had that thing about Blondie releasing the first video on the market.

"I kept ringing up and saying, 'look we have had one out for two months before Blondie' and they just wouldn't listen. Incidentally, that was our first video attempt; a short black and white affair that wasn't very successful. The new one is in colour and much better than a lot of big selling videos."

Chris Sievey and The Freshies are one of Manchester most interesting outfits. They combine experimental catchy pop with a ridiculous semi-Pythonesque sense of the absurd; they have released a string of instant and classy singles to resounding applause from their small band of devotees and, otherwise, universal apathy. Nobody ever said, "Yeah, the Freshies... they are alright."

Their move into the world of video is more than merely innovative... it is unique among the hoards of penniless independent bands. How on Earth did they manage it?

"It was simple," says Sievey. "We shot the film at various locations. At a couple of gigs and also at a deserted church we discovered in Wales. When Tony Wilson saw it he just couldn't understand how we managed it without the use of sound engineers and technicians. But we just hired one person who had a video camera and worked from there. Nothing to it. I am sure that soon everyone will be making their own videos as opposed to just making records.

"The real problem lies in the recording of duplicates. I have to sit at home and record every copy on a standard video recorder. This means sitting through every recording to make sure it all turned out fine. It is worth the trouble, even though we haven't sold many."

How many?

"Well three actually but it has only been on sale for a week. How do you promote it, though? It is too expensive to send out review copies to every mag and they probably wouldn't even bloody mention it anyway. What do you think of it?"

The Freshies video is – obviously – a must for fans of the band. It contains 15 razor sharp pop songs and successfully captures the celebrated chaos of *their onstage adventuring.*

It does suffer from a certain lack of technological expertise – or money perhaps? – offering little more than straight live shots of the band. It would have been improved by more natural photographic invention. Nevertheless, it is a remarkable achievement and a certain pointer to an oncoming medium and, once beyond initial outlay, a comparatively cheap medium.

However, The Freshies will be too busy to produce a third video during the next year of so. They are about to embark on a full year's intensive vinyl recording which will see a single released every month for 12 months plus a compilation album of old material and the release of their first album 'proper' in spring 1981. If this happens, they could be dubbed, 'Britain's most prolific unit'. One senses more glorious failure but it could... it just could finally reward them with media recognition (beginning here, now in The Face*).*

Anyone interested in The Freshies *video should contact Razz Records, 3, Oakliegh Court, Timperley, Cheshire.*

MICK MIDDLES. THE FACE 1980

CHRIS AND FACTORY

WHILE CHRIS AND TOSH seemed gloriously suited and, indeed, Rabid's edgy flippancy a perfect stable to allow for Chris's DIY beaverings, Sievey did attempt to pierce Factory Record's insular fortress on – at least – a couple of occasions. Yet Factory founder, the late Rob Gretton, who had previously set up his stall within the fledgling Rabid, just did not see Factory as a pop label at all.

Rob Gretton: "To be honest, I was never completely happy with The Distractions on Factory, let alone The Freshies. Not that I have anything against bands like that. They did approach us at some point. There is obviously a place for them but Factory wasn't the right label for them. It would have felt awkward. Plus I don't think that Tony – Wilson – was particularly keen."

True enough, Wilson wasn't a Freshies fan although he would later work extensively with Frank on television. Gretton was correct to claim that Factory would not have been the right home. Tosh and Rabid were certainly more attuned to the velocity and fluster of the pop market where the key is to get a song in and get it in fast... on Radio One and everywhere, establish an immediate presence within the lighter areas of the music press – *Smash Hits*, *Record Mirror* – and cash in before the particular bubble bursts. Rabid moved like lightning to secure the upward movement of Jilted John and one simply could not imagine the often bizarre and dysfunctional office at Factory doing likewise. It was simply not a pop label. Slipping out left field obscurities in the hope that they might attain cultish appeal – A Certain Ratio, Section 25, Minny Pops – sat closer to the Factory ethos sullied only by their infrequent lapses in taste by putting out records by friends and associates.

And there was another problem. Factory acts were asked to willingly submit to the sheen of Peter Saville's omnipresent design. Famously, the look would be seen as – at least – as equal importance to the sound. It is, therefore, impossible to see the naïve DIY design concepts of Chris Sievey finding any place within such an area. Oddly, this always fascinated Sievey and, in places, he would filter a gloriously juvenile take on Saville within his own design ideas. For an example of this look at Chris's poster and sleeve work for 'Dancing Doctors' and even, perhaps, just glimpse the initial shards of Frank Sidebottom. The 'Dancing Doctors' visuals always beautifully parodies early industrial indie sleeves by Cabaret Voltaire and Human League.

DECEMBER 2013

It was a postulating Friday evening in The Castle Hotel. The office-worker come-down from a heavy week. Somehow we managed to secrete ourselves beside the defunct bar in the rear room. The vibe began as raucous and increased in volume minute by minute. Even amid the garish Primark clothing of 2014, Rick Sarko seemed incongruous, his trademark tight white Levis and bulbous feathery topcoat, resembled a Disney bird plucked from the forests of Jungle Book. To his delight, he immediately turned heads and engaged in conversation with an unknown female after just four seconds. Perhaps he looked like some kind of rock star… which, indeed, he was. Intelligent, amiable as ever, he downed the first of many vodkas and recalled the wild days of Freshie-mania… and that was just within the band. Some things, it seems, just change shade slightly.

There were three of us at first. But after ten minutes I left Rick Sarko and Vicky Middles in the pub and made my way to the radio station. They joined me after sampling the myriad pubs that lay between Oldham Street and Portland Street. Once they had joined me at fabradiointernational, Rick's eyes widened with sheer delight.

"Chris would have loved this," he delightedly glowed. "Chris and Frank would have both done shows."

And Little Frank, perhaps? Rick sat inside the studio. The studio is situated within a large wooden Tardis. Upstairs sits the offices of sci-fi and genre magazine, *Starburst*. Fifty yards along Portland Street, sits The Fab Café, which helps govern this glorious example of multi-media escapism. It feels as if we have escaped to 'Chris World'.

Later that evening I interviewed Rick Sarko on the subjects of Chris, Frank and The Freshies. I had never before seen him so full of wonder.

CHRIS SIEVEY - 1980

RESPLENDENT IN SCARLET CORDUROY JEANS, relatively sober shirt and with an infectious smile; Sievey gently sipped his pint and proclaimed to the small world that gathered within The Ship Inn, Bowdon... "I have been listening to Van Der Graaf Generator. Does that surprise you?"

"Wouldn't have been the first band that springs to mind," I replied, before adding, "Although Van Der Graaf's Peter Hammill was seen in The Factory Club... working with Linder from Ludus..."

It was a statement that effectively summed up The Freshies conundrum. A pop band, albeit one with an intriguing artistic edge, lost within the aesthetic of a city scene where it seemed positively *de rigueur* to be seen working with ageing art school prog rockers. The flash of punk had been duly replaced, perhaps as the general musicality had improved, and a fascinating if insular art set had started to gain prominence.

Case in point – The Freshies had just turned down a support spot with the ironically named Bristol agit-funk outfit, The Pop Group. "Wouldn't have worked," admitted a thoughtful Sievey.

We were having an unofficial meeting here, attempting to see if we could squint towards some way forward, in particular within the inky and uninterested pages of the music press. I had been lucky; managing to prize four live reviews of the band onto the *Sounds* Reviews pages. It wasn't a difficult task. The gigs in question had been a disparate quartet, to say the least, from a support spot at the Ardwick Apollo; a gargantuan public house in equally unfashionable Swinton; a scout hut in nearby Bowdon Vale and that rather bizarre gig emanating out of unlikely Sale Town Hall, the place of Chris and Paula's marriage.

But little else, other than a slap in *Record Mirror*, penned by Altrincham's Mike Nicholls and a succession of hearty mentions from

MICK MIDDLES

New Manchester Review's Steve Forster. Chris was distraught and I knew, full well, that his letters to the *NME*, both from himself and his wry pseudonym, 'Beatles Band' – which ironically gained mythical status through the years - numbered in the hundreds.

"You told me that Dave McCullough (at *Sounds*) had been saying nice things about us. (He had and hinted as much in a recent single review). Couldn't he write a feature? Could you get us on the cover?"

The last question, I think, was somewhat tongue-in-cheek. Unlikely indeed that a magazine that favoured placing the likes of Iron Maiden and Def Leppard on the cover – thereby pushing its weekly readership beyond the 200,000 level - should opt for a tiny band from Altrincham who couldn't even gain a healthy following within their locale. Nevertheless, I promised Chris that I would take a copy of the new Freshies EP, the succinctly titled 'The Men From Banana Island Whose Stupid Ideas Never Caught on in the Western World as We Know it,' into the *Sounds* office and play it in the hope of catching the attention of writers rather more influential than I.

I glanced at the disc, mulling over the existential nature of a title that, perhaps, reflected the way Chris was feeling... as leader of a band of true outsiders. I knew precisely what he was thinking: that The Fall, who he deeply admired, had recently and successfully graced the cover of the paper. That had been the work of staff man Dave McCullough, when he suitably upstaged yours truly. Chris didn't like to say... but I know he wanted the same. To me, however, the reasons he wouldn't get it seemed woefully obvious. Nevertheless, I loved the band.

As such I was not overburdened with confidence as I strode purposefully along London's Long Acre, no doubt pausing nervously at the door which led to the *Sounds* and *Record Mirror* offices, situated evocatively above Covent Garden tube station.

To my surprise, the ragged sample of editorial staff in attendance that day seemed enthusiastic and I offered to slap the said Freshies EP onto the office stereo system. Editor Alan Lewis, Deputy ed, Geoff Barton, Gary Bushell, Hugh Fielder, Pete Silverton – alas no Dave McCullough – all gathered earnestly around, ears politely cocked. For reasons unbeknown to me, it was Gary Bushell himself who thought it amusing to place the needle on the final track. Sievey's words filled the office, even to the extent of creating attention with the non-Bohemian staff of *Yachting Weekly*.

*"An octopus, an octopus but how shall we cook it?
How about octopus stew, well, I am easy how about you?"*

Accusing faces turned towards me.
"Watch out Bob Dylan!" offered Lewis and I was hard pressed not to agree.
"You want us to put *them* on the cover?" asked Barton, exasperation flashing across his facial features.
"Well, it's not the typical Freshies song," I attempted, pointlessly as, one by one, they returned to their desks, leaving me to skulk out of the office, having rather wasted a day and the cost of a day return to London.
Recounting this story to Chris, I naturally expected a faint shrill of disappointment or suchlike. Nothing could have been further from the truth. Chris though it hilarious. "What a result!" he bellowed, much to my astonishment and my apologetic pleadings were batted away like flies. I think this was the precise moment where I realised that Chris Sievey wasn't like ordinary people... ordinary musicians... ordinary artists, if there can be such a thing. Chris had his own agenda... whatever that was.

The joke was... there was no joke. The singer could expose the heart of the song. While Frank could lampoon and flap and fail, beneath it all – and at all times – lay the stunning musicality of Chris Sievey. True enough, Frank could be a smokescreen to the talents of Sievey, and Sievey often hated him for it, but there were many genuine reflections and emulations on classic material. None more obviously than Frank's inclusion on the <u>NME</u>'s 'Sgt Pepper Knew My Father' compilation which also featured Sonic Youth – Thurston Moore attending Frank gigs! – Hue and Cry, Billy Bragg and Michelle Shocked. Arguably, Frank's version was the most successful of all these heady contemporary acts. His version of 'Flying', for the 'Revolution No 9' tribute album, was somewhat less successful.

MICK MIDDLES

Paul McCartney was not available for comment.

THE BABIES THAT BOUNCE

THERE IS A LOVELY SIMPLISTIC STATE. Having left school and taken up employment and existing in that carefree vacuum before marriage or maturity begin to set in. Many would prefer to remain in that lovely arena and the success of magazines such as *Mojo*, *Uncut*, *Record Collector* and *Classic Rock* strongly suggest that the male of the species likes to return to that state later in life.

Post-punk was the perfect period in which to enjoy such simplicity. Each week came a new collectable single, more often than not in coloured vinyl. Albums too. Nothing more important to think about than drifting down to a city centre record shop come Saturday, intent on choosing the following week's listening. A simple act often directed by superlative laden reviews in the *NME* or *Sounds*. No matter that Chris Sievey was very happily married. Something within him yearned for that state.

Despite being arguably the most ungainly song title of the past 30 years, 'I Can't Get Bouncing Babies by The Teardrop Explodes' was a clever little ploy of Chris's to forever link The Freshies with the considerably more successful Teardrop Explodes. Strangely, three decades later, Teardrop Explodes devotees – and some have survived the pop wars – would see the name The Freshies pop up whenever they Googled their favourite band. Not for the first or last time we see the hand of Chris Sievey reaching into the future.

This little ploy would still cause twists and panics some 30 years later within myriad radio stations across Britain. The 2014 use of 'Jazzler' radio playlist software being a case in point as the listings would often just state 'Bouncing Babies'. I do recall Freshies fan Paul Ripley of Manchester's Fabradiointernational, in an attempt to bring Sievey's star band to the attention of his Monday evening audience. Excitedly pluck 'Bouncing Babies' from the database, introduce it as The Freshies, only to be confronted with the earnest vocals of one Julian Cope. Sometimes, Chris's wry ploys twisted into reverse. Funny though.

Sievey's fan 'mail-outs' continued with extraordinary regularity during his time at Rabid. This one, 'All That Razz Issue One' seems particularly interesting as it deals with the seismic shift towards MCA and – the band hoped – a new long term relationship with a major record company at last. The distribution deal referred to would take away the legwork of, literally, wandering coldly and unannounced into record shops who wouldn't, by and large, express a great deal of interest in The Freshies. Although their forthcoming semi-hit 'I'm In Love with the Girl from the Manchester Virgin Megastore Checkout Desk' would change all this, it seemed to allow the system to take the strain, leaving Chris with a smaller mail out itinerary.

Not that he started to spend any less time in the Rabid office... it simply freed him to dream up new and bewildering forms of merchandising madness. While most of it would continue to fail, it might be noted that, again and again through his career, he managed to lock into a pre-echo of the future of the music business. Years later, at the start of the new millennium and given the global internet explosion, almost every band and artist on the planet would be firmly sold to the notion of 'merch'... to a ludicrous degree. Sievey never managed to perfect it, but he certainly glimpsed that new age... although admittedly The Grateful Dead had managed the same on a slightly larger scale!

MICK MIDDLES

ALL THAT RAZZ
ISSUE 1 £12.99

The Freshies,
20 Cotton Lane,
Withington,
Manchester,
M20 9UX

Hello Mail order fans,

Quite a lot has happened since Mail Order Sheet 1. For a start we have now signed a pressing and distribution deal with MCA Records for all our singles and tapes in the future which means basically we can carry on recording what we like, when we like and they stick it in the shops. Which is great for us because, although it's great fun running your own record company in so far as recording what you like and doing covers etc, the business side of getting into shops is very time-consuming and has always been our downfall. But now we can spend more time getting on with things like gigs. I will come to that in a min.

Right, we have just recorded a new single which comes out on the 27th March but, please note, it is not available from us. You will have to buy it in the shops. It is called 'Wrap Up The Rockets' and the B side is 'Gonna Get Better' (MCA 693). But there will also be a limited edition 12 inch single with an extra track called 'Tell Her I'm Ill' (Mcat 693), so if you want the 12 inch one, I'd order it now. We have also just completed RazzVizz 2 (On VHS only). I am afraid most of our Razz back catalogue has now run out. The only records or tapes left are>>>

Razz 6, 'Yellow Spot' single £1
Razz 7, 'No Money' / 'Oh Girl' single £1
Razz 9, ''Last' / 'Baiser' single £1
Razz 10, 'Razzvizz' 1 Hour video cassette £13
Razz 11, 'Virgin Megastore' / sing-along single £1
Razz 12, 'Certain Megastore ' / Bleep version (DJ copy) £2
Razz 13, 'Razzvizz 2' 1 hour video cassette £13

I'm afraid that all other records and tapes have now sold out but it is possible that we might press up the cassette LP onto plastic, but it won't be until 1982 at least. It looks quite possible that the records above will sell out soon due to the success (?) of 'Megastore'. So really we won't have anything to sell on record or tape. But we will still be doing the videos mail order, but we will carry on doing a mail out to you, so if you wish to remain on our list, please always include an SAE or you wont get a reply.

We have been asked by many people if there is a Freshies fan club but we are against the idea that you have to pay to be a fan, because you pay enough buying the records, don't you? So I suppose really that is a sort of fan club. So when records run out here we will carry on writing to you and sending you information but please don't forget the SAE. Anyway, if you send a large SAE to us next time you will get a photo and a badge UK. Please note our new address for ALL mail from now on and address it to The Freshies. Thanks for all your support.

Chris Sievey
PTO for gig info.

Christmas special – BBC Scotland's 'VideoGaiden' – a computer game television show; a perfect vehicle for Frank Sidebottom. (GaiDen, incidentally, is a Japanese word for 'Side-Show'). Perhaps this was Frank's most bombastic television appearance… although there have been a fair few. A sizeable chunk of Scottish schoolboys and nerds confronted by an extraordinary rendition of 'Christmas is Really Fantastic', even to the extent of knocking over the studio Christmas tree.

AVENUES OF INFLUENCE

TWO TOWERING PILLARS OF INFLUENCE served to dominate Chris, pretty much throughout his entire life. Both started to twist and stir his imagination in early boyhood and remained solidly in place, surfacing within all his work, casting obvious shards of brilliance or lurking in the shadows.

Chris was just six years old when The Beatles crashed spectacularly into the cultural spotlight, hanging in the air with omnipresent dominance up to and way beyond their split. No other musical artists affected Chris to such profound effect and even the disrespectful blast of punk would not be enough to untangle the bounds of connection within Chris' imagination. From a very early age (7 his brother Martin states) Chris fixated on The Beatles studying each and every song. By the time he hit his mid-teens, his knowledge of The Beatles had become encyclopaedic. The construction of songs, the eternally fascinating band dynamic – power struggles between Lennon and McCartney and Harrison and Lennon-McCartney – and the outrageous prolificacy that existed during their relatively short time as a band. All of this consumed Chris and his own songwriting always stood as a testimony to this fact. At one point, in 1986, his enthusiasm spilled into a large writing project which, from the examples he showed me, would seem to rival Ian MacDonald's imperious 'Revolution in the Head', arguably the greatest work on The Fabs and one which dissects every song, every nuance and places them in the context of the music, rather than the personalities involved. Needless to say, it was a worthy tome duly devoured by Sievey without, it seemed, a trace of envy.

The other influential strand, equally profound within The Freshies and, more obviously, Frank Sidebottom and areas of animation beyond, was unquestionably Gerry Anderson, the somewhat undervalued creator of, amongst many others, Thunderbirds, Stingray, Captain

Scarlet, Fireball XL5 and Space 1999, which was born from the ashes of Anderson's earlier creation, UFO.

Again, Sievey was consumed (almost) from the outset. He was surely too young to fully appreciate the complexities of 'Torchy the Battery Boy' or 'Four Feather Falls' , the latter emerging at the turn of the sixties. Although 1960's 'Supercar' probably caught his attention. But it was the futuristic space adventures of 'Fireball XL5' and the oceanic shenanigans of 'Stingray' that initially captured his attention before the big one, 'Thunderbirds' initially hit the flickery small screen in 1964 apparently inspired by the West German mining disaster of 1963.

Because of the comedic aspect of dubious sets and juddery puppet characters, many would latterly deride these amazing creations, believing them to be lost to a world of juvenilia. But this was precisely the aspect that most appealed to Sievey. They were, indeed, locked in a simplistic world that would never escape such boundaries. Sievey always knew that he could also work within those parameters.

Looking at The Beatles and the Anderson influences on Sievey, it might be easy to sense the emergence of a schizophrenic aesthetic state and, indeed, the suggestion that it was The Beatles who duly inspired The Freshies and Anderson who lurked within the creation of Frank Sidebottom. This is a little simplistic. Although disguised, Sidebottom's music contained many of the hooky pop twists he would have learned from his Beatles study while deep within the work of The Freshies, can be found touches of simplistic sci-fi: 'U-Boat' and 'Wrap Up The Rockets' both exhibited a juvenile take on extremely serious issues, for example.

Some aspects *are* unusual. The level of Sievey's obsession with both could certainly be said to be extreme and, in places, unhealthy. Not many 15 year-olds would stay up all night dissecting obscure Beatles songs. More obviously perhaps, while the rest of us left Thunderbirds behind and became fixated on more mature cultural outposts (James Bond, The Man From Uncle) Sievey's fascination for Anderson remained solid. I find it difficult to think of anyone else, friend or artist, so fiercely locked within a youthful passion.

Of course, to lock Sievey within these two dominant pillars is somewhat simplistic. Chris's cultural passions, if not obsessions, ran far deeper than that. One recalls detailed discussions with him on the subject of Lou Reed – 'New York', a particular favourite, Van Der Graaf Generator as stated, The Mekons and Subway Sect. Chris was fascinated by the post-punk era when a band's vision and ethos could be perfectly encapsulated within the release of a seven-inch single. In particular, that pre-album period where singles would be the only option for the band and the only way one could catch a glimpse of them. More often than not, the debut albums that followed seemed disappointingly fleshed out. The mere locking in within two and a half minutes was always a fascinating discipline. Just as well, really, as The Freshies – with a couple of concept exceptions – never managed to break from that minimalist heart. This subject would obviously surface within The Freshies 'I Can't Get Bouncing Babies by The Teardrop Explodes', the subtext of which is, again, an obvious obsession with format. Within this area, he also expressed fondness for The Skids, Undertones, Gang of Four, Human League (the classic version most obviously clasped between the covers of the single, 'Being Boiled' without an ex-cocktail waitress in sight) Cabaret Voltaire and The Passage.

On one occasion he listened to The Skids long lost 'Charade' six times on the run in order to understand Stuart Adamson's bubbling guitar interplay, presumably with himself.

"How has he done that? Don't quite get it," he stated with furrowed brow.

When I informed him, on the phone, of a band who had segued one song into another – can't recall which, I am afraid, although have a feeling it might have been something by V2 – he insisted that I drive immediately from Disley to Timperley in order for him to study said transition. This particular area of intrigue would later surface in the late twist within 'Wrap Up The Rockets' which flows into 'It's Gonna Get Better'. That particular twist was inspired by a Stiff Little Fingers gig. (On 16 February 1979. Chris was particularly aware that the Stiff Little Fingers album had kick-started Rough Trade and he loved the sheer energy rush of Jake and the lads.)

Other intriguing obsessions bubbled under the surface, later to become illuminated in the Frank Sidebottom era. A deep knowledge and love of certain variety characters is hinted at by CP Lee – another influence on Sievey. He loved the Lee led Alberto Y Lost Trios Paranoias – as Lee recalls, "Chris loved George Formby back in the seventies. But oddly we never got to talking about Frank Randle, so I don't know. He liked the humour in Formby's songs and all that Northern whimsy."

This, I believe, was apparent within the work of The Freshies, long before Frank made his appearance. At that point, the debt to Formby became obvious and was arguably reflected within the strong empathy Frank (nearly) always enjoyed in Lancashire.

I recall also talking to Henry Normal in the mid eighties. At that point he was a struggling performance poet, often sharing a bill with Frank and spending long hours in the back of cars with Chris, zipping up and down our beloved motorway network. Normal would later emerge as partner to Steve Coogan within the immensely successful Baby Cow film and television production company.

"We talked about the old days," Normal recalled, "The Freshies a great deal but he wouldn't talk about Frank. However, he would chat with great knowledge about George Formby, Les Dawson or Norman Evans. I had studied these people so we got along fine. I was surprised at the depth of his knowledge."

'MY TAPE'S GONE' (RAZZ 1980)
'WE'RE LIKE YOU' (RAZZ 1980)
'YELLOW SPOT' (RAZZ 1980)

The Freshies releases on Razz, under the guidance of Rabid, were arguably the area that, although not making any headway or providing necessary gravitas at the time, would eventually cement their cult appeal. However this would take many years to become apparent. Three releases in particular ushered in the beginning of the eighties and would gather a certain fondness from fans decades later. 'My Tape's Gone', 'We're Like You' and 'Yellow Spot' – all snubbed by a music press that was suddenly wavering precariously between the stark pomposity of post-punk and the garish new age of pop – remain proof that this was a band capable to pulling, tugging and messing with that notion of 'the pop single' in a manner rarely equalled at that time… at least outside the environs of Swindon, home of XTC. The two bands had much in common. While XTC were obviously the more successful outfit by far, it can be noted that they never compromised their natural aptitude for quirky invention much to the continued angst of their record label. Sievey had been an admirer since catching XTC live at Belle Vue playing 'Scooby Do Disco' in 1979. Chris mentioned meeting Andy Partridge on one occasion although, as far as I am aware, it was not at that particular gig.

While I remain particularly fond of 'My Tape's Gone', it was the third of this holy trinity, 'Yellow Spot' that gained a tangible notoriety and for a gloriously Sievey-esque reason.

What began as a sprightly song soon evolved into a single that typified both Sievey's attitude towards self-promotion and Tosh Ryan's mischievous muse. Ryan had been flushed by the success of Jilted John's 1979 hit, 'Jilted John'. Despite Ryan initially opting to stick the jaunty song on the b-side to 'Going Steady', he eventually bowed to pressure, flipped it and licensed it to EMI. He understood the power of a pop single etched from a gimmicky scenario and sensed a similar kind of precocity within Sievey to Jilted John's creator, actor Graham Fellows aka John Shuttleworth.

'Yellow Spot' was not a song capable of surging into the top ten in a similar manner, but both Sievey and Ryan were convinced that they could use the disc as a lever to lift the band onto the disparate roster at Stiff Records. Both Sievey and Ryan were strong admirers of Stiff and its tendency towards the idiosyncratic. What better home for The Freshies?

With this in mind, Chris devised a cunning and mind-bogglingly convoluted scam. During a speculatory visit to Stiff's London office, Sievey helped himself to a wad of Stiff's headed notepaper. Back home and ensconced in the Rabid office, he sat before his illicit pile and duly scrawled missives to all manner of journalists and music business luminaries, briskly informing them that '…something very big is about to happen at Stiff Records.'

To intensify matters, Sievey also sent two mock memos to Stiff bosses Dave Robinson and Paul Conroy, each one apparently from the other partner.

OUT OF HIS HEAD

"Dave, I can't tell you what is happening but be here on Friday at 5.30pm… and don't mention anything to anyone…" and vice versa.

Similar letters were also delivered to everyone who worked in and around the Stiff office. One can only assume that an eerie conspiratorial silence ensued within that esteemed office on the appointed day, with everyone pretending to be 'in the know'.

To Sievey's delight and considerable surprise, both the Stiff bosses appeared to eagerly fall for the set-up. Well, at least, they would have done had the Stiff phone lines not be completely jammed by feverish journos and mightily intrigued music biz folk. Typical of Sievey, perhaps, the resultant chaos was worse, far worse, than he could ever have intended or envisioned.

Down at Stiff, the chaos exploded into action. Sensing a rat, Conroy confronted his staff and a mass scrutinising of the fake missives took place that afternoon. All had one thing in common. They posed the mysterious question "What did you see?"

The answer should have been provided when Chris and Tosh arrived at the Stiff offices at 5.30pm that Friday, armed with a single with the catch line, 'What did you see? I saw a Yellow Spot!"

Perfect? Not quite. The mass scrutinising produced one letter where a biro impression word 'Freshies' could faintly be seen.

"I thought about this, afterwards," Sievey admitted to me in 1996, "and I remember writing a quick note to someone on a piece of paper that rested on my stack of Stiff notepaper. It was before I had written the fake notes. I must have pressed too hard with the biro… or something."

"Paul Conroy was angry," Sievey stated. "It was because we had caused his company to grind to a halt. It also happened to be a really busy afternoon at Stiff and the last thing they needed was a couple of northern idiots causing total chaos. He was screaming at us. Needless to say, we didn't get a deal at Stiff. Well, I would soon come to work with them so maybe it worked out in the long run. But on that occasion, we didn't even get to play them the record. Suddenly me and Tosh were sitting in a London pub getting absolutely ratted. We spent a lot of our time doing precisely that. What else was there to do? We started to see the funny side. So did Conroy… eventually. He half-heartedly even offered me a job in their promotions department. I thought about taking up that offer but I didn't want to drag Paula down to London. I didn't want to leave Tosh either. He had spent a lot of money on me... but then I did go... for a while."

Tosh Ryan: "I was always aware that, at any given time really, Chris and the band could have walked away, leaving me in the lurch. I should have worried more about that, knowing how fucking selfish musicians can be in terms of their own career. Actually, if they had walked away, it would have saved me a huge amount of money. As it was, I continued funding them... fucking insane that was."

And somewhat ironic, too, as the next single would be called...

'NO MONEY' (RAZZ 1980)

It might be noted that Chris saw his relationship with Tosh a little differently. On this endearingly catchy song, he rather sheepishly concludes:

"...there's no money, no money, no money for me."

Ryan: "No money for fucking Tosh would have been more accurate... the bastard!"

'No Money' is constructed around a simplistic revolving melody, punched into a faster gear by Spencer's spiked indie-guitar and the pulsating bass of Sarko's temporary replacement, Richard Maunder. 'No Money' is the blatantly honest tale of penniless musicianship and fading dreams. It nods towards the great lost Shell Silverston song for Dr Hook, 'Cover of The Rolling Stone', where the singer disdainfully glances towards fellow contemporary artists who had gained greater prominence by featuring on the cover of said organ.
So to Sievey who, in a state of wholly understandable envy, spent every Thursday evening watching a parade of – as he naturally saw it – lesser talents in thin ties and garish suits, leap gleefully about in front of the usual plethora of gormless girls in feather cuts. The

ritual of the British hit record.

Sievey knew full well the astonishing power wielded by the monopoly of Top of the Pops – and Radio One airplay - a situation unprecedented in subsequent eras. But still, The Freshies were left to distribute their single by hand. And it was, indeed, on such a jaunt of self-promotion that gave rise to the band's most successful single… a single that, despite going on to sell over 40,000 copies, would suddenly fade in a state of agonising inevitability.

INCIDENT AT THE CHELSEA SPACE GALLERY

NEXT TO TATE BRITAIN, JULY 4TH 2007

There have been a number of Frank exhibitions over the years. Mostly, they have been relatively modest affairs, attended by faces familiar from the front rows of his many shows. Rarely, if ever, did he manage to break from that occasionally suffocating circle of loyal fandom. No putdown intended. As stated earlier, Frank fans are almost always the loveliest of people, if often pleasantly unhinged. One thinks of two separate and gentle exhibitions at Stockport Art Gallery which did little more than reinforce standard notions of Frank. There would be, of course, a shed, heads and bodies of Little Frank, Little Denise and Amoeba Frank plus the standard selection of doctored Frank heads and sundry artefacts. Mostly these events were lightly supported by articles in the local press. If in Manchester, they would attract the attention of the now defunct *City Life* – the magazine and not the Friday supplement in the *Manchester Evening News*. In fairness, the *NME* would pitch in now and again. Rarely, however, did Frank or Chris find themselves taken seriously by more elevated organs.

The one exception was Frank's exhibition of drawings, animation, cardboard and wood constructions that courageously took place at London's Chelsea Space Gallery, next to Tate Britain, between July 4th and August 4th 2007. This event even gathered a splattering of supportive nods in the arts listing sections of several broadsheets. *The Guardian* even penned a short but profound piece praising 'the existential nature of this unique northern artist…' This became my favourite piece of Frank press, mostly because of the use of the word 'artist' rather than the lazy and much loathed 'Timperley funnyman'. Perhaps because of this exposure, and once beyond the opening attendees at this successful month-long exhibition didn't much look like Frank devotees at all. Perhaps they were merely curious and the kind of people who generally frequent exhibitions at art galleries on the Thames. I can't be sure, although it was a refreshing diversion. However, the entire affair was somewhat marred in true Frank style by an incident that occurred at the opening involving Frank, a wall and a pot of paint. This was archetypal Frank, of course, and is nicely reconstructed in 'Being Chris Sievey'. However, it didn't particularly please the management factions of the Chelsea Art Space who later descended on Sievey demanding an explanation. Sievey of course, merely shrugged and said, "…why are you asking me? Ask Frank?"

No two Frank Sidebottom shows were ever the same. Even the template for the basic show would twist and warp with elements of randomness and on-stage bravado. Chris could scrap whole sets and think nothing of staying up all night hammering a contrasting set together, cobbling up a few tight phrases although, mostly, he would allow the show to find its own way, punctuated by a string of favourite songs. These could drop through the floor at any given moment. Steve Sullivan recalled an evening when Frank simply turned up with a Subbuteo pitch and challenged members of the audience to a game.

"But Frank's team didn't have real Subbuteo players," he stated. "There was a Skeletor in there and he literally parked a bus in front of his goal."

RAZZ RECORDS PLAN OF STRATEGY

THE NOTION THAT THE FRESHIES, despite Sievey's personal and driven promotional nouse, were often held back by a hedonistic chaos – before and during the Rabid period – does carry some support, not least from the band themselves.

Barry Spencer: "Most of the time nobody had a clue what was going on. It was chaotic and we wouldn't have had it any other way."

Rick Sarko: "Mostly we would just turn up somewhere and play. It was difficult to have any other kind of input and we didn't mind because we left that to Chris. Whether Chris and Tosh really knew what they were doing was dubious, to be honest. Often they were off their faces. Again, we didn't mind a bit. We were never that kind of band. If we wanted more money or something doing differently then Chris would have done it for us."

While this is undoubtedly true and, indeed, while other local bands such as The Distractions, Joy Division and V2 seemed to employ a more steely attitude towards the vision of their own future, it was difficult to pinpoint this with The Freshies.

However, as this one month strategy revolving around the release of the Razz/Rabid double 'A' Side, clearly shows, an underlying seriousness did prevail. Unusual too, to see almost 1,000 singles reserved solely for promotional purposes.

Tosh Ryan: "Mostly I remember just flying by the seat of our pants. Very little was planned. I think we did get a bit serious around the time of 'No Money' though."

The reason for this might well be inherent within the very title of that song. Nothing so empowers a band and/or label more than an encroaching sense of desperation.

This was Razz 7. As stated, one thousand promotional copies were press and, transforming the Rabid office into something of a post room, the attack on all forms of media certainly seemed to be concentrated... to say the least.

FRESHIES PLAN OF STRATEGY:

Date to post	To whom	Qty
Mon June 9th	John Peel; selection of national fanzines	27
Tues June 10th	Rock DJs on IBA local radio	25
Weds June 11th	Rock DJs on local BBC radio stations	13
Thurs June 12th	Select producers of Independent TV shows	6
Frid June 13th	Rock DJs on Pirate Irish radio stations	15
Mon June 14th	Phil Sayers (BBC Radio Manchester)	1
Tues June 17th	Select overseas DJs and press/fanzines	18
Weds June 18th	Review copies for Music Week/Record Biz	4
ThursJune 19th	Review copies for local fanzines	7
Fri June 20th	Review copies for NME, MM, RM, Sounds plus Staff	43
Sat June 21st	Copies to major label A & R Depts	12
Sun June 22nd	Copies to directors of major labels	24
Mon June 23rd	Copies to Piccadilly Radio DJs	11
Tues June 24th	London gig venue DJs	15
Weds June 25th	Northern newspapers with bio, pics	18
Thurs June 26th	Select DJs at UK venues	48
Fri June 27th	Copies (without centres) for local juke boxes	15
Sat June 28th	Copies (without centres) for national juke Boxes	36
Sun June 29th	Programme controllers on independent Irish radio stations	13

Mon June 30th	Heads of BBC radio plus daytime Irish radio Station DJs	39
Tues July 1st	Programme controllers on all IBA radio stations	41
Weds July 2nd	ALL IBA DJs, Radio 1 producers, local BBC directors	322
Thurs July 3	all radio DJs	14
Frid July 4th	(Release date) 'Oh Girl' commences on tip sheet	1
Sat July 5th	Producers/directors/BBC/ITV/ music shows	47
Sun July 6th	Odd Radio 2 DJs. 25 to ATV Music	30
Mon July 7th	All local BBC Radio libraries (two copies each)	46
Tues July 8th	Daily papers/odd music publishers	13
Weds July 9th	Heads of BBC radios 1 2 3 4 and libraries	24
Thurs July 10th	All IBA radio libraries (3 each)	69
Fri July 11th	'No Money' on Tip Sheet for following week	1
Sat July 12th	Copies to record distributors	18
TOTAL		**937**

Remaining copies to be used for any forgotten.

Not too sloppy. The sheer physicality of this campaign seems exhausting. Especially by the standards to today where MP3s are reluctantly clicked out *en masse* and find further fire power by way of social media. One imagines Chris Sievey's daily wander to Withington Post Office, encumbered by multiple and often garishly decorated record boxes.

A dense swirl of blue cigarette smoke; eyes flashing through the night. It was a darkened room, upstairs at a Macclesfield pub. The lost days of 1992. The young comic Steve Coogan sat attentively by the bar, his pride flushed by a recent show at Manchester's Green Room where he had seemed unassuming and, perhaps, lacking the prevailing vitriol of post-Ben Elton comedic diatribe. He wasn't, he admitted, entirely sure which way to mobilise his act. Without doubt, his little skit on 'The Sweeney' – "There was one place he used to go… a deserted quarry…" had caused a ripple of amusement. On this night, he was accompanied by Manchester promoter Sandy Gort who would, one day, write an – as yet unpublished – book detailing the early nineties swell of comedic and musical talent on the small Manchester gig circuit. The agency he co-founded, 'Funnyside', would handle many of the acts – Coogan, Henry Normal, Johnny Dangerously, George Borowski – who would break through to greater artistic riches during the coming years. But this was an embryonic Coogan, wondering how his ability to flow into character could carry him to the glories of television.

Ten minutes earlier he been talking openly and sharing a pint with Chris Sievey. Coogan was fascinated by Sievey and the stark transformation from Chris to Frank. Frank didn't know Coogan and failed to acknowledge him as he walked past on his way to the lighted stage. There could have been 20 or 30 people there that night, it is difficult to recall. Frank was at his effortlessly shambolic best, however, throwing himself into a seemingly impromptu George Michael/Wham! medley which included the wearing of a leather jacket. Something that I never again witnessed. He might well have been loaned the item at the venue and tailored his act accordingly. Whatever, Coogan seemed duly impressed. Within weeks he had honed and perfected an alter ego of his own by way of a woolly hatted chap incapable of sensing his own irony. He was called Duncan Disorderly and, for a while, joined the flowering little pub circuit, adding deft touches of character here and there. Duncan Disorderly flickered briefly on Granada Television, unwittingly laying the groundwork for Coogan's hugely successful characters – Paul Calf, Alan Partridge and Saxondale – along the way. But back in the shadows of one of the most prominent film and television careers of the past two decades, flickered a man in a papier-mâché head.

MEGASTORE MADNESS

THE MANCHESTER VIRGIN MEGASTORE, rather like its London Oxford Road counterpart, was rooted in nostalgic '70s Bohemia. Back then, pre and post punk, it sat squarely on Lever Street, a hop away from the eternal circling throng of Piccadilly. It was downbeat, funky, mildly intimidating and terrific fun. Walking in you would be hit by swirls of dubious smoke. You could pause at the lively notice board – on which Howard Devoto once famously asked, 'Musicians wanted to play fast and slow music'. John McGeoch was one of the responders. Many times, Chris had posted similar requests. Every Saturday from 1972 to 1978 he would enjoy the shop's dishevelled charm.

And it was charming, too, You could drift to the rear and spend an entire day listening to the coolest sounds, swapping gossip and generally soaking into the heart of the Manchester scene, such as it was.

Certain rituals had to be obeyed. A completely up to the minute knowledge of the *NME* was deemed essential. Purchases, it always seemed, had to be passed by the critical eye of whichever hippy manned the counter. In 1975 you would be met with a definite nod of approval had you wandered to the counter clutching Little Feat's 'Feats Don't Fail Me Now' or, a year later, Nils Lofgren's 'Cry Tough'. Amazing albums both and both, incidentally, could be found lurking in Chris Sievey's album stack at home.

Should you ask for the same albums two years later, however, you would be met with a gaze of steely disapproval. Even the window was something of a barometer of cool. A hand drawn advert for tickets to Led Zeppelin's infamous Earls Court shows tempted many. Two years later passers-by were instructed to 'Watch The Sex Pistols tonight on Top of the Pops'. Everyone obeyed.

MICK MIDDLES

The opening of the replacement shop, the Virgin Megastore on Market Street, hailed a depressing new era for music retail ending the lovely pastime of lounging around record stores for hours on end, spending very little but soaking in the vibe. The vibe had been deliberately broken. For here could be found pristine racks, chrome and mirrors. The psychology was of the quick sell. Dive in, grab an album, pay at the checkout and back out to join the Market Street throng. Nevertheless, in 1979, a number of post-punk reprobates schooled in the ways of the old shop, started to irritate the hovering security guards by indulging in the subversive activity of standing around, enjoying the prevailing bonhomie and flicking endlessly through the racks, scrutinising sleeves front and back and generally using the shop as a social club.

Chris was a regular among them. The faintly subversive activity attained almost religious relevance. However, this was tinged with certain sadness. It was difficult not to realise that something had irrevocably altered, a corner had been turned. To some extent, this shiny new paradise signified the dying of post punk... it was the perfect palace for the bright new pop era of the eighties.

For Chris it represented something else. It was the physical manifestation of his endless quest to alert the record companies of Britain to the northern delights of The Freshies. For eight years he had steadfastly bombarded every London record company office... and for eight years derisory rejection slips had drifted depressingly back. Meanwhile, all manner of pop and rock acts, from those of blinding brilliance to hapless half-hit wonders had been snapped up by enthusiastic A and R teams. So why not Chris Sievey? Why not The Freshies? Could these people not recognise true artistic talent?

"I spent many years in a state of bitterness and bewilderment," Sievey admitted to me in 1982. "I became obsessed. The very act of mailing and winding up record companies started to become the heart of what I did and still do to some extent. I can't say that I wasn't bitter. Any songwriter who has been through that level of rejection would feel bitter. That's why I decided to make a bit of a nuisance of myself."

Sievey's one man crusade had changed shape, of course, with his merging with Rabid. And who better to accompany him than the equally devilish Tosh Ryan… an unholy alliance indeed.

To the casual listener, a song entitled 'I'm In Love With The Girl On The Manchester Virgin Megastore Checkout Desk' might seem to offer little more than gimmicky whimsy. A song, perhaps, deliberately created in order to catch instant attention in the vacuous manner of, say, The Piranhas 'Tom Hark' or 'Nellie the Elephant'. Indeed, gimmick hits had been featuring all too regularly on Top of the Pops in 1979, deflecting the attention away from loftier chart entries. But the song that was to become The Freshies biggest moment wasn't founded on gimmick at all. Almost a decade of hurt had been poured into that apparently lightweight lyric. The frustrating juxtaposition of a long-term songwriter drifting through the aisles at the Virgin Megastore, scrutinising endless artists seemingly effortlessly enjoying a record company home… studying the logos, the artwork, the song titles… all that pain served only to add spice and power to one of the most perfect pop singles of the era.

"It is a criminally underrated record,", Mike Doherty concurs, "it takes a particular kind of genius to string together a series of record company names in the form of a pop lyric. I just thought it was going to be a massive hit from the outset. That it wasn't is completely beyond me. Circumstance perhaps? Who knows? But it is still a brilliant record."

Chris Sievey's ongoing angst is the true heart of a lyric, even if it hangs on a title born from a moment of instantaneous lust. This proved to be one of the few times where a sharp blast of sex appeared in a Freshies lyric. It was a true story, too.

"It is what it is," said Sievey. "It was me and my mates in the store and my attention being caught by a beautiful girl. What more can I say. I didn't act on it…"

Well, other than write a song about it, one might conclude. Although Tosh Ryan seemed to believe that there was slightly more depth to the title than that.

"I seem to remember there being two girls," he stated. "He had written that song, 'Two of the Same Girl' and I am sure he told me that it was about the same situation. Chris was a man who fell in love a lot but to fall in love with two girls instantly, while of course being married, seems pretty bizarre."

The song was written on the night following a visit to the Megastore. Sievey sat piecing references to his multitude of rejection slips, fusing his angst with his new fleeting infatuation. The song took all night to form.

Tosh must have been duly impressed as he allowed Sievey to prize the final £74 from the dwindling Rabid fund to book time at Liverpool's Amazon Studios. The track took exactly one hour and fifteen minutes to record. Ryan's stack of 2,000 copies sold out within two days. As a second batch of the same number swiftly followed suit and with Radio One increasing its rotation, Ryan swiftly approached the one record company that didn't feature in Sievey's bulging rejection slips folder – MCA. The subsequent licensing deal was swiftly completed and 'Megastore' would enjoy an elongated 13 week run on the Radio One play list, even managing to remain in place throughout the typically swollen Christmas chart. The dark and cruel irony that unfolded, however, saw a postal strike prevent the chart return statistics from the north of England reaching the central computer in the heart of London.

I recall the shrill of my phone in Marple. Late night, oddly enough. Picking it up, I was met by the disembodied voice of David Hepworth, then editor of hugely successful teenzine *Smash Hits*. When *Smash Hits* called, and out of hours, you knew it must have been serious.

"Have you heard of this band, The Freshies?" he asked.

"Been writing about them for years," I replied, somewhat testily.

"They are going to have a big hit. We need a feature on them for next week's mag. Can you do it for tomorrow?"

It seemed that, at last, The Freshies were breaking through. Relief started to spread through my thoughts. Chris Sievey as a pop star? Perhaps it was inevitable that a bizarre twist of fate would suddenly intervene and place a barrier between Sievey and the success he had always craved.

"When 'Megastore' took off… or looked like it was taking off, we really did think 'this is it, boys'," recalls Barry Spencer, "well, we thought it would be an interesting novelty record, not necessarily of high artistic value but a good pop song nevertheless. And to an extent it was. But because of the problems at the BBC at the time and the Top of the Pops thing it was in the charts for a long time. Months. We were lined up for Top of the Pops for at least two weeks running... on standby. It was the guys who carry the amps who went on strike. The floor managers etc. Typical isn't it. At least three weeks went by with no Top of the Pops. But I believe that they played Top of the Pops out with the video of 'Megastore' filmed in Manchester. People today have no idea of what it was like to achieve that echelon of success back then. That you had to sell a huge amount of records - at least 70,000 - to get in the top fifty."

STEPHEN DOYLE

There are many ways to meet Stephen Doyle in 2014. One might discover him, stage-front at a gig by the mighty Kill Pretty, head lost to ecstatic concentration as the complex thrust of their late-age punk washes through the room. You might find him lost to the anguish that typifies the mental state of the contemporary Manchester United fan. Or indeed, you could find him in his Swinton abode, surrounded by the treasures of his obsession. For Doyle was the quintessential Freshies fan... Oh I know, there are so many. His story detailed in his own words is, at once, rather sweet and unholy. However, unlike many of his Freshies loving peers, he never fully made the transition to Frank devotee.

The best way, I suggest, to meet Stephen Doyle is to witness his staccato delivery during his excellent 'Sonic Diary' show on Salford City Radio. Even visiting the station proved neatly unsettling. Located to the rear of Swinton Town Hall, the station – which broadcasts way beyond the field normally associated with community radio - boasts none of the sexy dark confines normally associated with radio stations. Nevertheless, it is all the better for it. For a workmanlike aura of professionalism prevails... radioheads can be found sitting around the central room, pouring over newspapers and schedules. In the summer of 2013, Doyle had invited Barry Spencer and Rick Sarko into the studio to present a 'Freshies' special. It was one of the local successes of the summer and seemed to fall neatly in-line with the slides towards the Frank Sidebottom statue unveiling in October. Suddenly, people of a certain age, were desirous of a return to the pure driven pop typified by that particular band.

Stephen Doyle: "The first time I had ever seen The Freshies live… I had sort of read about them in the *NME* and *Sounds*… probably you. I saw them support The Undertones in 1979. Weirdly, I knew what you were called because you used to be involved with *City Fun*. I was obsessed with *City Fun* Fanzine and I hand wrote a little letter to it when I was 16. It was a review of The Undertones. They used to type out and print everything that everybody used to send. I knew that The Freshies were the support band. But I wrote, in the review, that although their music seemed good, I got a bit bored and went to the bar and came back. I wasn't a reviewer… I did that one and one of Joy Division at The Russell Club."

Despite his almost obsessive immersion in the local scene and, indeed, early exposure to The Freshies, Doyle had yet to become a fully-fledged fan. To be brutally honest, while 'Megastore' certainly swelled the audience levels, the very notion of a 'fully fledged Freshies fan' wasn't particularly feasible at that point. They just didn't seem like a band who could be your life, although Stephen Doyle might disagree.

"Then, kicking forward a few months to about the middle of 1980, Chris Sievey was on Piccadilly Radio, probably on the Ray Teret Show. A friend of mine, who was slightly younger than me, had got into punk, massively. He listened to the radio all the time. And he dropped off a couple of the earlier Freshies EPs and a few tapes. He said, 'have a listen to these!' Reluctantly, I did and I immediately thought they were absolutely brilliant. It was about 1980… so I went to see them at The Lamplight Club in Chorlton-Cum-Hardy. I was completely sold. I thought they were absolutely superb… what a great band. I remember speaking to Chris Sievey and Barry and Rick. Chris had been running his little fan club, sending mail outs and all that. He was totally ahead of the game, in that DIY aspect. I had never known anything like it. You could buy his singles from him. Buy Freshies videos, which I have still got. I still have four of them. Like many other people, I just started interacting with him and I became a massive fan. I might be wrong, but no other band, especially in Manchester, seemed to be doing this. In fact, the others seemed to be very aloof.

"About a year later, in 1981, I remember them playing four Tuesday nights on the trot, with George Borowski and the Fabulous Wonderfuls, they were supporting him. I even took a little £20 tape recorder with a microphone and recorded the gigs. (Steve, later, converted some of them to MP3s and played them on his Sonic Diary Show on Salford City Radio)."

It was the beginning of a mighty fandom.

"We just became obsessive fans and started following them all over. We went to see them at The Rock Garden, in London. The Gallery in Manchester. Stockport… I saw them about 40 times, more even, in that era although at The Rock Garden, that was a story. Chris Sievey did a coach trip from Manchester to The Rock Garden in London. It was typical Chris this, in those pre-internet days. Being on his mailing list, I got a little letter in the post every week. And one week he advertised for places on the coach. I rang him and booked four places on the coach for me and my mates. He said, 'Yes Steve, no problem.' We met in Manchester and I was with three proper scally mates, I'm from Ordsall, Salford. We turned up with loads of beer. And we got on the coach and there was Chris and Barry and Rick and Mike and wives and girlfriends and me and my pals who I had got into The Freshies, as such. And we go down the motorway, drinking and going mad. Bear in mind that we were pretty hardcore United fans at that point, so this seemed like any other weekend, really. By the time we got to London, I was absolutely pissed as a fart. I had been drinking since midday and we got there about 6pm. So we all paid our £2 or whatever and went in and I was really, really drunk. I got to the bar and was slurring my words while trying to order. And the barman refused to serve me. Can't say I blamed him but he shouted to the bouncer who grabbed me and flung me out of the club. Literally. So I am out in Covent Garden, totally out of it. But because I had spent time at the Manchester Apollo and those places, getting in free by blagging in the back way, I got the idea that I would do the same at The Rock Garden. But it wasn't like that there. There was no back door as such. So I wandered off around Covent Garden for hours… probably went in a pub and got more pissed. I ended up back there when they all came out and it was weird. It was like an incident.

"I remember a few years later, bumping into Chris at The Boardwalk in Manchester. He was laughing… saying 'Oh my god remember that gig at The Rock Garden? How did you even find the coach?' I didn't know, really. I just woke up in Salford and fell into the house. So we became really friendly with the band. We were like mates with them because we were just always there."

THE FRESHIES LAY THE TEMPLATE FOR MÖTLEY CRÜE

Barry Spencer: "These were just continuing good times. We all liked a few beers and still do. Occasionally we would get a bit too drunk but nothing more than any typical gang, really. Chris was no different to the rest of us. We had no indication whatsoever that he would one day becomes the hedonist that he is known for. He wasn't really so hedonistic back in The Freshies days. I think he was just young like us and we tried a few things. He tried drugs once back then, like we all did. We never did it again. We would have a drink and a laugh… just young lads. There was no real indication of how wild Chris could go."

PHIL JONES

Phil Jones has maintained a powerful presence on the Manchester music scene since the late seventies despite, as detailed by him here, the occasional stint in the capital. Originally from Leeds, he drifted into the role of promoter after graduating from Manchester University. Emerging through the eighties as one of Britain's premier promoters, he never forgot that his initial grounding came via two vital gigs with The Freshies. In later years, he enjoyed many encounters with both Chris Sievey and Frank Sidebottom. Latterly he has enjoyed extraordinary success guiding the career of a rejuvenated John Cooper Clarke and running the Manchester Food and Drink Festival.

Meeting him on a blustery February morning in 2014 proved suitably inspiring. For he lives on the hilly cusp where Cheshire meets Derbyshire's dark peak in a glorious stone barn building. Inside lay the heart of his obsession. Albums, CD's, DVDs and tapes furnish the room and beyond, in the angular hallway, a plethora of benign rock biographies and Wisden Cricket Annuals. In amongst this cornucopia sits a 'Sidie', the name of the Frank Sidebottom statuettes presented by Sievey to those who aided his career. Obviously a prized trophy, Jones' 'Sidie' proudly stands in its own display case. (If I had had the foresight to take a similar precaution, my cat wouldn't have sent mine crashing to the living room floor). On Phil Jones' family table, a scattering of Freshies and Chris Sievey solo singles, accompanied by a mid-eighties copy of Johnny Dangerously's immortal 'Black and Blue'. Dangerously, later retreating to his true name Bramwell, would lead 'I Am Kloot' and, later still, would come under the steely guidance of Phil Jones. Odd threesome, I thought. Bramwell, Cooper Clarke and Sievey/Sidebottom. Throughout their careers there remained powerful connections and similarities and not merely because they performed together on so many occasions. When I mentioned this to Jones, he immediately agreed.

"Yes, you would definitely link those three together... strangely. Maybe add George Borowski too. They are all more popular than famous. I seemed to have

specialised in that kind of artist."
    Huge and hidden followings. A soft and silent fondness that spreads across Britain and beyond. And it takes a promoter of rare intelligence and foresight to be able to unlock that following.

Phil Jones: "I don't recall the first time I met or promoted The Freshies. But there were two very significant gigs that I was involved with. One was at Comanche Students Union in Manchester, where the early New Order would soon play. I had started as a post-grad student in 1980 and this couple turned up at my door and asked me if I would get involved on their entertainment side. I had been putting gigs on since graduating in 1978 at The Garrick and The Squat Club. I kind of got to know everybody and got to know how things worked within live music. Anyway... these guys had heard of me and asked if I would organise the Fresher's Ball. So I did. Because of those Squat Club gigs and the Rock Against Racism gigs I had put on, I had got to know Tosh Ryan very well because he was running the fly-posting thing. I used to go and drop my posters round for Tosh. I think the next afternoon, I bumped into Tosh in Didsbury and told him what had happened. I told him that the hall held 1,000 people and wondered if the band he was looking after, The Freshies, would play and Tosh bit my hand off.

"So it happened. It was The Freshies and Ex-O-dus (a Factory reggae act of 'English Black Boys infamy') and it must have been around the time of 'Megastore' and the gig was October 1980. It was in the City College of Manchester refectory. And the pair of them just about sold 1,000 tickets and the college couldn't believe it. It was helped by the fact that we did these arty posters and Tosh posted them all over Manchester. You couldn't walk round a corner without seeing them. Tosh keep printing more and more. Must have been 500 of them all over Rusholme. And the gig did really well. In fact, that was probably the first time I ever made any money for me or anyone. I really enjoyed it. The Freshies were absolutely brilliant. The students couldn't believe what was happening in their refectory. From that we did a few more gigs and we ended up with New Order in that hall in 1981."

WRAP UP THE ROCKETS

Issued in 1981 by MCA, hot on the heels of the fading 'Megastore', it had been felt that 'Wrap Up The Rockets' contained enough hooks and dips to suitably cash in on The Freshies' brief flash of fame. It was, in fact, The Freshies' beautiful simplistic take on the somewhat serious issue of nuclear disarmament. The song's greatest achievement being the centrepiece of the band's set at the Tosh Ryan and Phil Jones' promoted 'Carnival Against Missiles' held in Moss Side's Alexander Park in 1981.

Phil Jones:"The other significant gig I was involved in was that was that Carnival Against the Missiles in Alexander Park. It was supposedly against the Greenham Common Missiles and somehow we managed to shoehorn rock music into it. We had an amazing bill lined up for that and one by one we lost the main acts. I still kick myself for that. We had Ronnie Lane's Slim Chance, Hawkwind, The Damned, The Freshies, John Cooper Clarke. But the week before, we looked at it and a lot of people were asking who Ronnie Lane's Slim Chance were. And we looked at it and decided to drop them. I was given the job of ringing Ronnie Lane to tell him he couldn't come and this was about eight days before the gig. He was really, really disappointed. I couldn't believe I was telling Ronnie Lane not to come (which, incidentally, would have been the last ever Ronnie Lane and Slim Chance gig). Then, about two days before the show, Hawkwind rang up and said they were in the studio and were stuck making an album and couldn't come. We were left with The Damned, who were great, Clarkey, who was brilliant and The Freshies, who went on first and were absolutely at the top of their game. Chris came on and he just blew this park away, he really did. They were a tight band at that point. Barry was a great guitarist, Mike a fantastic drummer and Sarko superb. There was between 10,000 and 15,000 people in that park. Yes a few were asking where Hawkwind were, because they were still on the posters. Those posters, by the way, which I fucking screen printed myself, were going for £35 on eBay last year."

It was a day of downbeat inebriation, heavy policing and street level polemic. Not, perhaps, the perfect vehicle for a set full of jaunty pop licks – hence the swift penning of 'Rockets' but a memorable mess of mud and dope, grass and beer, reckless, vaguely antagonistic dancing and supreme, if off-kilter, performances by The Freshies, John Cooper Clarke, China Street and Steel Pulse.

"Of course we even fucked that up in a way by choosing to perform in full combat gear," admits Barry Spencer.

"It did dawn on me that it might not be entirely appropriate to wear combat fatigues," Tosh Ryan concurs, "but I think everybody was too pissed to notice. It was a political theme close to my heart, but I'm not sure that it worked. Low level politics was everywhere at the time and, more often than not, it was an excuse for thugs from both political extremes to get their boots out."

If nothing else, The Freshies joyous set served to diffuse such tensions. One still wonders why a song as infectious and hook-laden as 'Wrap Up The Rockets' failed to fly up the charts.

"While 'Megastore' was plagued by problems outside of our control," adds Ryan, "Rockets had no such excuse. Everybody connected with the band felt that it would be a huge hit. It was even more obviously commercial than 'Megastore' and, what's more, was pretty much in tune with the way people were feeling at that time."

No greater subversion, one might conclude, than to wrap heavy and intense political – or sexual – feeling within such a light and rickety pop framework. While the charge of flippancy might hover near, it is still a masterstroke to be able to capture a song that so perceptively attacks both sides of the nuclear divide. It is a song that simply states, 'Fuck it... we can't do anything about it. Let's get pissed and have fun."

"From the Carnival Against the Missiles gig onwards I tried to get The Freshies as much work as possible," Phil Jones recalls, "but it just seemed to fall away from them. I eventually moved to London and Chris used to come and see me in my office down there and misbehave all the time. It was right down near Denmark Street and he loved the idea of the history down there and all that. So we stayed in touch... oh he turned up one day with Victor Brox, who we were looking after. I don't know. It just seemed to me that Chris's heart wasn't quite in The

Freshies anymore. He seemed to have other ideas floating around his head."

But how did the prodigious Sievey/Ryan partnership crumble to a halt? Did it dawn on Ryan that the bird had flown? Did they simply fall out? I recall one gig, mid-tour, at Manchester University. Tosh's son, Adam Ryan, was manning The Freshies drum kit. Packed hall, powerful gig. All seemingly well. I stood with Ryan and the impish impresario John Barratt at the rear of the hall. When I told Ryan that I thought they might finally be getting somewhere, he started to slowly shake his head in a disconsolate manner. After the show, Adam joined us.

"I have played the whole tour with The Freshies and they are not like any other band I have ever known, every other band goes on and on about how they are going to get somewhere... and they are going nowhere," Adam continued. "Playing with Chris, you get none of that. It is not about getting anywhere. He is totally mad but the band never have that horrible serious band meeting where the bass player starts to sulk and all that. It's very refreshing. None of us expect to make it." And all this from a man about to secure a lucrative multi-album deal with a major record label... but not with The Freshies.

Tosh Ryan: "Did we fall out? Not as such. We fell apart. He owed me so much money and I couldn't really go on... but I stayed involved for a while. I think Chris started working more in London at this point. He finally had this thing going with Stiff Records... Oh that was after he played on the 'Going Red' single ('Some Boys') with Graham Fellows (Jilted John, John Shuttleworth). I don't know. Things get a bit muddled. There may have been a spell when we didn't speak. But then he would just turn up and it would be ok. Personally, if not artistically."

As the eighties started to unfold into a garish new age of pop, Chris Sievey, as Tosh noted, had found himself working in a rather ad hoc capacity at Stiff Records. While The Freshies were holding firm, his mind, it seems, was wandering across new pastures. It was while still working with Stiff that the notion of dabbling with computer games and mixing such 'dabblings' with regular vinyl releases first occurred to Chris. He sensed that some kind of seismic change was about to occur and that Stiff might like to fund research into his innovative notions. Unfortunately, the idea was met with a lukewarm response from Dave Robinson and the powers that be at the record company.

It was an understandable reaction. The 'mad artist dabbles with new format' syndrome is guaranteed to bring forth giant and garish 'warning signs'. Not only does it immediately sound expensive, it surely arrives with little opportunity to recoup any initial monies. This is little more than the classic clash of artiste and financer. Even in the days when record companies could actually find returns for serious investments, it was a dangerous area, especially so for a small company armed with absolutely no knowledge whatsoever of the impending fiscal powers of computer graphics.

Nevertheless, Chris was distraught. He had spent weeks dreaming of this courageous, if rather ambitious, new venture and had sufficiently researched his pitch, or so he thought. The response to his over-active imagination was little more than a steely roll of the eyes and, during the following week, no phone calls came in from the company.

This wasn't the only problem. Although Stiff liked the Freshies song, 'Camouflage', they objected to the use of the line 'Sinking Americans' within the lyric. In addition, the company had showed a reluctance to instigate a follow up to 'Fasten Your Seatbelts' which had sold reasonably without creating much of a stir. Most artists are actively encouraged into a paranoiac state when the initial energy and enthusiasm of such a company suddenly begins to drip to a deadening silence. This is evident with those lack of phone calls; the fact that key people suddenly appear to be sitting in endless meetings and the nervous glance one gets from the office staff upon paying the company a surprise visit.

Worse still had been the gentle prodding by Stiff A & R personnel designed to guide him away from the more experimental areas he wished to travel and, on one instance, openly requesting that he should '…write more boy meets girl type material'. Chris had already decided that 'boy meets girl' type material was something he would allow to languish in his past. He had done 'boy meets girl' to death.

It was, admittedly, on odd situation. For this was 1982 and the British record industry, having surfed the myriad uncommercial traumas of the post-punk era, was seemingly entering the second age of pop. Powered by the new medium of the pop promo video – which, of course, The Freshies had helped to instigate – whole tribes of garishly clad bands claiming new romantic attachments started to flood the charts. Worse still for the serious indie music fanatic, essential organs such as the *NME* and *Sounds* had started to give less coverage to labels such as Factory, Fast Product and Postcard and started to champion even the most lightweight pop acts. So began Paul Morley's love affair with Trevor Horn within the pages of *NME*. A fact that even saw him hurling superlatives at the likes of Dollar and Bucks Fizz alongside emergent pop acts such as Haircut One Hundred, ABC, Culture Club and Spandau Ballet. *Sounds* soon followed suit, with their former indie champion Dave McCullough flirting inkily with acts such as the newly hyped Wham! Almost overnight, stalwarts such as The Fall were reduced to bit parts. The *NME*, now seemingly happy to hurl their energy at the major record labels, even openly asked of Factory Records, "...could somebody please shut the fucking place up?" No more Joy Division monochrome it seemed and new organs such as the beautiful Neville Brody designed *The Face* and the even more garish *Blitz* only served to encourage this axis shift towards a colourful new age of pop.

This is relevant here because Chris, in his own head if nowhere else, had moved from being out-of-fashion creator of brash colourful pop to take up – as he saw it – an exciting new ethos of pushing music and ideas towards new boundaries. With immaculate and not atypical timing, Chris' new found yearning for left-field innovation perfectly reversed the prevailing trends of the day. Typical.

Undaunted he decided, in his words, to 'hand in his notice' to Stiff and pursue his creative muse in his own way. Back in Altrincham, a chance meeting with the first Freshies bass player, Paul Burke and Paul's friend, Nigel Howard, led to a pint which, in turn, led to several more pints and an excitable threesome who exited the pub as owners of a new label called 'Random Records'. A new style of label and one that would not ask its one and only artist to 'write more boy meets girl type material'. Indeed, this company would actively seek out licensing deals to put out music and computer game packages.

Well, sort of.

And a few other things. Maybe? Ok, it was an ambiguous mission statement but something that, if nothing else, could allow Chris's imagination to fly. This is something that had started to become apparent back at Rabid. What once seemed exciting and new, full of possibility and wonder, had started to nurture traditional record company boundaries. On a day-to-day basis, the closer to success The Freshies edged, the more they became locked in the mechanisms of a traditional band. 'Camouflage' had been Chris's way of attempting to arrest this situation and, back at that Manchester University gig, Tosh knew it.

As such, Chris Sievey and The Freshies were in a state of disarray, with their leader pulling and pushing them in unfathomable and myriad directions at once. This flyer, from Sievey's own typewriter, hints powerfully at a new way forward.

CHRIS SIEVEY WORLD (MAY 1ST 1983)

"Chris Sievey... the man who made garage land audible cassettes acceptable as far back as 1974; ...the man who was one of the pioneers of the independent records boom in 1976; ...the very same man who brought out the first purpose made pop video in 1980 ahead of 'Eat to the Beat'; ...and the same man who for the first time in the UK publicly showed 3DTV... has done it again.

Yes, Chris Sievey gets another world first with the first ever computer-pop-promo!!! Not only that but it's FREE on the B side of his new single, 'Camouflage'. Confused? Then read on... when you buy a copy of Chris Sievey's new single, 'Camouflage', take it home and play the B side and all you will hear is '... beep... beep... beep... etc'. This, of course, will mean nothing to you at all ...unless you happen to have a 'ZX81' home computer. For if you play the B side into your 'ZX81' ...then turn over and play the A side, you will get the lyrics displayed on your TV set in sync with the song along with bits of computer graphics and patterns. A novel and unique idea which may prove to revolutionise the music industry, as Chris has already been approached by major labels to write programmes for other artists... but remember who did it first.

The B side also contains two more of Chris' programmes. A 1k and 16k version of an arcade type video game called 'Flying Train' the ideal game for those who can't decide whether they want to be an engine driver or an astronaut when they grow up - and all for the price of a single.

WHAT IS A ZX81?

For those of you who do not know what a ZX81 is (and if not, why not? It's no good sticking your head in the sand). It is a personal home computer that retails for under £40. Produced by Sinclair, it is about the size of a single sleeve and has a touch sensitive keyboard. It contains about 8k RAM (The brain, so to speak) and 1k RAM which is expandable (The space for storing memory). It uses basic computer language and can be used for education; keeping accounts; keeping catalogues; diary; mail order lists. As well as playing 'Flying Train' and watching 'Camouflage', so go and buy one. It is important for your future, especially if you are unemployed. We are all going to have to learn how to use them.

RANDOM RECORDS NEW LABEL

'Random Records' is the new label especially formed to launch Chris Sievey's new idea of putting computer software on record, with the average price of programmes between £5 and £10 on tape by other firms, Random's new low price should shake the computer industry up a bit and bring prices down to a more accessible price in today's inflation torn country.

IT SEEMS OBVIOUS to point out that gaming – and inventing, rather than merely passive playing – has always figured in the make-up of Chris Sievey. While this is clearly true, it is perhaps rather lazy to cast him, as many have, as a true innovator within the gargantuan ocean of electronic gaming. He perhaps could have been, had the main thrust of his working life not been gathered by activities elsewhere. However, and again, perhaps because of the pressures of being a father, attempting to become the front-man of a major international pop act and coping with the oncoming spectre of Frank, Chris delvings remained fleeting and rather sweetly lo-fi. More than that, the DIY ethos he had nurtured would be refreshingly infused within his computer work; a fact alone that serves to set him aside from the raft of intelligence of the big guns, beavering away in, say, Silicon Valley. As such, his entry into the world of computer gaming rather perfectly mirrored the tentative early steps of The Freshies.

Of course, as Paul Molyneux stated, Chris had always held a penchant for the magical creation of games and gaming.

"As far back as I can remember, I have always been surrounded by felt tip pens and crayons," Chris said. This was a fact that he carried throughout his life. Even in his latter days in Hale, the house would be bulging with packets of pens... some opened and scattered across tables, many still waiting patiently in their packs. Pens – often the cheapest possible varieties procured from the local newsagent, would always serve as Sievey's truest medium. The ultimate accessible aesthetic tool, be it for sleeve design, deceptively simplistic daubing, fan mail outs or, indeed, the invention of simplistic games.

"That is something I have always naturally done," he said. "Way back, I would gather my mates around from school and try out games with them. Sometimes they would be far too complex... sometimes just stupid. But I was learning all the time. Not just about the cleverness of the game, but by watching my mates trying to grasp it. It is not that different from writing a song, I discovered that quite early. It is the process of getting people's attention and stirring their imaginations. Got to be fun, too. I don't know if I was ever any good at it. It was just something that came naturally to me so, when I got a chance to put this into The Freshies output, even if only trying little things out really, I jumped at the chance. It really excited me."

As the link between music and gaming had yet to be visualised, let alone forged into a commercial reality in the early eighties, one can lay a claim for Chris striking a unique if somewhat modest course. As hinted by Chris's comments, the core of this largely unrealised desire and talent owes little to electronics. The history of computer gaming – which arguably stretches back to the 1950s – actually lies within more primal areas of gaming and, perhaps, warfare. There are only so many basic games, and many evolved neatly through the boom period of board games. Electronics served to accelerate these basic game themes into a dazzling universe, of course, and this seems to explode and evolve on a daily basis. I have no doubt that, had opportunities presented themselves differently, Chris Sievey could have enjoyed a highly lucrative career at the very peak of international gaming. There is a paradox here, of course. Would the celebrated 'out-of-the-box' vision make him too random for the unfolding process of commercial gaming intelligence? His comments above, delivered in 1992 but within retrospective thought, suggests that he had started to understand the principles. That computer game innovation is more rewarding if it picks up the threads of the players' imagination and gently stretches them to the horizon, rather than approaching from a completely new direction... if there are any completely new directions.

As this is now firmly in retrospect and, given the frenetic unfolding story of gaming, Chris's tentative dabblings now appear locked in a rather sweet world of sub-retro. Nevertheless, intriguing they remain.

In 1982, the computer gaming industry was comparatively pedantic. The Sinclair ZX81 had emerged as one of the first truly low-cost gaming computers. There were other embryonic strands, of course, but it was the ZX81 that first managed to capture Sievey's imagination and offer him a glimpse of the 'crystal cathedrals' that would emerge during the following decades.

In the late seventies, Chris had filtered his experiences within the music industry — albeit mainly in the areas of rejection — to build a complex overview which he filtered into a board game. He knew one thing. For all the rejection letters and prevailing arrogance, the music industry remained sexy and fun. They greatest fun he had ever glimpsed. A pathway of dreams and ambition. How wonderful, therefore, to filter all this hope, ambition, wild and extraordinary success and artistic brilliance... filter it all into a board game called... called... 'The Biz'. Early versions of this remain lost in a maze of hastily scribbled upon cards, boards and jotters full of rules. It didn't get beyond the kitchen table, however and, along with his myriad artefact collection, the embryonic 'The Biz' took dusty residence in the darkness of his loft.

Something changed the moment Sievey encountered the ZX81. Instantly he could see potential stretching towards a brilliant future. Despite having no personal money and, indeed, despite the competitive high price, Sievey managed to obtain one — Thanks Tosh! — and spend all his downtime, typically running through the night on many occasions, getting fully acquainted with this exciting new device.

MICK MIDDLES

His first attempt resulted in the game/video link called 'The Flying Train', which attached itself in a rather ungainly manner to the B side of The Freshies' extraordinary but largely ignored single, 'Camouflage'. While not entirely successful due to reasons of lumpen technology, Sievey would later defend the outing by claiming: "The Flying Train was the first budget game! The single only cost a pound and included the game while computer games at that time were £5 and up.

"Spurred on by the minor kerfuffle caused by 'The Flying Train' – I was never fully satisfied. I didn't really know what I was doing, but it was a first for The Freshies and it gave me the bug," he added – he started meddling with the idea of transposing the bare bones of 'The Biz' from board game into the electronic medium.

"The actual process wasn't that difficult for me," he explained. "It was merely a logical progression. The thing is that the game remained the same. It was just a matter of sorting out the technology."

Personally, I find lines such as "…it's just a case of sorting out the technology" carry a wearyingly dark inevitability and of course, this did prove to be the stumbling block. It wasn't Chris's knowledge that stalled, it was the fact that he just didn't have the necessary RAM. The ZX81 had, even in comparison with its contemporaries, a tiny memory and certainly way below the necessity for setting a complex computer game. Even when Chris managed to secure a 16 RAM back up pack, the process moved at a snail's pace, often freezing at breakthrough moments. It was frustrating in the extreme and provided Chris with a lesson he wouldn't forget. Even in later years, PCs would find it difficult to effectively cope with his continuous flights of fancy. Even when gaming was clearly heading for a golden age, he felt shackled by technological restrictions. Not a problem encountered by artists using more traditional mediums. He acknowledged this further paradox during an interview with *Muze* Magazine in 1986.

"Painters… or even people like me, who often prefer to just use pens, are never controlled by day-to-day technological advances. It's odd because, on the one hand, computers are fantastic and incredibly exciting, I mean, who knows where it will lead? But on the other hand, why should artists be controlled by their own computers? I found it, at once, restricting and incredibly empowering."

OUT OF HIS HEAD

In building 'The Biz', Chris found that the more he devised, the more he wrote, the more he became restricted by lack of memory. He started to search for a computer with larger memory. Again, attaining more memory is such an everyday activity these days. Back then, however, the available information and subsequent devices seemed inadequate and contradictory as computer manufacturers battled for prominence within the embryonic market-place.

It was fortuitous therefore that just as Chris was beginning to doubt his ability to pursue the game to its conclusion, the 48k Spectrum appeared in the shops. This employed a similar 'BASIC' system – much to Chris's relief – which meant that the sticky problem of converting files and programmes proved less traumatic. However, unable to raise the necessary finance, he borrowed a Spectrum from a friend and continued the conversion. It was obvious to Chris that the market for Spectrum programmes was opening out before his eyes, offering rapidly unfolding possibilities. For a while, Chris was bedazzled by the possibilities. Even given the ease of conversion, Chris struggled for "…a month or so…" to fully get to grips with the Spectrum. Especially as he realised that elements of each and every file needed "…painstaking tweaking. It was an immensely frustrating process."

While Chris had expected to bring the game to a reasonable and saleable standard within a few weeks, the reality of writing and conversion meant that 18 months passed before 'The Biz' finally appeared. The deeper he wrote the more it opened new possibilities. Even given Sievey's natural penchant for applying himself to endless through-the-night stints, this proved one of the most demanding projects of his career. His desire to make the game as 'challenging and interesting' as possible meant that he was constantly re-inventing his own ideas.

"I was my own worst enemy," he later admitted. "I was taking it too far and couldn't work out where the cut-off point could be. It is a bizarre industry, even back then as things were changing all the time. I could understand why some people go completely mad and I decided that my ventures into gaming would be occasional. I couldn't have done that full-time. It wouldn't have suited me."

There were other problems. 'The Biz' arrived with Chris's own music tracks that had to be cleared for publishing, itself a somewhat laborious process. In addition he forced himself to re-mix and, on a couple of occasions, re-record old work, making it suitable to fit within the Spectrum format. While all this was taking place, it must be noted that The Freshies were still an active band, attempting to build on the fleeting glimpse of success to which they had been exposed. In reality, this meant that his new found passion for computer gaming had to be interrupted by gigs and rehearsals for the band. It must also be noted that the 12 inch single that came with The Biz gently introduced a new character... a little known Freshies fan called Frank Sidebottom.

Not that this activity appeared to cause friction. As Barry Spencer notes, "We were always completely aware that Chris had other things going on in his life and, to be honest, we completely accepted it. Maybe... maybe we were actually relieved in a way because it took a bit of the focus off us. It did sometimes get intense with Chris... not in a bad way. But it could be hard work."

In truth, Chris's game had been rather hastily snapped up by Virgin; a company keen to forge ahead in this exciting new area. Clearly they saw something within Sievey that could have been beneficial. As Sievey noted to *Crash* Magazine. "Probably because everyone else would have turned the game down! Only joking, it's because of my involvement in the music business and because I know Virgin as a record company and how they operate. Virgin know how to market music as well as computer games, whereas if I signed to a games company they wouldn't know how to market the music. Virgin know how to market both at the same time and do a good job. I wanted to make it a complete package and good value for money. You've got a game, some music and an exclusive interview with me. I think games costing £5 or so are far too expensive — these new budget games are a great idea."

The computer generated video for 'Camouflage', to be found on the 12 inch single prior to the game, is claimed to be the very first such outing. It is certainly, given the pace of computer development, a veritable museum piece now. Nevertheless it is sweet, gloriously innocent, stark and simplistic. It should be placed carefully in a museum and perhaps, in a way, it has been. Check it out on YouTube.

★

OUT OF HIS HEAD

NOVEMBER 2013

Kraak is a small, dense, catacomb-like venue – yet it felt oddly cavernous, that night. In later weeks we would see the glorious ageing thrash of Kill Pretty and it would feel small, tight and hot. But not on this night. Three solo acts would play. We would see two of them. The first artist, Harry Sievey, seemed detached, cleverly aloof. The sparse audience watch with an air of curious somnolence. The sound of 'Lovechild' crashing messily into sparse brick walls. At one point Harry asked for a bottle opener and, with that prize in hand, he duly flipped open the lager. After the set, we offer to buy him another beer although the question seemed to cause him problems as he swilled it around his head and stared into space. The set had been a fine blend of electronica, golden funk and an echo of The Cure. Harry was using these gigs, we felt, as rehearsal time… as an evolving experiment, perhaps? Soon he was gone, dipping into the night with his gear clasped under his arms. He seemed so vulnerable.

ENTER FRANK

"The emergence of Frank was really Tosh's fault. You shouldn't give a movie camera to a fucking lunatic like Chris. I recall Tosh telling me, 'Chris has gone fucking mad. He is filming himself in a big papier-mâché head and all that.' It really did seem as if Chris had completely lost the plot. Tosh couldn't see any worth in this at all... and still can't. But there would be Frank making his debut on film. No doubt with Paula acting as cameraman."

MIKE DOHERTY

"Chris told me that he had got this new thing called Frank Sidebottom. And it was a papier-mâché head and, of course, I couldn't understand what he was talking about. He asked if I could get him some gigs. I just said, 'well, I don't really know, Chris'. Anyway, he went off. I think he kept ringing for advice. I was a good friend with him and Paula at that time. Anyway, I eventually saw him doing Frank in a community centre in Cheetham Hill. Can't remember much about it. I think he had other musicians with him but it wasn't that full band."

PHIL JONES

THE FIRST KNOWN SIGHTING of Frank Sidebottom took place, fittingly, on the streets of Timperley – actually, it was Broadheath, but that might be a moot point – on December 16th 1982. The head was in place although it had yet to be refined to the iconic globe we all know and love. It was a kind of simplistic version and is captured on camera as startled passers-by glared with suspicion as this noisy and unidentifiable comic creation of the future strode about. How could they possibly respond in any way other than sheer incredulity? Frank, too, wasn't fully formed. Maybe he had yet to climb out of Sievey... maybe the persona had yet to be fully constructed, for this was a trial run, after all. Where did this come from?

Nobody I have spoken to in preparation of this book could actually suggest that they had seen elements of Frank before his eventual emergence. As previously stated, Frankisms were in evidence all over The Freshies but they had yet to be distilled into a separate persona. But had they already done so in Chris Sievey's mind? It is a question that seems impossible to completely answer. One senses strongly, however, that Frank's roots stretch fully back into childhood. I am not an expert on this... *nobody* is an expert on the roots of Frank. Chris once stated that his goal was to create a number one fan of The Freshies - a totally devoted nutcase who could, say, arrive before the band at some radio station and proceed to completely 'wind up' the girls on reception. This happened, but the reality proved far more complex than that. For Frank is a one off.

However, it might be likened to the feeling of being born into the wrong body. Not unlike the intellectual rather than purely sexual journey undertaken by those who, later in life, choose to travel across the sexes and emerge as a more complete self. This might sound like cod-psychology but time and time again this can be traced to early childhood. The best example of this I can find being Jan Morris's extraordinary book on her own journey from James to Jan, 'Conundrum'. That, I suggest, is the most fitting way to describe the relationship between Chris and Frank. A 'conundrum'. Unsolvable and eternally fascinating.

Mike Doherty agrees, "Yes, that is an interesting comparison. I do believe that Frank started much earlier than anyone could know. Even Chris couldn't have known what was going on inside. That would explain a great deal but Chris was a genius. Everything he did, he did without any prior knowledge. I mean, Chris had no idea how to make a papier-mâché head and use wire and cast it and whatever he did. He made it up as he went along. It was also just one of a hundred ideas running through his head at any given time. Which one would take off? Nobody knew, least of all Chris. It's fucking amazing that it was Frank. So you're right, I'm sure. But even Chris couldn't confirm that theory that Frank extended back to childhood."

"I had seen Chris messing around with Frank with the videos," Barry Spencer recalls, "yeah after Tosh gave him that camera. I think that at that time Chris didn't want to be Chris on camera but we didn't really think anything of it. We went to his house to do a few songs and try some new stuff out. And near the end he came out and put that head on and introduced him. At the time I just thought it was another daft diversion. I dismissed it, really. I was staring at a man with a big head and saucer eyes. It was a bit disconcerting, I guess."

"Then Chris said he was going to bring Frank to a gig at The Gallery." Rick Sarko remembers, "Well, not really, it was pics of Chris at The Gallery and he edited himself in, plus pics of Tosh playing sax. Possibly Chris had it in mind that he would be doing Frank for a long time, but I don't really know. It wouldn't have bothered me even if it became a threat to The Freshies. I just thought, 'you know, if he wants to do that, fair enough'. We were all cool about it."

Barry: Spencer "I can't remember any ill feeling about Frank at all."

THE FRESHIES - 'CAMOUFLAGE' (1983)

'Camouflage', technically one of Chris Sievey's finest melodic creations – and, indeed, one that hints somewhat ironically at a brighter future for The Freshies, effectively served to end their creative output. On the single the song remains concise and clipped to a sharpness that, had any kind of promotional investment been forthcoming, might well have troubled the lower regions of the charts.

However, it is best known for the aforementioned Sievey video taken at Manchester's Gallery venue on Peter Street in 1983. The Gallery, being cubic and blessed with a square, rigid balcony, was often used for its filmic qualities. Bands as diverse as Marillion, Manic Street Preachers, Ignition, Stiff Little Fingers and A Certain Ratio filmed there. Chris probably understood that it offered many clear stage views, especially from upstairs, when he decided to filter pics of Frank from a different Gallery audience into straight forward shots of the band onstage taken by Tosh Ryan. However, when I showed this video to Tosh in his house in March 2013, he was astonished at the footage which, as mentioned, also included shards of himself playing saxophone as part of his own underground outfit, The Prime Time Suckers, that were not apparently filmed at The Gallery.

However, the somewhat elongated introduction to the song on that film, which stretched beyond three minutes, didn't sit well with Ryan. "Get on with it… get on with the bloody song, Chris… am I filming while the band are mucking about like this?"

I must admit to rather enjoying the slow, cagey build-up. It was very un-Freshies and, yet again, indicated that practice room sessions had seen the band taking unlikely directions.

Barry Spencer: "Yes, I only saw that clip recently. We start to bed in musically I think around that time. If we had managed to keep going then a very different band would have emerged. It was an odd time, because it felt like we had hit upon a real purple patch."

The infamous 'Camouflage' video at The Gallery was, obviously, a Sievey edit of two separate occasions. The Freshies show, taking place over two shows. The matinee at 4.30 pm on October 4th, has often been claimed to be the band's final show as a full band. However four further gigs would simmer in and around the city. A ferocious Manchester Poly (Cavendish House) appearance on October 23 – always good to see the band perform beneath a giant painting of Dennis the Menace… a visual effect that hadn't suited Killing Joke – now languishes fondly in the memory as one of the band's most spirited shows… indeed, it was a gig that, for once, saw a band displaying its punk teeth. They also performed at the City Fun Swing Club on November 5th, old stomping ground 'The Brookfield' in Stockport two days later and then finally… finally, an apt performance at Altrincham's less than hallowed Unicorn on November 8, which is generally believed to be the band's final performance with Sievey.

Barry Spencer: "I think so, probably, although I couldn't say for sure."

Rick Sarko: "Can't even remember that gig, mate. Perhaps they did it without telling me?"

The second 'filmed' evening at The Gallery didn't feature The Freshies at all, but did see the introduction of Frank Sidebottom to perform in the famous camera smashing incident towards the end of 'Camouflage' (Although it wasn't really 'Camouflage'… if you catch my drift). On display that day would be Stockport's erstwhile 'Syncopation' who, under the guidance of the ever-ebullient John Barratt, had secured the gig as a live filming to go out on The Tube. Thankfully, Frank didn't manage to destroy the Channel Four cameras as well.

Although Frank had featured heavily as an aspect of the band's promotional activities, this is often cited as his first appearance before the Manchester public. And he cut an intriguing figure as Gallery manager Peter Gresty led him slowly, step by step, downstairs from the venue's balcony, much to the bewilderment of the crowd (mainly Syncopation's mates, if truth be told).

"What the hell is that?" was the general consensus.

"This is Chris's new character from The Freshies… really funny, he is," exclaimed Gresty as if to assuage the prevailing sense of anxiety.

Frank was guided into general view before a Manchester music scene that didn't quite seem ready to say goodbye to the band who, to use an old cliché of local journalese, was Manchester's best kept secret.

Stephen Doyle recalls his feelings when he initially met with Frank. "I couldn't understand it at all," he admitted. "I just thought Chris was messing around. I mean I had been a big fan of The Freshies, going to over forty gigs and was really into the music. I wondered why Chris wanted to mess around with comedy, which I didn't really get at all. I remember most people feeling the same way. Just like, 'OK very good, when are you going to do some more Freshies stuff?' It came as shock to realise that Frank was replacing the band. I mean… why? To be honest, I liked Frank but I still preferred the music. The proper music."

John Barratt: "I can't say it went down that well. I kept asking Peter Gresty why he was doing this with Chris, who I didn't know. I was also being a bit guarded, as my band were being filmed and it was to have been their big break. Knowing what I found out later, Frank was the last person I would have allowed in that room, that night."

Now here's a thing. While I can understand and sympathise with Stephen Doyle's state of angst at the sudden demise of The Freshies and, indeed, their bizarre replacement, he is, after all, voicing the emotions of a fan who cared deeply for the band (and he reverses this opinion at a later stage). As such his understandable bewilderment is too warm to be taken as an objective view. So too, The Freshies. Despite Barry and Rick's admirable display of understanding – a more liberal rock band surely never existed – they must have felt a sting of disappointment even if it was dampened by Chris asking them to join Frank's as yet undefined circus. (Barry skipped into a ferocious punk band, in response).

Yet Chris saw things differently. For all the brilliance and bluster of The Freshies; for all their promise and DIY ethos, by the time Chris Sievey came to write 'Camouflage', he knew full well that, to re-use the phrase, the bird had flown. The band's stab at the charts had passed. Chris was also deeply indebted to Tosh, literally and emotionally. As such he was well aware that he would have to pull something extraordinary from the wreckage of a great, though commercially unsuccessful unit.

And here was another thing. There was always a sharp wit and depth of humour to Chris's writings and he was beginning to understand that a traditional pop combo was perhaps not the correct vehicle to carry this. Fine, when it exploded into a 'Megastore' or a 'Rockets' but how could it be sustained without the band falling into a state of gimmickry? The fact that they had survived for so long was miraculous in itself. The very framework of the music was starting to restrict his aesthetic ambition and the use of Frank as a Freshies über-fan, as he was initially conceived, was perhaps not the answer. His imagination was constricted but a full on Frank Sidebottom, sans The Freshies, would offer him a virtually unchallenged state of artistic licence. For there didn't have to be any rules with Frank. None at all; no boundaries, no constant search for chart status and, what's more, he wouldn't necessarily cost much money. Stage sets could be constructed quickly and easily while giving Chris a chance to flex his considerable artistic capabilities. After all, he had been building towards this, albeit unwittingly, for an awful long time. Stirling's Yellow Submarine bedroom being merely the tip of the iceberg.

MICK MIDDLES

It was the aesthetic possibilities, rather than comedic adventure, that truly excited Chris and his extraordinary imagination simply exploded out of the confines of the three minute pop song, much as he loved that basic medium.

As Tosh has stated, he hated Frank from the outset and, as I write in March 2014, he hates him still as he prepares to abandon Anglesey for the warmer climes of Crete. Despite having known Tosh on and off for 30 years, he contributed to this book with an air of resignation, if not reluctance. I also think it is fair to claim that I helped pursue him to be interviewed on camera for Steve Sullivan's film and he resisted for a long period. I know Steve was concerned about this but Tosh's angst remains intact because it stretched beyond the money. His involvement with Chris and The Freshies was deeply emotional. He truly believed that Chris was one of the great visionary musicians of recent times (and this, from a jazz loving saxophonist of note). As such he was rather embittered.

The irony is that Chris knew this and knew, also, that the twist into a whole new artistic vision would have to be swift and forceful. Some people would feel the pain.

IN MARCH 2014, I found myself in a curious window in regard to the Jon Ronson penned film, 'Frank'. Despite shovelling a few batches of words into his excellent book which, in a lovely ambiguous manner, charted his valuable time spent within the bombastic confines of the 'Oh Blimey Big Band', I had yet to see the film. Beyond, that is, the slightly disturbing trailer that had been bouncing around Facebook. I had many questions about the film that would stretch the information he has kindly supplied here. However, it was two months prior to general release and I was determined to conclude this book before that time. In a curious way, this seemed a good thing, for I was lost in a world where naiveté clashed with knowledge. A number of my acquaintances – Steve Sullivan, Dave Arnold, Neil and Sandra Taylor and, naturally enough, the Sievey family, had seen the film and were seemingly reporting it in contrasting shades of critique. While everyone appeared to enjoy it and approve of the existential nature of the central 'Frankish' character, some people seemed concerned about how it would fair with the Frank faithful.

It was fascinating to sit on this particular fence, watching the debate rage on Facebook. Many of the Frank Sidebottom aficionados were seemingly outraged by the Americanisation of the character although Ronson correctly and repeatedly noted that it "…it is not a film about Frank Sidebottom but it was inspired by him." It must be noted that none of the hyper-critical viewpoints came from the tiny gathering who had actually seen the film and most found their angst soothed by the conciliatory replies of Arnold and Sullivan. The general consensus was that, although it was dark, surprising and will not please everyone, it would succeed in drawing many people towards the cult of Frank and, indeed, physically to the village of Timperley. In short, it would add a powerful boost to the burgeoning Frank industry. No bad thing, surely? As two talks – from Sullivan and Ronson respectively – would take place in Manchester on consecutive nights at the end of the month, answers in regard to both films would obviously be forthcoming. However, I enjoyed the magic of remaining in blissful darkness. I actually toyed with idea of finishing this book without seeing either film or attending the talks, thereby sealing it neatly in an inconclusive state. Perhaps that would have been the correct way to fade away… to never, perhaps, actually watch either film or indeed, attend the talks. However, as the March days tripped speedily by, and as you will soon discover, my initially steely resolve continued to weaken.

"I gave Frank my granny's Blue Peter badge at The Hacienda one night."

LESLEY LEE

MICK MIDDLES

FRANKENSTEIN

IT WASN'T THAT CHRIS had grown weary of The Freshies' continual attempts to steal into the charts – indeed he was still writing potential Freshies material at this point – it was simply that the artistic opportunities supplied by the Frank Sidebottom character seemed to open up before him. Piecing together the multi-layered life of Frank was not unlike building a computer game. In fact, Chris's experience served him well, as he devised the character, his friends, his geographical setting, possibilities of further characters – and dummies… he was well aware that part of Frank's character might peel off and become manifest in some form of puppetry, although it was unlikely that this – these if you include Little Denise and Amoeba Frank, both of whom earned early mentions in embryonic Frank outings – would have been simple cardboard cut-outs in his mind. In an interview with Piccadilly Radio's Tony Michaelides, Chris admitted: "Working on Frank is the most fascinating thing happening at the moment. I keep waking up in the night with another idea. I have to dive out of bed and jot it down."

This certainly hints that Chris had been carrying a number of character possibilities in his head. It could be that he had previously intended these for some kind of game or, as he once mooted, "a kind of human challenge… an outside game for people." This is intriguing. Frustrating too as nobody I have spoken to can ever recall Chris talking openly about such an idea. The odds are that it was a simple build on the 'Frank as Freshies fan' wind up… he could have included other people – REAL people perhaps? - within the framework of that idea. It was never to get anywhere, though, and Frank would inevitably break free from that embryonic notion.

Rick Sarko: "I rang Chris up and said 'I have just seen an article in *Sounds* that says The Freshies are no more.' Chris said 'Yeah, but you can join The Oh Blimey Big Band if you want.' I said, 'Ok', so we started practicing and lined up a gig at this working man's club. We went onstage and I just couldn't believe it. The crowd were going mad and absolutely loving it. It was dead easy for me. I was playing one note every three days on the bass, which was too much for me, actually. The crowd were just going crazy. I remained in the band steadily for a bit then it was on and off. Mark Radcliffe was in later when I played and Patrick Gallagher, I think."

Reports vary here. Memories begin to mist. Take this recollection from promoter Chris Coupe which builds the aforementioned Henry Normal more full into the story.

"You probably already know that Chris never actually intended to be Frank, his interest (at the time) was in film making and the Frank character was supposed to be played by Henry Normal but the head didn't fit Henry because Chris had modelled the character using his own head measurements. So they had to swap roles. At the time of Frank's early development I was involved in a local band called Beau Leisure and Chris was experimenting with all sorts of ideas including singing to backing tracks while playing his bass to songs like 'I am the Walrus'. We were Altrincham based and he asked us if he could do a couple of support slots at our local gigs to try out one or two ideas. One of these gigs was at the social club at Wythenshawe Hospital where, after a few tunes using backing tracks (which in itself I suppose was groundbreaking) he proceeded to bend down, fix on Frank's head, and then turn to face a very bemused and puzzled audience for the very first time. It was Frank's debut on a public stage. To be honest, from memory, it was utter shite and people genuinely though he had completely lost the plot. Obviously for Chris it was nothing more than a work in progress but I'm almost positive it was the birth of Frank on the public stage and at a hospital of all places.

"Chris and I did bits and bobs including co-presenting a couple of shows with Frank - we even used to fake live links and hand-overs when he was gigging live so the audiences at his shows believed the performance was being broadcast 'live' on the radio while the radio audience would simply hear a pre-recorded show! (Genius) I'm a bit pissed off because just a few months before he died he agreed to be interviewed as Chris (which was very rare) to chat about all facets of his life including the Freshies and Frank! He shared loads of stories and we recorded about 2.5 hours of stuff including the fact that Paul McCartney literally hated him and just didn't get Frank at all, despite both Chris & Frank's love of the Beatles. He told the story of how I'm in Love with the Girl... could have reached number one in the charts if it wasn't for the national postal strike. (I think this story is pretty common knowledge) and how when in America he used to love rushing outside the theatres and venues when Frank had just finished a performance so he could listen to the comments of the departing audiences and get a handle on the bits they liked and the bits they didn't! Obviously they didn't have a clue that the scruffy git having a quick cig outside was the character they had just paid to see.

"Then there was the story of how Frank's hand and arm gestures had been acknowledged by Japanese Mime experts and promoted to drama students as a quality example of how mime could be brilliantly used in performance art. Obviously Chris just went with the flow on this! He was the first to admit that he never studied one minute of mime technique in his life. However, the experts had picked up on the fact that without facial expression the character either wittingly or unwittingly, was interpreting and insinuating actions, moods and gestures using limbs as a way of compensating for the lack of facial expression and therefore his actions were interpreted as brilliant mime."

Barry Spencer: "When Frank started, Chris did asked me if I wanted to join the Oh Blimey Big Band and I recall him coming over to my house and we had a few cracks at some of Frank's songs. Well, there may not actually have been a band at that point, it was more of a concept. To be honest, although I liked Frank, I wasn't really interested. I like to play and thrash out a bit... you know, play a bit of rock. So Frank didn't really appeal on a musical level. So I ended up playing with Ed Bangor for a while because I could rock out and he made me laugh."

Paula Sievey: "Chris used to take over the house. It would be covered in paint and bits of wood and stuff. Cardboard palm trees and stuff. It used to drive me crazy. I was just a woman who wanted a nice home, like anyone else. And there is Chris, wrecking everything. I would go out and come back and it was like, 'Oh my god… what have you done?' It wasn't just like doing a bit of art on the floor. He would have backdrops stuck to the wall and would be spraying stuff all over the place. He would often be up all night hammering and sawing and spray painting… it was impossible. I used to give in and help him. He was such a creative person I didn't like to suppress it. But then after I left him the last time and he lived on his own, it just went completely crazy. You couldn't move in that house. Because he had always lived with me and I could keep an eye on him. But, once on his own he just let rip."

MANCHESTER DIVIDED

THE YEAR 1985 WAS, IF ONLY SECRETLY, a big one for Manchester music. Even more secretly, it was a big year for Frank Sidebottom. It was a year of silent emergence. While London organs such as *NME* openly suggested that Manchester was 'a city without a scene' and this despite shards of truth from its own emergent writers, Sarah Champion and Bob Dickinson among them, strongly suggested otherwise, these were actually frenetic days in the city.

Frenetic days in a city divided. Booker, DJ and visionary Mike Pickering was filtering Chicago house into The Hacienda while, over in unlovable Longsight, Roger Eagle's perceptive booking policy brought in a new spread of bands... REM, Green on Red, Prefabs, Waterboys... a giant swing back to guitar bands, back to chords and riffs and familiar structures.

There was more. Colin Sinclair's ex-school venue, The Boardwalk attracted the indie injection and the new wave of breakthrough Manchester bands – Roses, Mondays, James, Easterhouse, Chameleons, Jazz Defekters and Kalima, Creepers – jostled for position in the wake of Simply Red's instant rise.

The big three (Smiths, New Order and The Fall) remained dominant as indicated by the success of their competitive sets at The Festival of the Tenth Summer in 1986. It would all bubble on until Madchester... after years in the wilderness, a city resurgent.

...and then came Frank Sidebottom.

I didn't notice him at first, to be honest, as he neatly surfed this divided city, popping up with ferocious regularity to offer support spots at all the major venues... The International, Hacienda and The Boardwalk. The precocious personality of Frank seeping with organic ease into the bedenimed, inebriated gig goers who, three Red Stripes into any given evening, gleefully accepted the bizarre act consisting of a man in a papier-mâché head unleashing a barrage of barbed juvenilia. Where did this fit in? Some would ask that question. The local listings magazine, *City Life*, not entirely buying the joke as their overtly 'PC' writers questioned the depth of this new mini phenomenon.

Many discovered and duly fell for Frank's charms via his interventions on the then powerful local radio. Although, for those blessed with alternative tastes, a number of options – Phil Korbel's 'Meltdown' on BBC Manchester, for one and Tony Michaelides' (Tony the Greek) 'Last Radio Programme' on Piccadilly Radio the other. It was the latter that most effectively voiced the local scene, mixing bands breaking to gargantuan size – REM, U2 – with a raft of Manchester acts from the true underground... Inca Babies, Bodines, Big Flame, Tools You Can Trust, Ignition (featuring John Bramwell, later of I Am Kloot), Stone Roses, Kalima, Marc Riley's Creepers, Easterhouse and so many more. In retrospect, it might seem difficult to see how Frank Sidebottom might fit into such illustrious and eclectic company... but fit in he did, and beautifully so. This even filtered into the many radio sessions that glistened from Tony's show, most noticeably Stone Roses and The Alarm. Frank himself enjoyed a session and, by all accounts, caused considerable consternation among the bemused Piccadilly Radio staff. Nevertheless, the core of what would become his Oh Blimey Big Band was forged from this relationship.

Among the staff at Piccadilly could be found one Chris Evans, then a sidekick to both Tim Grundy (Bill's son) and the effervescent Timmy Mallet and Mark Radcliffe, soon to become Head of Music but then working as producer to daytime presenter Suzie Mathis. Evans and Radcliffe were particularly drawn to Frank's wild juvenile humour and one can certainly see this seeping noticeably in such future Evan's escapades as 'Don't Forget Your Toothbrush'. Before that, Evans would gain local credence as the Oh Blimey Big Band van driver.

Frank and the embryonic band even performed a one-off concert within Piccadilly's studio complex on a memorable Sunday evening before an audience of local journalists, promoters and disc jockeys. What better way to surreptitiously enlist the help of this extremely powerful local media army? Once they were in, and happy to be involved, they became part of a little in-the-know Frank club. Indeed, in time, Frank would build on this courtesy with the creation of the one foot high 'Sidies', crafted from model clay and presented to media people who had proven particularly helpful.

In terms of self-promotion... Frank was not quite as daft as popular notion would insist.

Also related to this would be Frank's fleeting appearances within the local magazines. Having been rejected from *City Life*, he turned up at the shambolic offices of *Muze* Magazine, a loose but fun mag dedicated to the promotion of the city's music scene. Frank was duly enlisted as 'star columnist' and given *carte blanche* to produce his own 'Frank's Firm Page'. This eventually turned out to be a crazed Frank and Little Frank based comic strip, painstakingly assembled – no doubt through the night – and brought to the offices by a beaming Sievey. The page, created on a large storyboard, would be reduced to A4 format and sat neatly alongside articles on the likes of Ignition, Easterhouse, Stone Roses and The Smiths. Lack of funds in the local media meant that Chris received no recompense for his toils, although he was sussed enough to understand the logic of the shop window. (Local luminaries, if no one else, would devour this bi-monthly offering). Not everyone got the joke and, even within the office, Frank's emergence proved slightly controversial.

"Why have that when you could have an article on a serious local band?" came one comment. Another contributor, Ann Winder, even penned a scathing review in the national popzine, *Record Mirror*, stating, "The joke, if there ever was one, isn't funny anymore," which, at least, proved that Ann had an ear for The Smiths. Ann's belligerence filtered into the *Muze* editorial within a piece entitled 'Both Sides of the Fence'. The simple idea was to present parallel opinions on a number of Manchester acts – James, The Smiths, Easterhouse and Frank Sidebottom – in both supportive and critical viewpoints. It wasn't really intended to be serious although Sievey, visiting the office one Tuesday lunchtime, was less than impressed. Sitting sullenly in the corner for over an hour he reluctantly agreed to wander across the road, allowing the editorial to buy him no small number of lunchtime pints. After the fourth, he mellowed considerably and, for the only time I can recall, fell into a tumble of self-doubt and lack of confidence.

"Do people not like Frank?" he asked, repeatedly. "I don't know what to do. Should I retire him?"

The answer was that, although most fully enjoyed the Sidebottom experience, there would always be a minority who just couldn't get the joke. He left happier with the thought that the same could be said of Tommy Cooper or even the Pythons. Nevertheless, it was a moment of self-doubt that proved unsettling for the editorial team who, never again, played tricks with Chris's confidence. We had stumbled on his hidden fragility.

THE TRASH AESTHETIC

SOMETIMES THE COMEDY MASKED THE ART, hid the heart. Sometimes it just got plain in the way. Sometimes it made the work too openly accessible. That is the central theme of this book. Not really a battle between Chris and Frank, but a battle between what is perceived and what is intended. You could take any Frank performance from, say, the late eighties; take Manchester's International Club, slap bang in the heart of edgy Longsight. Black and red in the club tradition… fittingly so, for The International had survived years as Oceans 11 and Genevieve's; soft mainstream low-brow cabaret clubs run by the dubious. As The International, booked by Roger Eagle and owned, in part, by infamous Stone Roses manager, Gareth Evans, it served as the central calling card for a thriving guitar-based music scene. Hurling Frank into the centre of that and something interesting emerged.

Oh it was a laugh, wasn't it? Seeing the Timperley one cavorting onstage, parading through the hits of, say, Wham! "Last Christmas I gave you my heart…and the very next day you *threw* it away," he mimicked, placing emphasis heavily on the word threw. Perfect comic timing, actually and considerably cleverer than it initially seemed. For at the back of the heads of the inebriated revellers, so many of them in the latter stages of student hood, a loathing for all things light and airy, poppy and glib… a loathing for all that had long since started to manifest. And there was Frank, honing directly in for the comic kill. A northern comic with roots back to Formby and Randle, in a northern club with equally obvious roots stretching to the days when Manchester had been the 'night-life capital of Europe'. Could any scene be so intrinsically northern?

I wondered about this, as Paul Morley's sumptuous and exhaustive tome, 'The North (and almost everything in it)' appeared in June 2013. I had no problem with the book other than the selective elasticity of that word 'almost'. No mention within those 576 pages of Frank Sidebottom, arguably the truest northern outsider artist of the past 30 years. Odd one, I thought and then realised that Frank, it could be argued, often lampooned the very essence of British pop… the very stuff that Paul Morley had openly championed. It's not a hugely important point and, in fact, the book in question also refuses to acknowledge Elbow, Bury Market, Happy Mondays, Strawberry Studios, Bickershaw and Deeply Vale festivals, The Hollies and 10CC. All, with the exception of 10CC who were so significantly based in Stockport (the central town of the tome) profoundly northern.

As, indeed, was Frank. As The International audience swigged and laughed and forced their enjoyment to a crescendo that, again, echoed down the ages, it really did seem that so little had changed. There be a musical hall act. There be mischief and tomfoolery. There be a character bouncing off the stage after three glorious encores. There be the sad character of Chris Sievey, wandering away alone, Frank's head tucked in a bag under his arm. Chris Sievey wondering how, after years of diligent crafting and scribbling and plotting… after all that, he had emerged as an echo of a sepia-toned past. How ironic the world can seem.

As stated, many have tried but it remains difficult to pinpoint exactly where the source of the character, Frank Sidebottom lay. We need to briefly return to this theme. The Freshies – Barry, Rick, Bob Dixon – appear to be happy in the notion that he really did appear late in their career, initially as a promotional device for the band. In truth, Frank almost certainly started to form within Chris's fevered imagination back in the art department at Cecil Road High School. There appears to be no solid evidence for this. When I contacted the school regarding Chris's attendance, partly to inform them that this famous character who was about to have a statue, two films and book in his honour was an ex-pupil, they rigorously promised to seek out as much information as possible. I must admit, I presumed they would take a certain pride in having Sievey as an ex-pupil. Perhaps they do. On the other hand, it could be that the fact that such an intelligent and gifted pupil should leave as early as possible armed with no qualifications might not be seen to reflect too graciously on a school which harbours such a proud academic record.

In truth, I don't believe this to be a fault of the school at all. There are certain characters whose channel of intelligence is so random they fail to fall in line with any kind of curriculum. One can cite such icons as Michael Parkinson, Julie Burchill and Morrissey as comparative academic under-achievers; figures simply 'too bright' to fall in line. No bad thing. Had they done so then they would, no doubt, be top level civil servants or, worse, financiers by now. Thank God they didn't. Exactly the same can be said of Sievey. Well, almost. I find it difficult to believe that, given the excitable and colourful nature of his muse, he made no mark at all on the school art department.

Oddly enough, I visited the school at an 'open day' in the summer of 2013. Naturally, I had little choice but to allow my imagination to wander, sensing the young Chris running through those corridors, being forced to mime to hymns in *that* hall, playing football with Paul Molyneux and schoolmates on *that* grass. I didn't sense any lingering spirit of Chris, but felt happy with my own private little ghost of him. So this is where it began?

The notion of Frank seems to have actively featured in an early Bees Knees song and was born from two areas; Sievey's love of cartoons and, in particular, the innovative genius of Max Fleischer and his penchant for traditional northern entertainment. In this area it is difficult to look beyond George Formby.

Fleischer first.

Born in Krakow in 1883, which was then part of Austro-Hungary in the province of Galicia, Max was just four years old when his family immigrated to New York City where he attended public school.

Working alongside his brother, he started developing instructional cartoons for the US Army. His first noted innovation was to combine animation with live action. Through this development he created the internationally famous Koko the Clown. It is this early breakthrough that echoes so powerfully down the years and, obviously with the benefit of technology, would be echoed by Sievey with the creation of his 'Frank's World' animation film and DVD.

Fleisher's story is complex and ultimately rather depressing. His innovations and characters, who included Betty Boop and Popeye, served to cast himself as the main competitor to Walt Disney, who he later worked for. But Fleisher, who died in 1972, remained trapped in a powerful and oppressive state of bitterness towards his rival who, he believed, used superior finance and technology to select and enhance his basic ideas.

The George Formby connection is perhaps the most obvious. Formby-philes are extremely precious, particularly whenever anyone attempts comparisons to a man they regard as unique (although devotees of Frank Randle, Professor CP Lee among them, vigorously tell a different story). Formby, and his father, Formby Snr, both stood proudly for the power of the talent of the ordinary man, betwixt music hall and film, between the wars and, at all times, Formby remained profoundly northern. Or profoundly Lancastrian, as might be considered the case. Although Formby was born in Wigan, he is actually buried in Warrington, a town unceremoniously shunted into Cheshire and, it might be noted, just three bus stops away from Altrincham. It is not relevant for me to dig too deeply into this complex tale here, for although there are many similarities between Formby and Sidebottom, there are also many differences (savage and buried innuendo being a Formby trait which would, frankly, be somewhat above the Timperley man).

Yet Formby's strength was that initial look of innocence; of ordinariness; the look of a simpleton armed with a sharp and disarming brain. Therein lies the connection. That and Frank's tendency to emulate Formby's talkative ukulele style. Of course there are obvious similarities and one wonders, as Chris began to construct his first papier-mâché head (later heads would be fibre-glass in construction) if he had Formby in mind, as he crafted those big, baby blue eyes and an open mouth, intended to convey childlike innocence... more than that perhaps, crafted a softener for the unaccustomed audience. For, as Formby's smile made him seem like the daft but loveable kid at school who might never amount to anything (beyond cleaning windows), so Frank would give the initial impression of one who could mean no harm.

"Whilst working for a little known music magazine Muze, *in the mid-eighties, I remember collecting Frank and delivering him to a reader's door who had won a 'private gig' in a competition. I then returned him from whence he came. He remained in character throughout and caused consternation at traffic lights."*

PETER GILMORE

MICK MIDDLES

FRANK HITS THE STREETS

MEETING FRANK, RATHER THAN CHRIS, at the Timperley flat proved an unsettling experience. I had arrived with photographer Karen with the simple premise of spending time with Frank on the streets of Timperley and Broadheath, photographing and recording him for the pages of *Muze* Magazine for a 'Frank spread'. By this time – mid 1985 – Frank had already become part of the fabric of Manchester music and, as we were about to discover, on the streets of his locale.

Odd though, as I had spent time with Chris on the previous day, skipping across for pints in The Ducie Bridge while plotting this little excursion. But Chris wasn't there, twenty-four hours later. While I felt that I knew Chris well and could relax in his company, Frank was an unknown quantity. Again and again, you will read in this book, about the transformation from Chris to Frank and back again. The moment the head was placed, the change was total. Not merely a change in attitude or outlook. It never seemed like a performance, no mere showbiz gimmick. It was a journey; a visionary and intellectual journey not unlike, I sense, the travelling involved when someone changes sex. I have known people who, by the age of six, knew they had been born into the wrong sex. Absurdly, this is more of an intellectual than purely sexual journey. So it was when Chris became Frank. A journey from one person to the other. I completely believe that Chris was born as two people. It was not an aspect of his personality, either. I guess you had to be close to it to realise the true extent of the divide. Most people interviewed for this book found themselves close to this remarkable transformation. It is something they will probably never encounter again. It is the rarest of journeys.

And so to the streets of Timperley and Broadheath. With Frank literally pointing the way forward, striding through the estate, playing with an ice cream rocket plucked from the freezer of the newsagents.

Remarkable, indeed, to witness the level of acceptance that Frank had attained in his locale. Aside from the wit of a knot of schoolkids who bellowed "Hey, big-head" as we ambled past, several people of no identifiable age or style merely offered a polite, "Hi Frank... you OK?" I found this to be almost shocking. No longer a daft man in a papier-mâché head, but a genuine local character with a fully formed personality and, it seemed, a full set of local friends. I couldn't help wondering if these same people also knew Chris Sievey. I guessed not. Chris would have melted. Chris was never so much 'out there'.

MARK RADCLIFFE

Mark Radcliffe's broadcasting career and subsequent musical ethos is firmly cemented within Manchester music's legacy. One recalls him, back in the early eighties, fronting Piccadilly Radio's late night 'Transmission' programme which, like a localised John Peel, proudly served the disparate and nationally ignored Manchester scene. The fact, that the Morleys and Penmans of this world were lost in a swirl of flash Londonisms, hit Radcliffe hard. He would, begrudgingly, move to London for a short while, although his heart lay in the north. His mantle as radio spokesperson for Manchester would change as he handed the baton to his good friend Tony Michaelides. Radcliffe spent time as a mainstream producer before gaining the position of Head of Music at Piccadilly and Key 103... a position he held while performing anarchic gigs as Mr Emerson-Lake of Frank's Oh Blimey Big Band.

When we met for this interview, in Spring 2013, it was within the JG Ballardian spread known as Salford Quays and, in particular, the BBC's pristine complex known as Dial House, complete with it's modern glass frontage and metallic sheen interior. Radcliffe had just finished the hugely successful BBC 6 Music Show he co-presented with Stuart Maconie. A giant poster of the pair of them, plus a gnomic looking Marc Riley, adorns the front of the building. How things have changed, I thought, from his days spent within the cave-like darkness of Piccadilly Radio. How odd too, perhaps, that two of the three presenters chosen for the honour of fronting the Beeb's lovely if bewildering new home, should have been members of the Oh Blimey Big Band.

MICK MIDDLES

Mark Radcliffe: "Funnily enough, I think the first time I met Chris was in London. Because I went down to work at Radio One. I had worked at Piccadilly and our paths had never crossed then. I went to London and he brought out that record, 'The Biz', which was a record with a computer game on the other side. I just thought, 'what a funny and daft idea' and everything. As in so many things, in his own mad way, he was completely ahead of the curve. He came down and did that… I think he did an interview on a programme we did called 'Saturday Live', with Richard Skinner and Andy Batten-Foster on Saturday afternoon on Radio One. After that we went to the pub and started talking. I told him I was moving back. He said he was launching this character called Frank Sidebottom and we arranged to hook up when I got back.

"I was aware of The Freshies and I knew who he was but we hadn't met. I definitely played some Freshies stuff when I had my show 'Transmission' on Piccadilly Radio and he used to send me lots of things. I don't think we ever met."

Which is surprising, given the lack of opportunities for local bands during that era. Also, given Sievey's fascination with radio and the astonishingly penetrative powers of local radio at that point – the monopolisation of stations such as Piccadilly created stars within the city; a fact borne out by the giant presenter posters that overlooked Piccadilly Gardens, although this latterly seems rather absurd. I have no doubt that Chris and, later, Frank forced their way into that plush Piccadilly/Key 103 reception on many occasions, armed with inventive paraphernalia of self promotion.

"When I did get to know him, I thought he was a kind of loveable person. One of those people who were kind of lost in their own world. He was totally sold on an idea and was determined to see it through, whatever happened. Also he had a completely irresponsible streak. I mean. That day we went for a drink he was supposed to get the next train and he missed that and probably missed all of them. So it became clear that time didn't really matter to him. And I found this a lot, much later, when he would be doing things like colouring in Frank Sidebottom comics and things like that. Doing all the artwork. He would just stay up and do it all night… or stay up for three days and three nights doing it. He would sustain himself the best way he saw fit."

Radcliffe's comparative sobriety didn't appear to affect their relationship. "He was a bit of a party animal, Chris. He was a bit of a rock'n'roll animal. He really liked to drink but, as I said, he had no concept of time and this worsened when he had a drink. You could see why he was someone who had never been able to hold down a nine-to-five job, although he had tried. In fact later in life he came back to it a bit, when he was doing the 'Bob the Builder' thing. I remember when he got that job, all of us who knew him were relieved and thought, at last he'll be doing something he really loves and getting paid for it. But Chris would always find absurd ways of fucking things up."

Comedic ideas pinballed furiously between Sievey and Radcliffe, not all of them hinged on Frank. I recall Radcliffe telling me that the pair had stayed up all night working on the idea of an 'alternative English dictionary in which, for example, 'ensconced' would mean, 'surrounded by scones'. When Radcliffe told me this, his face clouded with a jolt of sudden angst. "You wont nick that, will you?" he asked. 'Why', I thought, 'would I 'nick' 'surrounded by scones?'

"We did all kinds of things... before I took on the role of Mr Emerson-Lake, the greengrocer, and become part of the band, mainly on drums. But although he was so easy to work with on one level, there were frustrating elements. He was very friendly, very smiley, always good company but obviously there was a kind of mad driven streak that could take him anywhere. Also he wouldn't rely on people. He was always very reluctant to let anything go. He couldn't delegate. He had to do all the artwork. He had to colour everything. He always had to do it. Even though he had been in bands like The Freshies and even though there were a lot of us who helped him, he really was always a one man band. With The Oh Blimey Big Band, he did tend to move through people. People came and went. He simply couldn't delegate and that is why that was always an extremely transient band. I didn't mind because I had another life. I was Head of Music at Piccadilly Radio and had to get to work on time the morning after gigs. I am glad about this because I might have become lost in Chris's world. I always remained capable of pulling back."

Which seemed to work. The initial Oh Blimey Big Band was a loose affair with Frank often straying to perform solo gigs. He once told me that he had no idea whether the band would survive or where Frank was going. He accepted gigs... *any* gigs it seemed, as a kind of artistic test. Hence, a wholly unsuitable working man's club in, say, Bradford, appealed to Chris (if not the tentative band members) as an experiment. This would factor in with Radcliffe's later anarchic work with Chris under the guise of the artless Billy and Barry Belly.

"Some people in Manchester in the mid eighties didn't get Frank at all. But I understood Frank instantly... the moment Chris explained it to me because he had it so fully realised I thought, 'Oh yeah, that sounds great'. He had the papier-mâché head and everything but he had the whole story of who Frank was, where he lived and all his friends and he started to sketch in that when we did the Radio Timperley thing at Piccadilly Radio. That was a nice idea; that within Piccadilly was this little pirate radio station... I mean, why would Piccadilly ever give a radio station to someone like Frank in Timperley? But it was fully realised, with jingles. Chris was very productive."

Almost overnight, Frank had forced himself into position on the often insular Piccadilly Radio. An immense achievement, even if his working partner was head of music. But the radio medium allowed Frank to develop as a character... his mum's imaginary garden shed becoming a tangible base, a studio perhaps where he could play with props... where Frank could simply muck about and discover himself.

"Chris asked me to open the fire exit door for him, back-stage at The Green Room once. He was leaving the gig and had all Frank's gear in a big case on wheels. I said the door looked like it was alarmed, but he told me that he had had a word with the manager and he had switched it off. I let him out and pulled it closed again only to have very stressed bar/venue managers as the fire alarm was sounding which, I think, rang the fire brigade."

TONY WALSH

THE CURIOUS AND SECRET WORLD OF ANDY WRIGHT

Housed within the cavernous void of Manchester's Piccadilly Plaza, directly beneath the Piccadilly Hotel, Piccadilly Radio – and later, Key 103 – was a warm vortex of local celebrity. To reach it, one had to meander through the ghostly aromatic monstrosity of the Plaza, by this time a largely defunct and eerie place. All of which made the reception areas and studios beyond appear all the more glamorous. Chris loved Piccadilly... at least until the sheer force of his artistic notions pushed the boundaries with a little too much force. But he did love it and, even during the days of The Freshies, often dreamed about creative use of the twin studios... a use that extended way beyond the parameters allowed by commercial radio. However, while his Radio Timperley exploits became etched into local notoriety, thereby gaining cult status, some of his other work for the station remained largely unknown.

As David Dunne, presenter, producer and executive at the station later explained: "Chris was amazing when he came into Piccadilly Radio. He was just exploding with ideas. So much so that we kind of gave in and allowed him to do what he wanted. That was the start of Radio Timperley which was pretty much unparalleled, especially in the field of commercial radio. I produced quite a few pieces on Frank for Piccadilly and enjoyed it very much. It was always anarchic and I also knew that there would be a body of listeners who wouldn't get it at all. That makes it a risky venture for a station like Piccadilly. Some people would take Frank completely at face value.

"But, and this was the time when Piccadilly was splitting frequency and doing something different on the AM and FM frequencies. It was also the time when they changed the name of the FM station to Piccadilly Key 103. The split frequency opened up the airwaves, making it much easier for Chris to get new ideas accepted. There was simply a lot more time."

The dream had reached fruition. Increased airtime meant a greater hunger for new style creative in-put. For a while, Chris had found his perfect medium.

"Chris had many ideas but the one that got through was the invention of a new character called Andy Wright. Wright would be a failed Manchester musician and obsessive who had been given a Sunday morning show. Musically he would play a bit of new wave, punk, guitary stuff really and he would be a bit mopey. It started off quite straight but, as the weeks went by, things would start to get increasingly odd and surreal. Things like… well, he would have to bring his kids into the studio while he did the show because he couldn't get a babysitter. They would start interrupting him during his links… or his wife would call him up and start telling him off or he would have a row with his producer – me – and I would storm out and he wouldn't be able to work the equipment."

Although born from public reaction – and occasional indifference to Frank – Wright was a much more controlled character. While Frank would be increasingly bombastic, the anarchy within Wright would be more subtle and allowed only to seep gently through the airwaves. The basic idea was to slowly pull the listener to the heart of the show, before starting to play the tricks. Subversive, indeed.

"As the weeks progressed, it would get stranger and stranger. The idea was that nobody would know it was Chris at all and there would be no connection to Frank. I think we must have been on air with it for about six months and absolutely nobody had cottoned on that it was him. Paula and the kids came in a few times to do a few bits and Caroline Aherne came in and played his randy neighbour. This would have been about 1988-89. It was a strange interlude in his Frank adventures and many aspects of it were Chris sending up his own life as a musician as well.

"I must add that this show has never been written about or even mentioned in any interviews. Sadly, I don't have any tapes of it at all."

DARREN POYZER

Honest, mischievous, talented: be it as performer, songwriter or promoter, Darren Poyzer has flitted amiably around the Manchester gig circuit for the best part of 30 years. One harbours fond memories of his days in the mid-80s, running and living about Ashton-Under-Lyne's lively Witchwood venue, unquestionably one of Frank's favourite gigs.

Darren is a rarity... one of the few people who simultaneously promoted Frank while performing alongside him, most notably at the series of 'Manchester Busker' events which he believes were very much "...the catalyst for UK alternative comedy" in the 1990s.

His love of great eccentrics took him to two General Elections as one of the most successful Official Monster Raving Loony Party candidates of all time; ventures into the absurd that were, in no small part, inspired by his love of Frank Sidebottom.

Darren Poyzer: "I considered it a coup when I first booked Frank Sidebottom. The shows were either sell-outs or near to capacity. The audience was quite partisan so I quickly learned not to book a support act. The occasion was Frank and Little Frank and little else survived the chaos. We had the pleasure of bringing to the club a wealth of increasingly popular comedy talent: Steve Coogan, Caroline Aherne, John Thomson, Henry Normal and many more had already taken to the small stage and helped create a magical place and performance space. Then there was the wider circuit that we all shared and enjoyed. The Manchester Busker shows, a fledgling new comedy club in Manchester called The Buzz Club and a number of alternative cabaret events and small clubs dotted around the country that created and nurtured a wonderful approach to comedy. It was a great scene and a wealth of lovely people with fresh, cutting edge writing skills.

"I don't think that, other than bellyaching laughter, you could compare Frank with alternative, never mind mainstream, comedians. He was, for me, out there with the rare, great eccentrics of our era, most notably Lord Such and Wild Willi Beckett. Frank wasn't political, though. He didn't need to be. There was enough absurdity around. You just had to celebrate it and he knew how to help you see it. I would say that, outside of the locality, you would have to reach out to Charlie Chaplin via Tommy Cooper, add a touch of Theatre de l'Absurd and Monty Python, drink fizzy Vimto through a straw up your nose during a food fight and listen to everything by The Smiths played on a kazoo, before you could anywhere close to describing the wreckless child-inspired magic of a Frank gig.

"For me, his indie music mimicry was genius. However, the Match of the Day song maybe unfairly took Frank out of the comedy intelligentsia and made him the king of the Saturday night football crowd. They took to him very easily. If, despite his success, you are looking for reasons why Frank didn't go global, I always felt that this association did him no favours. It's a bastard of a business and you get all too quickly labelled and left to one side if you are not in the trendy comfort zone. Maybe the cold, harsh truth is that not everyone got the joke. Safe people can't be doing with absurdity and football.

"Some people are completely different on and off stage; indeed, there is the cliché that you don't wish to meet your heroes for fear of disappointment. With Chris though, I found that I enjoyed the bonkers-headed Frank and level-headed Chris in equal measure. When I had an episode of great personal tragedy – my flat went up in flames, I lost the lot – he came forward and volunteered himself as compere, performer and media face for a benefit concert organised by friends to help me out. As I understand it, he was originally asked for a signed item for a raffle, a request that others of his ilk ignored, but Chris jumped in with both feet. On the night he was amazing, worked the whole four hour show and raised the bar for a thrilling occasion enjoyed by all.

"There is one story that tells of how we were sharing a chat and a drink, stood at the bar as people were piling into the venue, pre-gig. I was repeatedly accosted by a very excited male punter who wanted to speak to Frank without his head and get to know him as he was in real life. Much to Chris's straight-faced amusement, the guy made me agree to do whatever I could to make this happen. Needless to say, this continued as a theme at every show so, then Chris would set up with a mate performing a peg nosed sound check, before driving away from the club, only to return either as Frank already or a back door pimpernel plotting and scheming any amount of diversions to avoid identification.

"My lasting memory has to be one very low-key Manchester Busker anniversary gathering of a handful of performers at The Castle pub, probably around 2008. I had had many conversations with Chris, but never with Frank. As I was nudging my way to the bar, Frank was making his way in. He greeted me personally by name asking how things were going. For a moment, I froze. I truly didn't know what to say. Whether to engage in conversation and discuss the performer politics of the gig or make some outrageous, loud, diabolical response. I think it is fair to say that, whatever my lines were, I fluffed them. It was the closest I came to that place where Chris and Frank existed together. It kinda blew my mind…"

There was the time me, Chris and Stirling went to the Isle of Man to watch Man City and Chris spent the weekend wearing his City slippers which didn't give much grip on the cobbles after a full day on the beer."

SIMON HEYWOOD

Mark Radcliffe: "It is difficult to recall the timeline. But we were going out and doing gigs as Frank before he came on the radio and me being Emerson-Lake, the character was my idea. I loved the name and the idea of this greengrocer who was obsessed with lard. I remember when I went to Chris's wake at Castlefield and I had never seen the new Oh Blimey Big Band and they were all dressed like Emerson-Lake… like me in a brown overall and a fez. Cos Emerson-Lake used to come straight from the shop in his overall and to make him more showbizzy he used to put a Fez on. In my head, showbiz meant Tommy Cooper.

MICK MIDDLES

The joke was that we were going to be Emerson-Lake and Sidebottom but Frank used to insist that it was Sidebottom and Emerson-Lake, so the joke would kind of be destroyed. It made us laugh every single time. So he started doing some gigs. I came back to Manchester from my spell in London and my old band had gone. I didn't really know anybody at the time. I wanted to play and do some gigs and things. I had played in all kinds of bands, like Bob Sleigh and the Crestas. I didn't want to be famous, I just wanted to be in a band so I could go out and get pissed, like we used to do. And Chris seemed to offer a very good way of doing just that.

"There was only me and him and the manager Mike Doherty, who was involved. Mike is an incredible guy. He was the sensible one, really. Mike used to drive everywhere and they were always full of enthusiasm and plans. They were always disorganised and in the end I used to get frustrated because, if we were doing a gig, they would arrange to pick me up at a certain time. So I would get washed and brushed and get ready for, say, five o'clock and they would turn up at half six and would say, 'Oh we've got to go and get some T-shirts'. So although we had a gig in, say, Stoke on Trent, we would first go to Preston to pick up some T-shirts and then about 8 pm they would be coming back past the top of my road. Mike was as bad as Chris in that respect. You could really lose days. Total days because of this stuff."

I asked Mark if, during those formative days, there was a noticeable barrier between Chris and Frank. How soon did it become apparent that they might be two separate entities?

"He always travelled as Chris. Once he was Frank, you couldn't talk to him as Chris. We would wind Frank up. We would say the dirtiest and foulest things we could to wind Frank up who was an innocent, to try and make Chris crack up. Occasionally you would see him shake but once he was in character, you just couldn't talk to him. If you talked to him onstage, because he couldn't see very well with the head on, you had to stand in front of him and talk through the mouth. So it looked like you were kissing him. You had to talk through this bit of nylon stocking in the mouth area. But you are correct. There was no connection between Chris and Frank. You reacted differently to them both."

★

Frank makes an incongruous and somewhat worrying appearance within the pages of Irvine Welsh's booze and drug riddled detective yarn, 'Filth' - here is the sentence.

> *"After a while I, we find that we have become aroused again. Still, she'll be back. Nothing surer than that. We put on our Frank Sidebottom 'Timperley' EP then we, I, we put on a video where this big blonde 'hoor' takes on a couple of lumberjacks in an Alaskan forest."*

Mark Radcliffe: "We played The Rock Garden in Covent Garden and ULU where Jon Ronson was the social sec. He started booking Frank there and The Cricketers Arms, in Kennington, by The Oval cricket ground. So we would just get in the van and, well we weren't young guys, and we would drive to Kennington. We never stayed in hotels. So we would drive down there, play the gig, get slaughtered, great fun and have a few more drinks then, at half one in the morning, we would realise that we were in Kennington. Mike would always drive. He never drank in those days but then we would go to someone's flat. It would go on and on. Then we would drive back up the motorway, I would be thinking 'oh I'm nearly home now' and Chris would say 'Oh let's go to Knutsford Services?' I would say, 'Shall we not'. But we would go to the services and buy egg, chips and beans for £17.50 and then Chris would go on the machines. He was like a child in that way."

Mike Doherty's guidance and influence over Frank started to fully form at this point.

Mike Doherty: "I had been working as a tour manager. I hadn't planned that. It was a guy at Kennedy Street Enterprises who suggested that I should do that. He told me that I knew the business and he would hire me. It is not an easy job. At one point I was trying to look after Hawkwind. I mean, they were fucking horrible… a fucking horrible bunch of hippie degenerate bastards who had all moved to the country and hated each other. Well, I will tell you something, even looking after Hawkwind, who I despised, was often easier than attempting to control Frank. Worse than Hawkwind, he was."

It should be noted here that Kennedy Street Music Management and Promotions Agency was based in Altrincham and run by Harvey Lisberg and Rick Dixon. They were largely responsible for a lot of Manchester acts from Herman's Hermits through to 10CC and Sad Café.

"But I worked with a lot of comedians on the road," Mike Doherty continues, "Bernard Manning, people like that. Really professional people and it seemed a lot easier than attempting to organise articulated lorries and PA systems for some massive horrible band. Unbeknown to me it provided me with the perfect grounding to be able to work as Frank's manager… well, as much experience as possible because, believe me, *nothing* could fully prepare you for working with Frank.

Phil Jones: "I was working with JMP Concerts in London and word started to filter down that he was doing lots of gigs and was on telly and the radio… basically that it was all starting to happen for Frank. So Mike Doherty came to our office which was in Kentish Town and asked for gigs. So, we were a little team of promoters. We sat down with Mike on a Tuesday afternoon and went through and we decided to give it a go. We gave him Leicester Poly and Manchester Ritz. I think it must have been leading up to Christmas '88 and we started feeding him gigs. I recall that gig at The Ritz in Manchester with Big Jim White's 'Presley in Mind'. We got about 575 people in to that just before Christmas. Not too shoddy although it probably lost a little bit of money. And Leicester Poly and that one actually made money and encouraged us to try him at a number of places. In 1988 I had met my future wife Barbara and I was in Manchester more and more. Frank was all over the place at that point. For my stag do we went to the pantomime at Timperley Labour Club. Barbara actually came with me. It must have been the 17 or 18 January 1989. He also came and did my wedding party at the town hall. I didn't tell Barbara about that and he turned up and presented us with a lovely 'Sidie'. I later discovered that, because of Frank, people were actually buying tickets outside the Town Hall to my wedding party. Chris came as Frank and he appeared during the speeches and was absolutely brilliant. The entire place was in stitches… honestly."

Mike Doherty: "Chris was the most extraordinary person I have even known. No one else could ever be remotely like him. He was a complete one off. He was also a mass of contradictions. He was a lovely sweet guy on the one hand… and yet he was also a beast far beyond any rock star I ever worked with. He was a raging alcoholic, drug addict and sex addict. Don't get me wrong, he always loved Paula and would do absolutely everything for his kids. But beyond that he was totally mad. And as for Frank… Frank was utterly out of control the whole of the time."

SUNDAY APRIL 30 2014.
MANCHESTER DANCEHOUSE THEATRE

JON RONSON'S TALK, which centred on his time spent within the Oh Blimey Big Band and the initial creation of the film, 'Frank', had been punctuated by snaps and pops of intelligence and wit. His natural self-effacing character had been allied to warm comedic timing. At half time, myself and Vick were – literally – leapt upon by an ebullient Paula Sievey and her friend, Sandra Taylor. She seemed delightfully lost to the thrill and glory that Frank, albeit posthumously, was now attaining.

"This is all I ever wanted," she gleefully stated. "Isn't it fantastic?"

I resisted the urge to reply with, "it really is."

At the show's conclusion there came a brief set performed by varying members of the Oh Blimey Big Band, all garbed in Mr Emerson-Lake outfits. Jon Ronson briefly resumed his keyboard duties, Dave Arnold took up bass, 'Jailbird' Roche, was on guitar and Harry Sievey, bounced around frenetically on vocals. Eerily, a Frank Sidebottom head peered at us from the stage front. It proved suitably shambolic and not, perhaps, one of the all time classic gigs of Mancunia, but a neatly placed full-stop to an evening when, time and time again, my eyes darted around the room, studying the vast crowd. I wondered who all these people were - where were they, back in those lost gigs of mid-term Frank?

The emergence of Jon Ronson within this story is intriguing and nicely detailed within his book - Frank: The True Story that Inspired the Movie.

Mike Doherty: "It was me who introduced Jon Ronson to Frank. Jon was working as booker for London Poly and happened to mention that he could play keyboards a little bit. So we basically got him into 'The Oh Blimey Big Band'. It was always difficult to get people to play in that band because there was absolutely no kudos. I mean, who the fuck wants to travel to Bradford or somewhere like that just to play plinkety piano? There is no artistic merit at all and you are hardly gonna get any groupies are you? So it had to be a certain kind of person, someone who has absolutely nothing to prove and understood Frank completely. Mark Radcliffe was just perfect for that - for playing Mr Emerson Lake the greengrocer and drummer. Who could be better?"

Jon Ronson: "It wasn't ULU as people have claimed, it was PCL - the Polytechnic of Central London, which was just down the road from ULU. I was the social secretary - it was a year's sabbatical for the student union, not a full time job. The ULU social secretary at the time, or roughly the same time, was Ricky Gervais. But, otherwise, yes. That's how it happened. I can't remember how I first got talking with Mike Doherty, just that I did. And I used to really enjoy getting calls from him. A lot of agents and managers would sense how naïve we student social secs were, and would milk us for all we were worth, but Mike wasn't like that. He was genuinely nice and friendly and fun to talk to. I remember seeing Frank a year earlier. He'd been booked by my predecessor to play the union bar. One of my friends said we should turn up early to see him get out of his tour van without his head on. So we turned up early and we waited for ages. Finally a transit van pulled up and Frank got out. "HELLO!" he yelled. He was wearing his fake head. It was both disappointing and thrilling. Then I became the social secretary. One day I was in my office when my phone rang. It was Mike.

"'Frank's playing a show in London tonight and our keyboard player can't make it,' he said. 'Do you know any keyboard players?'

"'I, um, play the keyboards,' I replied.'

"'Well, you're in!' he shouted.

"'But I don't know any of the songs,' I said.

"'Can you play C, F and G?' he asked.

"'Yes,' I said.

"'Well, you're in!' he shouted."

One of the very few true things that made it to the heavily fictionalized Frank movie was that exchange. Although in the Frank movie it happens on a beach. For the record, Ronson had not been aware of the existence of The Freshies at all. "The first time I met Chris was that night – the night I was the stand-in keyboard player. It was at the Cricketers pub by The Oval. Frank was preparing to sound-check. Even though the concert was a few hours away, he was already wearing the fake head. I knew his real name was Chris, so I approached and said, 'Hello, Chris. I'm Jon.' He ignored me. 'Hello Chris,' I said again. He continued to ignore me. 'Hello, uh, Frank?' I tried. 'HELLO!' he yelled.

"Later that evening – before the gig – I met Chris, instead of Frank. I remember he was quiet and quite serious. We ran through the songs, which didn't take long because they were all C, F and G. In the flesh he wasn't ostentatious at all. His brother Martin is much more ostentatious. Chris was more invisible than that. I remember one time someone barged into our dressing room and said, 'I'm not leaving until I work out which of you is Frank!' She went round the room, saying, 'It's you! It's you!' The only person she didn't ask was Chris. This is, I swear, a true story.

"Anyway, that first night at The Cricketers: 'We'll put you over here' said Mike, setting up a keyboard stand for me at the side of the stage. Then the audience came in, and the show began.

"Being on stage with them was just the greatest experience of my life. I think the film we've written – 'Frank' – really captures the magical, 'Alice through the Looking Glass' feel of that night. I was Alice, plucked from the suburbs, to join this mad band. Getting up on stage was like going through the looking glass. That's the feeling I wanted to capture when we started writing the movie.

"Anyway, at the end of the show that night Frank introduced the band. 'On guitar, Rick Sarko!' The audience cheered. 'On drums, Mike Doherty!' The audience cheered. 'On keyboards, Jon Ronson'. Nobody cheered.

"'What's gone wrong?' I thought. And then I realised. Concerned that I didn't know any of the songs, they had turned my keyboard right down and positioned my stand so far behind the speaker stack that, unbeknownst to me until that moment, the majority of the audience had no idea I was there.

"'Why did they even bother asking me?' I thought miserably on the journey home. And then, a few weeks later, Mike called and asked if I wanted to join the band full time, and so I moved to Manchester."

One recalls the young Jon Ronson, flitting through Manchester venues such as The Boardwalk and The International alongside journalist Sarah Champion. He spent time, also, working as an evening DJ on

Stockport's KFM Radio, co-presenting with Craig Cash, a painter and decorator from Heaton Moor who would, one day attain astonishing fame via The Royle Family. Radio adventures became an activity that provided him with excellent grounding for Ronson's future media career. However it was sometime before I realised he was the keyboard player of the 'Oh Blimey Big Band'. But I wanted to know if, like Mark Radcliffe, he 'got' Frank in an instant.

"Yes, that first time I saw him play I got him straight away. I loved it. I loved the absurdity of it, the repetition. And I loved the head. From time to time Chris would keep Frank's head on for unexpectedly long stretches. I used to love those times. It was so strange to be sitting next to a man with a big fake head on as we drove down the motorway. It was fantastically mysterious to the young me who craved enchantment. Chris would only do it if, say, he was doing a radio interview the afternoon of a gig. Then he'd continue to be Frank in the van, through the sound-check, and into the show. But he'd take the head off as soon as we were back in the dressing room."

That early version of the band from 1986 through to the early nineties, was something of a shambolic and transient unit. Indeed, you never quite knew what you were going to see... or hear. Where was this band going? What were they, as opposed to Frank, hoping to achieve?

"Actually, I don't remember much about the first band," Jon admits, "the plinky-plonky band. I don't have too many memories of that. I have far more memories of when Chris decided to make Frank more professional sounding. The less good band, if you ask me. The dynamic got worse. He hired an overly suave bass player called Richard. Richard played in that indie band The Desert Wolves (managed by Mark Radcliffe's best friend, Piccadilly Radio DJ Tony Michaelides). I believe he now manages The Pixies. Richard took an instant dislike to me and, two rehearsals in, threatened to take me outside and 'break my keyboard playing fingers'. Suddenly, we were rehearsing a lot more than we used to. We were building virtuoso sax and guitar solos into 'Timperley Sunset' and 'Anarchy in Timperley'. I don't want to sound wise after the fact but it was clear to me that this was heading for disaster, and only I had the foresight to realise it. 'The audience don't want a note-perfect Oh Blimey Big Band,' I urgently told Mike. 'Yes,' Mike replied, 'but we can't just spend our lives sounding bobbins. We need to move it forward.' 'The audience isn't going to like it,' I warned.

"I booked Frank a huge 30-date tour. It was decided in rehearsals that I'd begin the show. I'd walk on, alone, into the spotlight, and play a powerful C. This lone note would last a minute or more, a simple but compellingly forceful C pulsating through the venue. It would ignite the audience into a frenzy of anticipation. Then the rest of the band would join me and we'd open by thrashing out a power-rock version of 'Born in Timperley'.

"The audience was noticeably perplexed. Where had our beloved sound gone? What were we thinking? We sounded like John Shuttleworth being backed by Survivor. A few days into the tour we got an extremely caustic review in the *NME*. Previously, they had always liked us. Now they expressed astonishment at our new musical direction. Word got around that we had lost our talent. By mid-tour, our audiences had dwindled from 500 or so to 30 if we were lucky. Chris always said that his favourite shows were the ones where everything went wrong. There were lots of those in the latter half of the tour. In Dudley, there can't have been more than 15 people in the audience. Midway through, someone produced a ball. The audience split into two teams and, ignoring us, played a game. As we came off stage that night, Chris took off the head and said: 'That was the best show ever!'

"Well, I say that but there were many highlights. There are great stories of the times he supported Bros and Gary Glitter. Glitter's roadies were extremely rude, cornering the band and issuing a list of dos and don'ts: 'You aren't allowed to use our lights. Stay away from our hydraulic stage.' And so on. Under the head, Chris was seething. As soon as Frank went on, he jumped on to the hydraulic floor, which set off smoke bombs and rose dramatically above the heads of the audience. 'Come on! Come on!' sang Frank, 'Do you want to be in my gang?' Within 20 seconds Gary Glitter's roadies were pushing their way through the audience towards him. He jumped off stage and ran down the corridor, pulling off his head and costume as he went – he had his own clothes on underneath – just as the roadies caught up with him they demanded 'Did you see Frank Sidebottom?' 'He went that way,' said Chris.

"The Bros story was that he was booed off, this was at Wembley, and the minute he got off stage he went straight up to Harvey Goldsmith and said, 'I'm thinking of putting on a gig at the Timperley Labour Club. Do you have any tips?' I remember us supporting Jonathan Richman at the Town and Country club too. Nothing funny happened but it was an incredible thrill."

The beauty of Frank and, indeed, the best versions of the 'Oh Blimeys' was the element of risk… a band teetering on the verge of collapse and held together only by the sheer bravado of its leader, is a hilarious sight to witness. It might be noted, also, that Frank's true comedic genius was the ability to convey an element that flies between naiveté and, deliberate this, blatant stupidity. Because of this, Frank could step beyond firmly patrolled boundaries. At this point, the persona becomes the artist. At this point it steps beyond mere entertainment. Frank's continual use of the word 'showbiz', as in 'my fantastic showbiz career', is one of the true ironies of this story. It was mostly beyond showbiz and, therefore, impossible to control or contain. Frank would have fared badly within the tight confines of 'X Factor' or 'Britain's Got Talent'. It could also be the reason why, whether appearing on Yorkshire TV, Granada or London Weekend, his tenure rarely lasted long. Sooner or later, 'the suits' would pull the plug. Always.

Jon Ronson: "Yes. I really loved and admired the way he aimed low, played by his own rules, did everything homemade, and was very happy to not reach for the stars. I loved that. Concentrating on the minutiae the way he did - assiduously building everything himself etc. That was a great work ethic. Aiming low: I really admire that. And he was just incredibly funny and mysterious and a bit insane. I'll never forget his stories about how he created Frank. He told me he recorded a terrible version of 'Anarchy in the UK' and sent it around the major record labels with a covering letter that began: 'Dear …, I'm thinking of getting into show business. Do you have any pamphlets?' Someone at EMI found this funny enough to invite him in. He arrived, dressed as Frank, and as he walked in the A&R man asked: 'Have you been in show business for long?' Frank looked at his watch and replied: '10 seconds'."

The lifestyle, within the confines of 'The Oh Blimeys' was, as Radcliffe previously hinted, an anarchic roller-coaster in its own right. Tight, controlled and professional are words that would not feature in any description of these wild days.

Mark Radcliffe: "The other thing about Chris is that he never had any money. Never. But if he did have, he would be incredibly generous. I had come back from London and had a good job as Head of Music at Piccadilly Radio. I remember one gig at The Flagship Showbar in Blackpool, with the big parrot outside. It was a foggy night. Chris had no money and his things would get cut off occasionally… so we would go and do the gig and perhaps we got £200, quite a lot of money in the mid eighties. But he would divide it in two and say 'that's yours'. I'd say 'no… no, they've come to see you.' If he had money he would just spend it immediately. Mike used to try and do the accounts. But it was hard. If he got money he might take Paula and the kids to Blackpool and they would just blitz Blackpool and buy loads of tat… rubbish. But still not put any aside for the electric bill.

"Occasionally you would see him and have to bail him out because he would have no way of getting home. We didn't mind because he was always generous."

Jon Ronson: "I do remember some nights when it was just him, Mike and me, and instead of driving back to Manchester we'd go off to someone's house and they'd get trashed and sleep with women while I just sat there on a chair in the corner, desperately wanting to go home to bed. Those are my only bad memories. And they're not especially bad. I just wanted to go to bed!"

Mark Radcliffe: "I do regret the fact that Chris never actually got a load of money to be able to do something really crazy because he would have blown a load of money on some mad scheme. Me, him and Mike Doherty were sitting round one night and agreed that it all went wrong we would form a company and call it The Great Big Company. We would have a massive office block in Manchester that would be designed to look like just the front door and doorstep of a terraced house. We would have a seventy five foot pint of milk on the doorstep. Chris, if he had come across millions of pounds, he would have done it. Me and Mike would have said 'no let's buy a car or a nice house.' Chris would have done it. Definitely. That is what I loved about Chris. He had a sense of the absurd that would just run over the normal rules of life. It must have been very entertaining but also very difficult for Paula to live with. He could never ever ever change. It would never happen, whatever the circumstances."

PATRICK GALLAGHER

Ghosts in the garden; echoes by the patio. Deep in the estate sprawl of Burnage, close to Kingsway, famed by the brothers Gallagher... and little else. It was August 2013, at the sweet end of a quiet cul-de-sac, a lawn flattened down to a garden shed, trees and undergrowth stretched from an enormous rectangular kitchen. Dowsed in sunlight, I imagined the scene on the same lawn, some 16 years earlier, with Chris and a five year-old Harry running among the shrubs. Thunderbirds models scattered on the grass. Balls would be kicked, air punched. From a distance... a distance of one and a half decades, all might appear perfectly normal. But apparently normality hides a truth blessed with a more diluted innocence. Chris, estranged from Paula, spent six months living at the house with its owner, Patrick Gallagher, himself bringing a story of depth, intrigue and considerable comedic success to the tale.

Gallagher's tale could perhaps begin at school, where he distantly befriended the future Fall bassist and Radio presenter Marc (Lard) Riley. Once Riley had leapt from the bizarre tutelage of The Fall, in 1984, alongside local impresario Jim Khambatta, he launched 'In Tape Records', a Manchester label primarily aimed at releasing a series of excellent singles by Riley's band, The Creepers.

A chance meeting in a Manchester street saw Gallagher — a humorist, cartoonist and animator by trade... amongst other things — designing sleeves for Marc Riley and the Creepers singles. The liaison between Gallagher and Riley would extend beyond May 1986 when Gallagher took hold of the successful editorship of anarchic children's comic, 'Oink', among whose contributors were Private Eye cartoonist Tony Husband, Riley, Viz Comic creator Chris Donald and future satirist Charlie Brooker. It attained a lovely controversial slant during its 68 glorious issues and, as it folded, Gallagher, Husband and Marc Rodgers were offered television work while Riley worked in the music promotions office run by Tony Michaelides.

It was several issues into 'Oink's' success when Gallagher sat on top of a Manchester bound bus, heartily chortling at the 'Frank's Firm Page' that graced the local music magazine, Muze.

"It was instantly brilliant," stated Gallagher. "As soon as I saw the bottom of Frank's page on which he left a note for the milkman – also in Frank's band – that stated, 'Three gold tops please... and gig tonight!' I knew I had to get Frank onboard 'Oink!' I asked Marc Riley, who was playing in Frank's band at the time, to make the connection and Frank fitted perfect into place within the comic's highly creative and juvenile content. It was a creative marriage formed in Heaven... or, at least, in Burnage, which is the next best thing.

When Chris and Paula decided to part company, albeit temporarily, it seemed both natural and safe for Chris to move in with Patrick. Wandering through Patrick's house in 2013, it was easy to see how Chris and Patrick would instantly embark on countless creative adventures. For in Patrick's workroom alone, I discovered a cornucopia of television and radio paraphernalia. Basil Brush – Patrick wrote six episodes of the esteemed fox's show – and racks of videos, CDs, DVDs, books and embryonic cartoons... many nights were spent here, and in the kitchen and lounge, excitedly talking up new notions, pushing new ideas. Other nights, perhaps lost to cloudy inebriation, would be rather more soul-searching. It would be an elastic six months that glittered with brilliance on many occasions and became fraught with tension and inner demons on others.

Patrick Gallagher: "I remember the time when Chris and Mark Radcliffe were doing things together and they really sparked off each other. Mark is very sharp and put that with Chris's endlessly searching mind and you had an incredibly creative combination. I must admit I found it a bit odd when Mark Radcliffe and Marc Riley started working together as Mark and Lard. I always thought Mark and Chris had a lot more in common and would have made a more artistically fertile partnership. It was when Marc Riley got introduced to Radio One at the time and his career just rocketed. It was just about that time when Chris kind of hit the rocks. Deep down Chris was a bit bitter about all that. It was the same with Caroline Aherne. But it wasn't Caroline or Marc Riley's fault. The fault lay with Chris and his self-destruct button. There were a number of times during his career where he could have taken more control and been more responsible. More than that, there were precise moments when he was poised on some major breakthrough and he seemed to deliberately take a step back, perhaps allowing people with more ambition in terms of career rather than artistic ambition to get ahead of him."

Mark Radcliffe: "We didn't fall out. We just stopped doing it. I left Piccadilly and I was producing some shows at Radio Two. We used to go and do interviews, as Frank, for Radio Two. I remember going to see Viv Richards, the legendary West Indies cricketer, who was playing for Rishton, in Lancashire, so we went to the hotel and I explained to Viv Richards and explained who Frank was. So, for the interview Chris puts a peg on his nose but not the head...Viv was very cool...he was like 'Whatever'. Frank's first question would be 'When you go for tea, do you get a choice of cakes?' Viv went with it. We did him, we did Cheryl Baker, Barbara Windsor, Michael Barrymore. They all went with it. Michael Barrymore took some persuading. Cheryl Baker knew Chris from Saturday morning television.

"The thing with Chris was that it was always going to be the next big idea that would work. During the time I knew him he never lost that belief in himself. I think the rest of us, at different times, would tire of it. I think I left The Oh Blimey Big Band, which expanded and became quite a good band. I was playing keyboards. Mike Doherty was the drummer. The guitarist was Mike Taylor who was a cartoonist on the Oink! Comic with Marc Riley – Marc was in the pantos we did at the Brooklands Trade and Labour Club. He wasn't in the Oh Blimey Big band. Once we did a Big Band gig and Marc Riley supported us as a Country and Western band where Chris played bass guitar, without the head on. Richard Jones was on bass (he manages The Pixies now and lives in Marple). He was the bass player but gradually as people got jobs it became a bit much. That was a good band technically. There was some kudos because the halls were packed with people who loved it. So we were all in it to find a little adulation. Everyone seemed to get it even though we did some odd gigs. I don't personally remember it being very confrontational."

Gallagher's entry into this story is twisted with Marc Riley's elongated emergence into the Manchester scene.

Patrick Gallagher: "I had known Marc Riley at school, obviously just before he joined The Fall. Then I didn't really see him until after he had left the band and I bumped into him in town. He had started the In-

MICK MIDDLES

Tape record label with Jim Khambatta, mainly to promote his own band, The Creepers. I think Marc genuinely believed they were going to be bigger than The Fall, which I can understand. After I met him, I started doing sleeves and things for In-Tape. It was funny how things kind of fell into place. Marc started working for Tony Michaelides Promotions and it was a time when everything seemed to start happening again in Manchester. Tony had an office on Princess Street. Dave Haslam had an office in there... as did Mark E Smith for a while. Nathan McGough was there with Happy Mondays... it was a great place and you could feel the energy happening. You would walk in that building at any given time and you might bump into Mick Hucknall, Mark E Smith, Marc Riley, Shaun Ryder... it was all bubbling up. It was just a great place to be in 1985/86. Frank would go in as well... and Chris, depending on how he felt. Chris liked to be around the buzz."

Patrick Gallagher's exposure to Chris's idiosyncrasies remains both shocking and piercingly accurate. There is no better way to gain an insight into the artistic and personal psyches than to live and work with someone. While Chris's amenable nature might have helped ease this situation, the dark side cannot be discounted. I was touched by the painful honesty of Gallagher's account. "Chris had visions but he couldn't control them... in fact he was totally out of control. Whereas, say, Caroline Aherne had a single vision and could just pursue that, Chris might have a fantastic idea, spend some time gaining interest and developing it and then, just at the point where it might actually get somewhere, he would spin off onto something completely different. That's okay for a while but it tended to piss people off because they never knew where they stood."

John Barratt, then working as office manager at Pete Waterman's church studio on Manchester's Deansgate agreed. "Chris was his own worse enemy. He really was. I am not sure he understood his own genius. The problem is that he was all over the place which made him very difficult to work with. I liked him and wanted to do lots of things with him... the scope was endless, but you never knew what he was going to do next. It was impossible. At one point I was getting a lot of interest from people at Granada TV, among others, for shows featuring Frank. It wasn't huge money but these ideas came with budgets of, say

£20,000. These shows were pretty much ready and waiting to go. But I just couldn't trust Chris. Would he turn up? Would he ruin the sets? I liked him so much and dearly wanted to work with him but, in the end, I just thought, I don't need the aggravation. It just wasn't worth the risk."

Ironic, perhaps, as the element of risk was part of the reason that Frank seemed so appealing in the first place. But Chris's lifestyle was beginning to consume him. There is little doubt, also, that the hedonistic bent was beginning to govern his life. The split from Paula was the most blatant indication of this.

Patrick Gallagher: "What you have to remember is that drugs and alcohol played a big part in Chris' day-to-day life and that was a big part of his problem. For years people accepted this as part of his make up… you know he could get away with it on that controllable level. But then came a marked deterioration. That is when things started to really change. Suddenly it affected his health, his thinking, his concentration and people would get annoyed with him. When I first started working with him, he was doing a lot of cocaine. When Mick Doherty was looking after him, that didn't matter too much in terms of his work because Doherty was brilliant at pinning Chris's workload down. He would get him to shows, get the money in and develop Frank in a very intelligent way. He would just tell Chris what to do financially and sort all that out for him. I felt sorry for Mike, really. He had done a lot of hard work to get Frank to a certain level. They were getting decent gigs, radio, advertising, Match of the Day… really lots of work that Chris could never have got. The world really did open up for Frank at that point. But his imbibing increased alongside his workload. That is the irony here.

"When Chris and Mike eventually had a fall out, I think it was because Chris eventually became too much even for Mike to handle, Chris's work just completely fell apart. Chris fell apart. It was a terrible thing to witness."

Mark Radcliffe: "The hallmark of genius is… well some of his stuff was fantastic and groundbreaking. But other stuff was complete rubbish. Chris seemed to have no real way of deciding which was which. He couldn't quite see the merits. If you look at the people who went through that band, like me and Chris Evans and Jon Ronson… I think the greatest compliment I can give Chris is that all of us came out of our association with him thinking that there is an alternative way of looking at the world. There is a different way of assimilating all the information that came to us. None of us wanted to be quite as reckless about it as Chris. But all of us thought that you could take these things and do something different with it. That you could be in a band but it would be different to every other band or you could write something that would be different. However, unlike Chris, we were prepared to conform and turn up on time for work and hold down relationships. Chris didn't really obey any of those rules. I know people tried to help him by giving him work. He had a couple of jobs down at Granada during that time when satellite telly had started and there was a bit more access to television then. I think Patrick Gallagher got him doing some edits or something. But Chris decided to see how long he could live on cloves of garlic. So he stank of garlic and would turn up in a little editing booth and nobody would work with him cos he stank. God knows why? He probably had a character in mind… The Garlic Kid or something and decided to live it and see if it had any resonance."

Patrick Gallagher: "I know for a fact that Mike Doherty put a great deal of input into Frank. He was the one person, really, that was able to motivate Chris, both in terms of getting things done and on an artistic level. Mike has a very lively mind that is very similar to Chris's and I think he understood Chris and Frank in a way that nobody else really did. They would be on the same level. Mike was a great musician too and he understood how to guide the 'Oh Blimey Big Band'. That might sound easy but, believe me, it wasn't. You had to think on the same musical level as Frank. Mike managed to get Chris a lot of work that would have been out of reach for most agents. He had that special way of thinking… of knowing that Frank would be good in certain situations. Like those advertising things they did. He was always trying to find new areas for Frank and I know that excited Chris. Well, for a while it did. The relationship was a bit like a marriage and, unfortunately, it broke down towards the end. But they were really good together, Mike and Chris."

I still believe that Chris was at his best, and indeed happiest, when firmly lost in some confrontational set performed before an army of unbelievers. The Bros gig was arguably the finest example of such an event although he was equally capable of breaking the rules in some small pub before a trickle of disbelieving pensioners, leaving bar staff open-mouthed in disbelief. At such a gig, absolutely anything could happen at any time. You could catch Frank at his best when no one turned up – apart from yourself. While I was watching the Jon Ronson talk at The Dancehouse, the audience, sweet as they were, noticeably sighed with fondness as Ronson flash up back projections of Frank in various guises. 'This wouldn't have been a good audience for Frank', I decided. He was better when lost to the world and left to his own devices, free from the shackles of speculation.

Mark Radcliffe: "One of the most confrontational things was when Chris and I did this thing called Billy and Barry Belly. We were a comedy act with no material, really. We would go on and hope for the best. I remember doing a working man's club somewhere, with Chris. I don't even think Frank was on the bill. In fact, if Frank was on, that would be fine. Once we did a panto at Brooklands Trade and Labour Club and Billy and Barry Belly were outside, selling pirate programmes for more than the programme were inside. Also they directed all the parking. So all the cars were jumbled up. But Chris was screwing up his own gig. One time we played the Baxi Social Club in Preston – we had a small pocket of fans who worked there and put Frank on and Billy and Barry Belly were roadies. So before Frank came on they would be setting up the equipment and abusing the audience. So we tweaked all the levels, turning everything up full. So when The Oh Blimey Big Band came on, the sound was horrendous. Feeding back all over the place. So Chris was quite happily sabotaging his own gig. I can not think of anyone else who would do that.

"So we did this gig… I think Chris said that we should 'try out' Billy and Barry. One of the first gigs was at Blackburn King George's Hall supporting Jerry Sadowitz. But we did one at Preston and Billy and Barry had a drum kit. That was it. We would do songs like 'Baby Come Back' by The Equals. So Chris would sing and I would drum.

Then we would swap over. Chris would go on drums and I would sing one. It was horrendous. So we could smoke fags while playing we would have the drumstick for the cymbal stuck on the bottom of my shoe. We did this University in Yorkshire somewhere which went down really badly…because it was awful. But Chris seemed to thrive on the danger of it."

I recall John Barratt telling me: "I have just met Chris… he is living with that Patrick Gallagher in Burnage. It's mad in that house, two lunatics running around playing with toys. That's all that seems to happen."

Patrick Gallagher: "Chris and Paula had split up and Chris had nowhere to stay. I had this big house in Burnage and loved working with Chris so it seemed perfectly natural for him to come and stay with me. I would charge him a small rent because I had to pay the bills somehow. But not much. It was a good time and, at first, I thought it would be the making of him. Harry was very young and I reasoned that Chris would have to get his act together a bit for the sake of Harry, really… that would be a perfect reason for him to knuckle down and get on with things. That was the theory. And Harry would come and stay at the weekend and the two of them would play together in the garden… great? Problem was, it had the reverse effect. Chris suddenly reverted back to his childlike ways. He'd suddenly go out and have a reason to spend all the money he had on toys for Harry. I thought, 'Oh fucking hell, what have I done? I have made things ten times worse, giving Chris a license to completely indulge himself'. Poor Harry didn't really have any options other than to learn music… he'd have a drum kit here and was just immersed in this stuff. Harry had no choice. He had no fucking choice. Chris was very close to Harry because, I think, he and Paula had had Harry quite late in life. That was great but Chris could be a very selfish person. He would indulge Harry in all his passions, whether it would be Thunderbirds or The Beatles or whatever. Luckily Harry responded very well and seems well grounded but, at the time, he did seem swamped as Chris unleashed everything on him. It concerned me greatly at the time. I am not saying it was totally intentional, it was just the way he was. The selfishness came because he devoted so much to Frank and allowed Frank into his private life. Most people in that position would have done the professional thing with the act, then put that to one side and have a private and family life as well. Chris could not do that. He allowed Frank to seep into his private life... well, not just Frank but all his artistic ideas. This meant that he relinquished his responsibilities. He never compromised in that way."

The tale darkens considerably here. Much has been made of the fact that Chris had a so called 'golden touch'. That people around him would go on to do very well in their respective fields. Whether this is a result of his ability to inspire, his charismatic nature or simply that talented people would gravitate towards is a matter of some debate.

Phil Jones: "I think it is endlessly fascinating to note just how many people around Chris went on to really do well. Obviously people like Mark Radcliffe, Marc Riley, Chris Evans, Caroline Aherne and Jon Ronson. It is a long list and sometimes unlikely. I remember Jon Ronson... quite shy and nervous really, saying that he wanted to be a journalist. I couldn't see it at the time but look what happened. I know for a fact that he was inspired by Chris. He was in awe of Chris, really. It was interesting that they all did so well while Chris, who probably inspired them, fell away and seemed quite a sad figure for long periods of time. The thing about Chris was that he was always a lovely fella and he loved working as Frank, but to be totally honest, it did become a bit of a job for him. He started churning it out and it was really difficult... so to keep doing it he did chemically enhance himself a little too much.

Mark Radcliffe: "I don't know if he was materialistic or not... you couldn't say he was not materialistic because he had attics and garages full of stuff. He was materialistic about the kind of things that most of us had sort of grown out of. Toys and things. He never drove. Maybe they had a car that Paula drove at some point. But the toys thing is quite interesting because Frank obviously had that childlike thing and Chris had it as well. Chris absolutely adored Thunderbirds and Gerry Anderson. He loved it. He also had a very good pop brain. He should have been Head of Marketing for a major company. He had all the marketing ideas and campaigns in his head. Like he saw computer games before anyone else."

Phil Jones: "He became represented by 'Off the Kerb' agency in London. By Addison Cresswell, who sadly died recently. He went on to be a serious producer and manager of people like Jack Dee, Jonathan Ross and Michael McIntyre. I knew Addison from doing Red Wedge in the eighties. Anyway, Addison would ring me up at the beginning and say – adopts Cockney twang – 'who is this crazy fucking cant? What can I do with him, Phil?' One day, I was working in Manchester and I got a phone call from Addison who asked 'Can you lend Chris £60… he will give it you back tomorrow… no worries.' That would be about 1991 or 92. And I didn't see him then for years. Well, I saw him but every time he saw me he dodged away. Unfortunately that caused some kind of rift… not a lot of money but I was annoyed with this. It was a shame that that happened and we lost touch. However, I started to see Chris years later and he always kind of distanced himself from me. I felt like saying, 'let's just forget the bloody £60'. I was annoyed about it. I could tell, even from that distance, that a good deal of inebriation was going on."

Mark Radcliffe: "There were times when he had money coming in. He had that deal with EMI when he got them to re-start the Regal Zonophone label. I went to London with him because we had the budget to a video in which a shed exploded and things like that. I went with him to see Malcolm Illey was the head of that division of EMI and we sat in his office and drank all his drinks. Malcolm had to take the video to the boardroom to get it cleared. But it wasn't, it was banned, so it never got shown."

Patrick Gallagher: "In terms of drugs and drink, Chris had no cut off point at all. One night I came back to the house with this big bag of… well it was kind of a mixture of coke and speed. Incredible gear that would induce this tremendous rush of euphoria. But you had to treat this with respect. Just take a little at a time. But Chris being Chris, went into the kitchen and took the whole lot. I was stunned. I thought, fucking hell… if that is indicative of what Chris actually does, that is not just indulgence. That is completely another level. It really scared me because it showed what he was capable of. Which was basically going the whole way. There were times when I remember people who were big drinkers coming out of a session where Chris had drunk every last drop in the kitchen and saying, 'Fucking hell… that guy… who is he?'"

This didn't always get in the way of the performances. Although Chris's imbibing certainly enhanced his idiosyncrasies.

Patrick Gallagher: "I recall one gig in London. I was to play guitar and Jon Ronson, who would join us in London, would be on keyboards. I was somewhat nervous about this because I didn't know the songs at all. I also knew that Chris could be a bit cavalier when it came to things like this, but I am not built like that. I need to know what I am doing before I go onstage. The gig was a big one. We were supporting Jonathan Richman at Camden, I think, so it was a bit scary for me. Chris told me that there would be no problem because he and Mark Radcliffe would have to go off and do something when we got to London which would leave me a couple of hours where I could just go through the songs with Jon. He said I could just follow Jon. When we got there it was typically chaotic. Chris asked if I wanted to go to the pub, I said 'No, I want to learn the fucking songs.' When I got together with Jon it seems that he didn't know them at all. In fact, Chris had told him that I knew the songs and that he would just have to follow me. I was absolutely furious and terrified, to be honest. I think there were times at that gig when we were playing completely different tunes. Chris was right in one respect. Nobody seemed to notice at all. Still, it wasn't the way I liked to work. I think this illustrates a fundamental different in the way we approached things. Chris could unsettle people and this was a problem when it came to television. People need to know where they stand or they become nervous. You can't do that when you are trying to get a television commission, which is difficult at the best of times."

Throughout this period, Gallagher was practically supporting Chris; emotionally, financially and artistically. "While Chris was staying with me and it was for six months or so, Chris would talk about Paula a great deal," he stated. "Sometimes deep into the night and the next morning. He obviously still loved her and wanted to get back together with her. My relationship with Chris started to suffer a bit. I was helping him a lot. I would lend him money. Get him gigs. Do a bit of driving to gigs. I took on a lot of responsibility. He wasn't just living here… he was living here and I was looking after him and, it seemed, his career. He was intriguing to live with. He was practical in the way that he could build a shed but he couldn't pay a bill or whatever.

"I think on the early days, Martin didn't get enough credit. Martin has a lot of things going on in his head and was every bit as creative as Chris. He was also every bit as hedonistic... but then we all were. I remember when me and Marc Riley were working with the 'Oh Blimey Big Band'. Chris had the 'Shed Show' in Yorkshire and Gerry Anderson came on the show. He had a couple of sci-fi sketches. We all went over to Yorkshire. Mark Radcliffe was there as Mr Emerson-Lake the greengrocer and Martin was there. Barry was there. It was a fucking great day out. Everyone getting pissed. It was often like that. Not really with Jon Ronson but certainly with the others.

Mark Radcliffe: "I also think he was a good songwriter. He adored The Beatles, along with his brother, Martin. If you listen to those Frank songs, a lot of them were really catchy. They were great pop tunes. 'The Robins are Not Bobbins' of The Freshies stuff."

Patrick Gallagher: "Chris had a tendency to be over-protective of Frank, I think. He always tried to keep that gap between Chris and Frank as wide as possible. But he felt it difficult to let other people do some of the mundane work. I used to tell him that he could let some of Frank go... let other people help a bit more. We could have done more together but Chris would sometimes pull back and be very selfish in regard to Frank. It didn't always work both ways."

The situation ultimately frustrated Gallagher – indeed both Gallaghers, as his brother, Michael, also featured heavily in 'The Oh Blimeys' – who remains an artist fired by a desire to go with the flow. It would have made a more productive partnership had Chris allowed Patrick's considerable talents to help in a less pedantic fashion.

Patrick Gallagher: "It was funny when Chris was staying with me. Towards the end there were some good opportunities for us to do some really good work together. I had television work waiting and Chris would be really enthusiastic but then would pull away. I couldn't understand it. It is odd because he has this well deserved reputation for being a really hard worker and, of course, he was but he could also be incredibly lazy. I think he could only really work on the one thing that was in his head and it was difficult for him to take on other people's suggestions. He would be given an opportunity but didn't seem capable of fully applying himself to it. He would take too long and opportunities would die on him.

"Plus, towards the end, he was wanting to go back with Paula. She would be ringing up and asking how he was and I would say, 'He's fine… he's listening to The Beatles' or whatever and then I would try and get him to talk to Paula. Eventually he did go back and we kind of drifted a little bit.

"He would waste so much time. He would spend ages doing all the new artwork for a Frank gig. He would go and do the gig and, at the end, he would give it all away. So, for the next gig he would have to start all over again. I used to tell him to stop giving stuff away. He was making things difficult for himself. He would go to B&Q, spend hours building stuff for the gig and, at the end of the gig, he would be completely pissed so he would give it away, come home, take drugs and start again building stuff for the next night. That was it. Was it the drugs and drink leading him, or the other way around? He would have a lot of coke and whiskey and be quite happy making stuff for the next gig."

★

"Backstage at an Icicle Works gig, after he had been on, we spotted him having an argument with Little Frank about how crap he was on stage that night. We were roaring laughing."

MARK REVELL

"Frank told me to go stand at the back of the classroom with your nose against the wall, for a song at Hull Adelphi in 1988. The song I asked for was 'Being for the Benefit of Mr Kite' which he had just recorded for the NME album "Sgt Pepper Knew My Father'. Needless to say, he didn't play it."

ARASH TORABI

★

"Playing a gig the night before Freddie Mercury died, Frank introduced 'Bohemian Rhapsody' as a tune by 'someone who is about to croak it'."

SIMON HEYWOOD

19th July 1986

On the occasion of the Factory run 'Festival of the Tenth Summer', on July 19th 1986, 8,000 people attended the central event held across 11 hours of mayhem and brilliance at Manchester's G-Mex.

Many words in many books and magazines have pinned this momentous occasion down in Manchester's enduring mythology. Some of them, like James Nice's majestic Factory tome, 'Shadowplayers', rightly claim to have nailed the happenings on that day... a day intended to cast a nod back to the Sex Pistols' ultra legendary two gigs at the Lesser Free Trade Hall in the late Spring of 1976.

Throughout these articles, most people now understand that the G-Mex day featured performances from New Order, The Fall, The Smiths, John Cooper Clarke, John Cale, A Certain Ration, OMD, two Buzzcocks, Wayne Fontana and the Mindbenders, Virgin Prunes (why?), The Worst, Sandie Shaw and a suitably anarchic cameo by one time Sex Pistols taunter Bill Grundy.

But Patrick Gallagher recalled a stripped down version of the Oh Blimey's performing; "perhaps with a taped backing... there was something weird about it".

In addition, Chris Sievey performed alone, sliding effortlessly through 'Megastore'. How touching and ironic to see so many of the attendees mouthing the words, lost to a state of nostalgic delight. Nobody, not even Chris, could have sensed that such blanket fondness hung in the Manchester air. Certainly not Factory boss Tony Wilson who, intriguingly, telephoned the *Manchester Evening News* during the run up to the gig to pose the question, "The Chameleons and The Freshies. Should they be on the bill? I know so little about them."

A NIGHT TO REMEMBER

THE VOICE OF HISTORY, it has been often stated, is composite. The voice of musical history, more profoundly so. The voice of Manchester musical history, thunderously so. Many voices; loud voices, filling the air, vying for attention; a demanding, often vacuous, cycle of self-promotion; shouts and screams at the time and then later, as history passes, voices screaming from retrospective media, be it a book, film, podcast, Wikipedia or a personality that remains, late in life, fixated on self-promotion. This warps the truth, wrestles the limelight, reshapes history. True enough, stories become entangled with other stories, become snagged and torn... and some fade enigmatically into the obscure.

There are other forces. Dark forces for some, brilliant shards of fortune for others. But it is, always, more than merely random and more, much more, than obvious force of talent. There are some occasions where the dark forces seem to flicker all the more obviously; seem to hang ominously in the air.

The evening to which I refer in this instance took place in the unlikely setting of The Offerton Palace nightclub on the fringe of Stockport. Oddly, The Offerton Palace was the only Stockport venue that The Beatles ever played on 13th June 1963. Strange, considering the myriad venues in the time during the Meseybeat period.

Normally, attending such a place would see the drinking of a gallon of ale followed by loud shouting and 'handbag' altercations at the late night bus stop. Not so on this occasion as the venue had been booked by Stockport's KFM Radio, to celebrate its transition from ersatz and oft-raided pirate stalwart of the area to a licensed and financially backed going concern blessed with a pristine and sexy new studio just off the town's teeming Mersey Square. Through the bizarre lottery of radio licence appropriation, KFM would be turning legit and join the harsh radio marketplace. Inevitably, they would fail and, as most often happens, they would be hurriedly sold to some vulturous corporate. Before then however, and before the station softened into lucrative mundanity, a period of glorious unholy local anarchy would prevail.

However the evening was to play a part in the story of Chris Sievey and, indeed, the dark and mysteriously twists of fate that happened around him, around Frank. And it was Chris, rather than Frank, who attended this strangely low key evening. He was in good and mild humour, too, sipping pints of bitter – though not copious amounts – and accompanied by a witty, talkative Paula and her nervous companion, Caroline Aherne. The significance of the moment couldn't possibly be apparent to anyone and yet… and yet… it was an oddly reflective affair; as if something was just about to change; something beyond the inception of a new local radio station.

Caroline was a funny girl, obviously so - although not particularly on this occasion. She had certainly impressed station manager Steve Toon who, after one meeting, offered her the lofty role as co-presenter of the new station's breakfast show. Her counterpart in what would become a joyously frenetic stomp around the retail establishments of Stockport town centre, would be Heaton Moor painter and decorator Craig Cash who had presented occasional shows at the pirate KFM's home in Goyt Mill, Marple. We all knew Craig well; natural, witty, precocious and wholly unpretentious. Toon had known him for years and his appointment seemed to make perfect sense, even if some of the housewives of Adswood struggled to grasp his vivid sarcasm. What we didn't know at the time and what Chris couldn't possibly have known, is that they were beginning a journey that would carry them to BAFTA winning success and, flanked by the likes of Henry Normal, emerge as one of the true cornerstones of British comedy. The very idea would have seemed absurd.

Yet there did appear a shift, back there at Offerton Palace. Chris, freed from the bombastic shackles of Frank, seemed politely pensive and certainly curious about the attention afforded to Caroline and Craig. Nevertheless, and despite his position on the outside of the rival Piccadilly Radio, Frank would often feature on KFM's unsteady platform. Not least on the show presented by Jon Ronson, up in

Manchester to enjoy and endure his role within the confines of the 'Oh Blimey Big Band'.

After Caroline had tentatively answered my questions for an upcoming *Manchester Evening News* feature, I settled next to Chris and asked him what was on his mind.

"I feel a little odd, like I am locked in a little box… with Frank, anyway. Don't know. Beginning to wonder why I put so much energy into Frank… beginning to wonder what is happening."

That was it, really. A small and apparently insignificant quote that hinted at a brooding sense of insecurity. It was the most vulnerable I had seen Chris since that day at *Muze* Magazine.. However, I had yet to witness the full extent of his hedonistic bent. I always had a feeling that this obscure little night proved to be a vital hinge moment.

Mike Doherty: "Caroline Aherne was living next to Paula's parents. I remember Chris telling me about this girl who was really funny… a natural. So eventually she took on the name Mrs Merton, who was a character in Frank's World. But it is wrong to say that she stole from Chris. That wasn't true. All she took was the name. I have no doubt that, somehow, Caroline would have made it to the top. It just so happened that she did it with a Frank character's name."

Barry Spencer: "Chris could be very lackadaisical with his material. The Mrs Merton thing, I can remember how it happened. He came to me, because I was an actor, and said 'Do you know anyone who can do Mrs Merton?' Paula was sat next to me and said, 'Caroline… Caroline, she could do it.' So Chris said, 'Well can you ask her, because Katie Puckrick, (the Canadian comedian) said she could do it'. Caroline went for it and said, 'Can I do this, Chris?' He said 'Yeah, go on then'. The rest is history of course because she took Mrs Merton onto the stage and got a TV series out of it. He was like that, Chris. I don't know if that was a period where he was drinking heavily but he let Mrs Merton go, really'.

MRS MERTON'S FIRST TELEVISION APPEARANCE

CAROLINE AHERNE HAD BEEN WORKING as The Mitzi Goldberg Experience in and around Manchester clubs. John Barratt, then working as studio manager at Pete Waterman's Church Studio at the wrong end of Deansgate, remembers taking Craig Cash – a long term friend from their locale, the Bohemian district of Heaton Moor, Stockport, to see Caroline as Mitzi Goldberg at Fagin's. Craig had already started to work with Caroline at KFM and was keen to gain a more rounded view of his new friend's talent.

Craig and Caroline, locked in their role as co-presenters at KFM, visited John's Heaton Moor home and interviewed John's wife, Rosemary. As Ro Newton, she had already built a powerful career in the media. While in London she had gained a position as co-presenter of The Old Grey Whistle Test while simultaneously presenting a Radio One music gossip show, 'Back Chat'. As such, and as a Stockport resident, Ro proved perfect for KFM's loose listenership. In recent years, Ro and John had been working on a BSB daytime television show called, 'Cool Cube'. With its roots planted firmly in the 'Tiswas' school of anarchic children's television with a cult student following, 'Cool Cube' had been chugging away at the idiosyncratic edge of satellite television for some time. John and Ro invited Caroline to bring Mitzi Goldberg to the show, which she duly did. She also mentioned that she had gained the role of Mrs Merton on Frank's Fantastic Shed Show at Piccadilly Radio. As such, a kernel of an idea formed. Mrs Merton could appear on 'Cool Cube' as a regular agony aunt. A perfect way of encouraging viewer interaction.

Caroline duly turned up at the Granada based studio, keen to develop the persona further. Unfortunately, as Mrs Merton had only been a cartoon character and radio personality up and until that point, she arrived with no Mrs Merton costume. Unabashed, John and Ro rushed Caroline down to the Coronation Street wardrobe and managed to find a suitable 'old lady' garb. As such, the visual character of Mrs Merton was born.

'Cool Cube' also provided rich pickings for Frank Sidebottom, who made regular appearances for £200 a show – a huge amount, considering the small scale of the embryonic satellite television station.

John Barratt also recalls meeting Chris and Caroline in the Horse and Jockey pub in Didsbury. The pair were clearly lost in a conspiratorial huddle before Chris suddenly proclaimed that he was "…going to manage Caroline and take care of her career."

It was a brave notion although, with the best will in the world, one found it difficult to imagine Chris Sievey having the singular focus necessary to manage a burgeoning television career. Needless to say, the idea never seriously took off. Nevertheless, the Mrs Merton character was in the ascendancy. An appearance on 'The Legendary Manchester Busker Show' at Manchester's Green Room, was witnessed by a team of Granada producers who included the show as part of their celebratory night out. The audience apparently seemed unusually aged that night which led to the notion of a Mrs Merton chat show complete with a audience of pensionable age. Whether that is a simplistic version of events or not is perhaps irrelevant. What did transpire was a complete reversal of fortunes. While Caroline's Mrs Merton, who undeniably began life as a Chris Sievey invention, gained instant and massive success on Granada Television before spreading to cover the country, thereby laying the foundations of a great if troubled career, Chris appeared to fall by the wayside, dragging Frank to perform tirelessly before dwindling audiences.

"There was a story going around that Chris had got completely wasted and turned up in the middle of the night in Caroline Aherne's front garden in Burnage," John Barratt remembers. "He was shouting that he had 'made her everything she is.' It was a sad part of his life, really."

★

John Barratt: "We asked both Mark E. Smith and Chris to take part in our video for The Sweeney back in 1998. We took them both down to the Fab Café in Manchester, which was kind of our base for a while. The owners were really pleased at first until they realised just how much these two could consume... immense amounts. Free drinks all over the place. I think it was the first time that Chris had met Mark and it surprised me that Mark seemed aware of Chris and liked what he did with Frank. I never saw any connection before but I realised that they were quite similar personalities. Both lived by their own rules, really. It could be said that Chris was a nicer character than Mark, who could be so difficult, but Chris wasn't always so nice. When he was really drunk, and he really did get absolutely leathered, he could be impossible. I remember picking him up one Saturday morning and taking him to Moulah Rouge Studios in Stockport. Chris was recording a song, 'Stockport is Really Fantastic' for me that was going to be placed on the other side of Frankie Vaughan's 'Stockport, That's Where It's At.' But he was sensationally drunk and had a child with him, when really he shouldn't have been in charge of a child."

IT DIDN'T ALWAYS WORK. Frank. Not always. And it wasn't merely a question of territory, either. Sometimes, for no apparent reason, a perfectly good and liberal student audience would fail to rise to the joke. This bore absolutely no relation to how funny Frank was on a particular night. I have seen extraordinary, side-splitting performances that dip and sway into the truly surreal... performances that would have made an embryonic Vic Reeves appear staid by comparison. I have seen some of the finest shows of his career faced by stony silence. I have seen Chris wandering backstage chatting freely with Little Frank, seemingly wholly unaware of the oasis of a stage he had just exited.

Frank: "Well, I thought that went well, Little Frank... what did you think?"

Little Frank: "I thought it was bobbins."

This not uncommon exchange more often than not would explode into a full blown argument, regardless of whether the dressing room would be empty or not. More curious still would be the transformation back to Chris Sievey. I have seen him troubled by ecstatic crowd reactions in, say, Manchester's International Club and yet seemingly completely unbothered by hostile receptions in some distant club or college. Almost as if the performance would be judged solely by Chris… and only Chris really understood what made a good performance. Truth is, and the Billy and Barry Belly moments were born from this, that Chris found things within his own performance that would go unnoticed to all but the carefully trained eye. A lead perhaps? A thread that might carry a joke into a contrasting area, an exciting thread that could be further explored on the following night. Something that sparked within Chris' imagination, keeping him content throughout the night as he followed the Frank thread. This forward movement was always considered far more important than instant audience gratification. Almost as if Chris was surfing at an entirely different level. Almost as if the performance was total… a 24/7 affair between the two entities, rolling on and on and spreading with ecstatic glee, further and further into the absurd. Truly a dangerous place to linger.

As it was with Chris, not everything was sweetness and light with Frank. Whether getting the joke or not, not everyone found his company inspiring. Some girls, I noticed, believed him ever-so-slightly… er… creepy. Not in any kind of sexual way. In fact, possibly the opposite was true. His sexless nature unnerved them, robbed them of their power, perhaps? Certainly, the bulk of his audience would always be male. One woman of my acquaintance found his head to be 'completely unattractive'. When I replied, 'well that is kind of missing the point… you are not supposed to fancy him', she just looked at me with cold unwavering eyes, disdainful as a cat's. I don't think she got the joke, but couldn't be sure. Even Paula, as Tosh Ryan remembered, 'Couldn't bloody stand that Frank' although she has more cause than most to dislike his bombastic nature. Tales of people having sex while wearing Frank heads hang intriguingly in the air.

Weirder still, I guess, Chris often expressed exasperation where Frank was concerned. I do recall him chuntering, "He is really getting on my fucking nerves today."

"Who is, Chris?"

OUT OF HIS HEAD

"Frank, pain in the fucking arse."

Well, of course, he could be but, again, that is kind of the point of Frank. Wasn't he specifically invented to be a professional wind-up merchant? Who in the world could be more annoying? Chris had started to worry that Frank's mercenary attitude – for example supporting any football team that would pay him more money – might spill out into his own life. Well, it did, once or twice, when life became tough and there seemed little option other than to take the hard line and join the bastards who ripped you off at every stroke. But Chris had managers and agents to do that. His biggest fear; his very *real* fear was that Chris and Frank might merge into the same persona. That Chris might even fade beneath Frank's sheer dominance. A real fear indeed for Chris, given his insecurities and swings of hedonism, could never compete with the single-minded pragmatism of Frank.

As time went by, Frank also became increasingly 'un-PC'. What place in society for a 35 year-old who lives with his mother and remains completely in fear of her? Who talks about her at every given opportunity? That is not just creepy, it is faintly perverse. Had he lived on, one imagines him – Frank – being arrested to 'help the police with their enquiries' over some heinous sex crime.

"There are some strange stories of Frank at his most extreme. One example is a gig in Northern Ireland at a Catholic pub, I believe, where he was singing 'The IRA are really fantastic.' That is unbelievable, really and maybe only Frank could get away with that."

DAN PARROTT

FOOTBALL FOCUS

Frank and football will forever remain synonymous. On the surface, this is obvious. The Timperley Big Shorts FC, Frank's own team, still play in the Altrincham and District Amateur Football League - lying third in the table, as I type, below Navigation Bay and Partington Village. Below them sit such teams as Buck Inn, Pelican, FC Broadway, Bricklayers Arms and Bird Ith Hand. They formed in 1990 and still wear the crest of their 'El Presidente', Frank Sidebottom. Their motto, 'In Big Shorts We Trust'.

Frank's immersion in football was gloriously archaic and embedded in the days of footballer cigarette cards, *Charlie Buchan's Football Monthly*, *The Topical Times Football Annual*. Evocative artefacts from the childhood days of Chris Sievey. Back then, footballers had craggy, lived-in faces, smoked Woodbines and didn't really earn much more than the average Joe. It was more fun, of course, and effortlessly romantic. Big Shorts evoked the lost spirit of football in an era before the multi-millionaire players of United and City would park their Lamborghini's in Chris's home village of Ashton-on-Mersey, the village lying close to the Carrington Moss training grounds of both teams.

Steve Forster: "I met Chris by chance one day at White Hart Lane. Spurs were playing Altrincham in the FA Cup (January 7, 1995. Spurs won 3 – 0). Frank had been on the pitch before as the Altrincham mascot. But I was under the stand at half time and Chris came running up saying, 'Did you see Frank? He was on before the match.' He could only speak of Frank as another person, even in a situation like that. It was like Chris and Frank had both travelled separately to the game. We shared a meat pie. It seemed slightly surreal."

Chris, of course, was a die-hard Manchester City supporter, although his love of the game extended beyond such singular loyalty. Frank, by contrast, could change allegiance at the drop of a hat and support anyone in a wholly sycophantic manner. Paula, too, remains fiercely loyal to City.

Steve Forster: "When Chris had a gig in London, we would tailor our Saturday afternoons to take in the football match that was nearer the venue he might be playing. We would just decide to go to Leyton Orient or Brentford. He loved relaxing at football… any football. I think it took him away from his worries."

Steve Forster: "When Little Denise's head went missing, I remember students and fans from all over the world sending in pics of the head that they had made them themselves… photos from Tokyo and everywhere."

In Steve Sullivan's 'Being Chris Sievey' film, Dave Arnold, holding the cardboard body of Little Denise, makes a plea to finally discover the whereabouts of her head. Some people, it has been said, are still looking. The last time I saw Little Denise was at Manchester's Boardwalk where Frank supported The Membranes. Little Denise received a better reception than either Frank or Little Frank, even to the extent of a post set chant, albeit delivered with a sense of inebriated irony. One story was that Frank became jealous of this attention and stole the head, perhaps burying it under a patio in Timperley. When I visited Steve Sullivan's set for 'Being Chris Sievey' in Timperley, I didn't even recognise the headless cardboard body of Little Denise.

Steve Forster: "There was this mad shop near my house in Woolwich next to a bus stop. They just sold crazy and useless items. We were looking in the window and Chris became absolutely fascinated by a pineapple scraper. He really was genuinely transfixed. 'Imagine that… a pineapple scraper…' But it was Sunday and the shop was closed. I just knew I had to buy it for him and I did. In fact I took it up to present it to him, Paula and the family. I remember they were all equally transfixed and rushed out to buy a pineapple."

MICK MIDDLES

★

Chris once told me that he could quite happily have spent the rest of his life living in that flat on the Brooklands roundabout with Paula. He seemed perplexed that anyone could wish for a more prestigious abode and quite rightly so. Whenever I visited I was struck by the aforementioned familial atmosphere. It always seemed colourful and oddly creative, with Paula and the kids seemingly understanding and enjoying the sense of artistic release. This seemed unusual to me, as most families I knew tended to settle down to artless mundanity, submitting to the sundry distractions of early evening television. That never appeared to be the case in that flat.

Paula Sievey: "As mentioned, we had Asher and Stirling in our old flat on The Brooklands roundabout. Those were our happiest times, really and we had stayed there for about 10 years but the council, in their wisdom, told us that we couldn't bring up two kids there, so they moved us to this council house off Wythenshawe Road. It was awful. We hated it. Really horrible place. We lasted there about ten years and then we rented a house on Park Road. We were there for four years but after a couple of years I got pregnant with Harry and that was when his drinking got really bad. He had an office in Timperley village and it kept getting broken into and they kept stealing all his stuff. I think it did his head in. I kept finding whiskey bottles in his pocket. I would ask him 'why are you drinking so much? You have a gig at Timperley Leisure club, tonight?' and he would be there, absolutely pissed out of his head. But he would say, 'oh it'll be alright'. He was completely out of control at that point.

"We eventually got evicted from that house because the rent never got paid. But the sad thing was while we lived in that house he got the deal with Yorkshire Television to do the Shed Show, and we had loads of money. He just started doing loads of drugs… cocaine, drink… oh he was probably spending it on prostitutes. So we got evicted from there and I found a house on Manor Road, where Tesco now is in Altrincham, on the corner. We lived there but he was getting worse and worse. He would disappear for days and days on end… weeks. Just go and stay with people in town or wherever. He would come back absolutely trashed. Harry would have been about two and a half then. It was as bad as it gets. He wasn't giving me any money to pay the bills. I was going out doing cleaning jobs to try and get by. But we didn't. Something had to give. In the end I just scooped up the kids and went and lived in a hostel. I just left him there. Of course, he got evicted from there and went to stay in the Isle of Man for a bit. I was in a hostel for about three months and then I found a house in Hawthorn Road, Hale and me and the kinds moved in there."

★

MICK MIDDLES

DAVE ARNOLD

On a windswept and saturated corner. Deep, leaden skies, rows of solid terracing... on the fringe of Wigan. On such a Saturday, deep within the dank unstable January of 2014, the area seemed to evoke early 70s austerity. What light had seeped into the afternoon was now fading fast and I felt it difficult not to imagine it a scene from some black and white cinematic glimpse at a dark age, with piles of rubbish – not there in actuality – and a gang of local skinheads kicking a tin can in the road... the skinheads weren't there, either.

At first the bungalow didn't seem at all appropriate for a skate boarding punk skate park designer such as Dave Arnold. Until, that is, one wandered around to the rear of the property to discover a gargantuan skate park dominating the garden.

"We built that ourselves... that's what we do," offered Arnold. "If you wanted one in your garden, it would cost around sixty grand."

I couldn't quite see, unless one lived in Venice Beach, how such an item could significantly add to the value of any property.

"Doubles as a swimming pool, in summer," he added.

It must be stated that the true heart of Dave's house was undoubtedly the loft space. An area stacked and furnished with the ephemera of a punk, skateboard and Frank Sidebottom obsessive. Single sleeves lined the walls and appeared like benign old friends. Familiar visions of The Adverts, Blitz, The Ruts, UK Subs and, slightly more obscure, the Rabid recording of John Scott and CP Lee's Gerry and the Holograms, the record that, it is often claimed, formed the rhythmic base of New Order's Blue Monday. To the left, the headless bodies of Little Frank and Little Denise shuddered eerily on the wall. A small pile of faded Sounds magazines sat on the floor, inviting perusal. I always like to discover piles of Sounds magazines.

Three days earlier, Dave had attended a miniscule screening of Jon Ronson's 'Frank' movie among a gathering of assorted Sieveys, with Neil Taylor and Steve Sullivan.

"I am worried that it might be a bit dark for me," I meekly offered.

"Well, it is extremely dark," he agreed. "There is a suicide in the first ten minutes... but it is really good..." he mused, "...really good although not what any of us ever envisaged. Some people probably won't connect with it... old Frank obsessives and people like that."

One could sense that Dave Arnold, stalwart Frank tour manager, bassist and a kind of artistic dynamo, felt relieved to discover that the film would carry Frank into a whole new and unexpected area, teasing out myriad possibilities that had not, before, been evident. Taking Frank – at long last – out of Timperley. I wondered how the Arnold and Sievey stars managed to collide.

Dave Arnold: "Being in bands is all I have ever done since being a kid. Since 1976. Punk rock in Wigan. Stupid bands really. Influenced by American punk, really. Dead Kennedys, Black Flag. So harder, faster than what was going on in the UK at the time. Got into the whole thing. English stuff too... Blitz, Discharge. Got really into the Crass anarcho thing. All that. It never left me. At the same time I was always skateboarding. These were my two passions. I would read magazines like *Maximum Rock'n'Roll* that would champion what was going on in America. I started seriously seeking out American stuff, which was hard to find in the UK at the time.

"The first time I got to know Chris was when I had this shop in Affleck's Palace. It was clothing and mildly collectable records and a lot of toys. I loved toys. In the shop I had a Frank head that I had made. It was pretty good, too. I had it on a dummy, high up in the shop. One day this guy walked in and pointed to it. He said, 'That's Frank Sidebottom. He is my mate, he is... I will have to bring him in.' Sure enough, a week or so went by and in he walks with Chris. Chris inspected the head and said 'Oh yes, it is good... can I borrow it off you?' This would have been in the early 1990s. He wanted to borrow it to put in his art exhibition at Stockport Art Gallery. He was going to put a shed in there and a dummy Frank with a head. But he only had one head at that point. So that is how we first met."

The Frank Sidebottom exhibition at Stockport Art Gallery was, I suggest, quite unlike any exhibition that had ever previously occupied that space. Naturally, the usual exhibits were in place... Frank heads in a variety of guises, cardboard bodies, a shed… standard Frank ephemera, really and the initial swell of attendees included most of the usual devotees of Frank. No surprises there and it made for a fairly pleasant opening, drinking bad white and chatting Frank stuff. More interesting, however, would be later days, once the flurry had settled and Stockport Art Gallery regained its regular somnolent state (a Tuesday afternoon, perhaps?). At such times, the exhibition took on a different life, as random and regular attendees wandered into the heart of the exhibition with no prior knowledge of Frank whatsoever. Imagine their astonishment to discover a row of Frank heads! This also provided Chris with the perfect opportunity to wander amongst these little knots of local art lovers and note their gazes, their conversations (it hadn't been like this with the Bob Dylan exhibition which preceded it). Unwittingly, Stockport Art Gallery had provided Chris with a glimpse of a possible future. One day, maybe, the perfect venues for both Chris and Frank might be gallery space rather than students union bar.

Dave Arnold: "I was aware of The Freshies, of course. But – I will be honest – only really 'Megastore' and maybe 'Bouncing Babies' when it came out. It was the guitarist in one of the bands I played in who got me into Frank. I didn't know the connection at first. This would be early 1987, that I became aware of Frank, so he had already been going a couple of years. I think I first saw him at Timperley Labour Club and from that moment onwards, I was completely and utterly wrapped up in Frank. Totally obsessed. I would go to his gigs all the time. Living in Ashton-on-Makerfield, you are close to everywhere… only ten minutes to St Helens from here and Frank played at The Citadel. Just like in Timperley he would play like four nights in a row. He did that in Liverpool too. Or he would do like four consecutive Thursdays. So I just went to the lot. It was extremely convenient and I got to know his stuff very well. I was just always there. I remember Paula used to say 'are you not sick of *this*?' whenever I turned up. So I gradually got to know Chris well, too. But I was never sick of Frank at all. There was always something different going on. Every set, really."

OUTPUT

WHILE THE OH BLIMEY BIG BAND may have expanded, the 'live Frank experience' became an increasingly bizarre aural show, nevertheless his recorded output remained largely the work of one man… or two, if you catch my drift.

As a body of work, Frank on CD or cassette or vinyl, has few equals. The reason for this belongs to the simplicity, cheapness and availability of the performer in question. A peg on the nose and a state of hangover not too crushing was often all that was needed for Frank to enter the world of the recording studio. And how he loved it. The darkness. The little lights. The befuddled sound engineer and completely dumbfounded producer. Sitting in the studio with Frank Sidebottom is an experienced denied to all but a select few. And, I must admit, I only fleetingly enjoyed this unique sight. And what a sight! At Cavalier studios, I seem to recall. For a recording managed by a producer and engineer who simply had not fully bought into Frank's warped world (Timperley) view and, frankly, would rather be suitably engaged in the task of polishing 'serious music', be it a Puressence single or something by Big Flame. Not this ranting idiot! The in-studio dynamic was extraordinary. Frank, of course, would leap on any opportunity to irritate both engineer and producer by leaning over the mixing desk, fiddling with whatever knobs or buttons came within his grasp – very Mark E. Smith, I thought – and asking questions of an unusual variety.

"If it is sixteen tracks does that mean I have to sing it sixteen times? Blimey!"

I sense that this is the reason that much of Frank's recorded output was completed with a degree of haste. Not necessarily a bad thing, for we are not talking 'Dark Side of the Moon' here, but I often felt that certain opportunities were missed.

Frank could lampoon anything, and more often than not, did just that. From The Fall - 'Hit The North' – to Queen – 'We Are The Champions' and most things in-between. However, and despite one or two notable excursions – 'Hey You, Street Artist', being one memorable moment - the energy flash world of rave and dance existed chiefly without the inclusion of Frank Sidebottom's iconic voice. What a pity as one always felt if rife for sampling. If Rick Astley can hit such heights without re-recording a line, why not Frank? Rapping too would have seemed the perfect tool even if the concept of Gangsta Rap might have been somewhat beyond his world view. However, I would have loved Frank's voice to filter through the Balearic air. It would have melted perfectly to the prevailing vibe, I am sure.

While I suggest that Frank Sidebottom should be remembered more firmly as a live and living phenomenon, here are a few personal favourites.

'ANARCHY IN TIMPERLEY'

Chris Sievey was of an age still inspired and invigorated by the initial explosion of The Sex Pistols classic debut single in November 1976. Chris said that he initially heard the single one evening on a Radio Luxemburg broadcast that also featured an interview with Johnny Rotten and Malcolm McClaren. He was particularly struck by their slow paced cockney drawl, which seemed so exotic, at least when listened to in Sale. As to whether the first hearing changed his life… Probably not, as he was already five years into a career attempting to catch the attention of the record companies. Nevertheless it hardened his attitude towards song-writing – the embryonic Freshies becoming the lightest possible version of a punk band – and probably hardened his attitude towards life as well.

Of course Frank would famously dismantle the soaring intensity of The Sex Pistols. 'Anarchy in Timperley' is exactly what you might expect of a song written about a suburban town with a caravan on every drive and an unholy amount of the colour beige. A touch of genius, is the Frank method of comedifying the infamous Rotten smile, turning the whole affair into something one might encounter at a primary school end of term disco. Performed live, it always raised a cheer and often caused a pseudo-mosh pit. Not least at Manchester University which became a swirl of regurgitated lager and badly dressed 21 year-olds. It was most impressively performed at Blackpool's 'Rebellion' punk festival in 2009 where Frank, complete with safety pins and Mohican, became the perfect embodiment of ageing punkdom. Killing Joke, on the same bill, would never quite be the same again.

'TIMPERLEY BLUES'

In which Frank attempts to capture the spirit of the original genre, beautifully tearing away at the framework of the very music that provided the template for American – and subsequently British – music for the next sixty years. It is not known quite what John Lee Hooker, John Mayall, Eric Clapton or Jack White made of it. However, Blues aficionados Gary and Gillian Atkinson, twin owners of the massive blues archive label 'Document', both professed a strong devotion to Sidebottom. Although Mayall hailed from nearby Macclesfield and Cheadle Hulme, it is difficult to discover any further connections the area has with the blues. (Be quiet, pedants, Chorlton station is too far away).

'TIMPERLEY SUNSET'

Controversially chosen as the lyrical subject of Frank's blue plaque in Timperley – a number of local papers even claimed the melody to be entirely the work of Frank. One wonders quite what Kinks leader Ray Davies, a notably litigious character if myth be believed, would make of it all. Perhaps best to keep quiet as Frank uses this famous and delicately rolling melody on which to place his offbeat vocal take. It doesn't work… and it does work, to superb effect. Of course, the Timperley factor weighs heavy here and, while one can imagine that romantic liaisons have taken place between Terrys and Julies on Brooklands Bridge, it doesn't seem to carry quite the same level of intrigue and mischief, although Barry Spencer might disagree.

'BORN IN TIMPERLEY'

Springsteen's '80s thumper remains arguably the most misunderstood single of all time, with American political parties, television stations and even the US military refusing to understand the fact that it is so obviously dipped in the heavy glue of irony. So it came as no surprise at all to discover that Frank, likewise, fails to grasp the concept of irony with this ferocious statement of intent and love for his homeland stretch of tedious suburbia. However, the site of Frank's statue will grant Frank the eternal bond he always openly desired.

'SURFIN' TIMPERLEY'

Difficult indeed to successfully envisage this lively take on The Beach Boys vision of early sixties Malibu. Where, indeed, in Timperley could this vision be placed? One senses only on the banks of the Bridgewater Canal which slices through the region, latterly flanked by the yellow beauties of Metrolink. Given a little Sunday sunshine, the canal transforms into a veritable frenzy of weekend escapism. Frank, however, may have been recalling his trip down Washway Road to the gargantuan shell of The Pelican pub in nearby Sale. This writer once accompanied Frank's creator plus Paula, Asher and Stirling, then of tender ages, to The Pelican's hilarious 'Beach day on the car park' which saw the local children sprawling over 20 tons of imported sand while the parents extended the pretence of a Spanish holiday. It didn't quite work although much beer did indeed flow. Years later, at an identical event, Frank Sidebottom apparently performed this very song on the same car park. I sense his appearance added a juvenile frisson to the occasion.

OUT OF HIS HEAD

'OH TIMPERLEY'

Obvious really. Nicely inelegant take on Ultravox's stylish 'Vienna', complete with Frank's hilarious slicked back Midge Ure stance. Timperley is not quite the Bohemian home of the original, although it does have trams and, along the leafy extension of Park Road, a certain architectural grandeur. In addition, of course, the exclamation 'Oh' is famously a Frankism. In addition, and for many years, many people actually believed that Frank Sidebottom was Midge Ure. The reason for this, according to Jon Ronson, was that Ure was often seen at Frank's gigs. However, this theory does break down a little when one could see Ure in the audience while Frank was performing.

'THE ROBINS ARE NOT BOBBINS'

Mystifying, one senses, to anyone living beyond the boundaries of Trafford, 'The Robins are not Bobbins' proved such a perfect theme song for Frank's beloved Altrincham FC. Whether in his honoured role as official mascot or, as happened on several occasions, storming uninvited onto the pitch, Frank often made a colourful distraction from the all-too-often dour clogging and hoofing taking place in the penalty areas. At one point, the ground was mooted as the site for the Frank statue, which would have made sense, although central Timperley gave him a more universal presence.

'GUESS WHO'S BEEN ON MATCH OF THE DAY?'

From the moment Chris moulded his first Frank head in his Timperley bathroom, the character was always destined to one day make an impact on Britain's favourite football show.

Frank and 'Match of the Day' were made for one another - the celebratory and anthemic nature of the theme tune made it a favourite at Frank gigs for a number of years. More than that, it would grow into a feature moment, where Frank would throw the question to the crowd who always simply loved to offer the unified answer, "You, Frank, in your big shorts." Few sights in popular entertainment manage to equal the sight of 150 mature people – teachers, doctors, solicitors and professional surfboarders – all gleefully adding to Frank's open and honest braggadocio. On record, as is the case with much of Frank's output, it didn't quite match the strange thrill of live spontaneity. It is a song also sung – still, to this day – whenever the Frank inspired Timperley Big Shorts take to the field. A fact that has attained poignancy over the past three years.

'HIT THE NORTH'

Probably best known for its appearance on MTV, complete with a bemused David Soul and ex-Happy Monday man Paul Ryder, Frank's tribute to The Fall's Mark E. Smith improved with age as Frank attained a greater grasp of Smith's infamous idiosyncrasies. As such, he would love to stalk the stage, verbally abusing and, on certain notable occasions, sacking Little Frank from the band, hanging his coat on any piece of musical equipment, sitting at the back of the stage with a stack of lyrics and coming as close as Frank ever could to the art of the inebriated grimace.

'I SHOULD BE SO LUCKY'

Incredibly, Pete Waterman claimed to be a huge fan of Frank. Speaking from his church studio at the Castlefield end of Manchester's Deansgate, Waterman stated: "I love Frank Sidebottom... always found him funny but I also enjoy the way he arranges songs. He is extremely underrated. He manages to take a popular tune and turn it inside out, taking the piss and creating something unique. Always thought his recordings were excellent... not that I sit at home listening to Frank Sidebottom."

Intriguingly, even the most devoted Sidebottom fans rarely spend time listening with intent to his recorded output. Perhaps that would miss the point, somewhat. Frank albums are an appendage and never central to the character.

'I Should Be So Lucky' is a case in point. The sight of Frank

Sidebottom taking off Kylie Minogue, arguably his true antithesis, will live with me for many years.

'MULL OF TIMPERLEY'

Well it is easy to suggest that Frank used this as a kick-back to Sievey, for it certainly offered the chance for him to climb in and mess about with Macca's hugely successfully and most critically loathed moment. Where better for Frank to tread? Lovely to think of the 'mist rolling in' from the beleaguered expanses of Broadheath. Simplicity itself. I'm sure McCartney would heartily approve.

'XMAS IS REALLY FANTASTIC' / 'I WISH IT COULD BE CHRISTMAS EVERY DAY' / 'OH COME ALL YE FAITHFUL' / 'OH BLIMEY, IT'S CHRISTMAS' / 'LAST CHRISTMAS'.

Obviously perhaps, Frank came into his own at Christmas. Indeed, Christmas *belonged* to Frank. Not the Christmas of packed raucous pubs, binge imbibing and rolling around in the gutters of Warrington, but an old-fashioned Christmas of toys and models and shimmering lights. One always loved his statement within the 'Magical Timperley Tour' DVD, as the bus drove slowly down the village's Shaftsbury Avenue'. "Every Christmas, a war breaks out between the rich people on that side of the road and the poorer people on the other side of the road. On that side they buy a massive reindeer for like a million quid… on the other side they go to Poundworld and buy every Christmas light and just leather the garden with them."

Such a battle would be hugely engrained within Frank's vision.

Frank's live show would warp brilliantly as the Festive season dawned. 'Xmas is Really Fantastic' was, of course, the standard template Frank number and has appeared in a variety of forms, from 'Stockport is Really Fantastic' to his ironic 'Man U are Really Fantastic'. Best of all was his take on Wham's 'Last Christmas' with Frank hamming "..but the very next day, you *threw* it awaaaay!". Near genius.

MICK MIDDLES

'ELECTRICITY'

Always an admirer of Wirrall's finest export, Orchestral Manoeuvres in the Dark, this version of their debut Factory single allowed Frank to fully utilise his keyboard skills. The effect, not dissimilar to a Les Dawson piano sing-along, proved to be one of the finest send ups of the electric nuances of the 80s that I have ever heard. (It is probably the *only* 80s send up I have heard, but no matter).

STORIES WE COULD TELL

Loose night, warm gig; Salford University. A man now lost to the mists of disgrace, then loveable uncle. Many had evolved through teenage years with an Uncle Gary Glitter in sight. Loathed by the proggers; mocked by music press... loved by those who loved the flash of pop. Chris saw the artistic worth in Glitter's daft flash. Felt proud too, he did, to take a supporting role for Frank at many venues. For Glitter and Frank made for the perfect anarchic Fresher's Ball. All this, of course, before the soot black truth dawned on a nation.

But before that violent loss of innocence, what could rival a gallon of ale and Frank and Gary: wall-to-wall daftness on a Friday night.

Of course, the reality wouldn't be so perfect. It didn't take too many gigs for another truth to dawn. The egotistical aloofness of the said Mr Glitter. Perhaps the only man at the gig... perhaps the only man in glam Britain of the seventies, who didn't get the thrust of his own joke. A serious artist? We are not talking Bob Dylan here. We are talking about a warped out extra from the fringe of the sixties who got lucky via the flash insanity of the glam era. Good old Gary, eh?

At all gigs, there would be a stairway leading down to the stage. The prefect prop for the startled-eyed, elongated entrance of Gary Glitter, strutting slowly – ever-so-slowly down to stage front. Teasing the inebriated throng, stoking up the atmosphere and effectively so.

There would, of course, always be the darkness, perhaps here paraded as the symbol of the diva. No one in Frank's entourage was allowed to speak to Glitter prior to the performance. And under no circumstances should the entertainer known as Frank Sidebottom, or anyone else for that matter, be allowed to descend those stars and take the stage the Glitter way. How inevitable therefore that, come Frank's stage-time, he would be seen in Gary Glitter mode, slowly descending the stairs, flashing his own version of startled eyed Glitter glory. Working the joke to the extreme. Frank as Gary. Camping it up to the max. Leaping from the stairs into his own act at stage front. Perfectly stealing the Glitter glory and backstage, ignoring the grim requests not to disturb the one once called Paul Raven. Rick Sarko, pushing down the corridor, pushing into Glitter's dressing room, amazed to see Glitter sitting their in a state of complete baldness. The true horror of the situation beyond him.

At least, on that occasion, Frank would be the wizard, the true star.

At the BBC's New Broadcasting House, the commendable if insane orgy of well intentioned mischief, bad jokes and mistimed reporting known as 'Children in Need'. Frank and Rick Sarko are down there… Frank to perform (answering the phones?) fully enjoying the raw flash of mainstream celebrity, even if only from a localised BBC outpost: "And now to Manchester where we meet a man with a big head… FRANK SIDEBOTTOM!!!"

Well, it was all for the cause. Celebrities wandered everywhere, that day, through the catacombs of New Broadcasting House. Famous faces looming from the gloom of the corridors, most of them not recognising Frank or his colleague, Rick Sarko as they bundled backstage, happy to discover a jug of single malt, which they swiftly devoured. Only later did they feel a mite sheepish, as the voluminous, commanding and ever-familiar voice of Les Dawson screamed, "Who has nicked my bloody whiskeeeee?" Rick Sarko: "We both loved Les Dawson but we could never admit that. We fled home and carried on drinking, buzzing off the incident all night long."

FRANK IS DEAD

"I got to know Patrick Gallagher through an entirely different set of circumstances, which was…we design and build skate parks and we had just built one in Stockport. We built the park but we were left building one of those things outside, in wood. It was taking ages. The skate park was open but we were still working. I looked over and I saw Patrick and I recognised him from his part in 'Frank and the Beanstalk'. Patrick was the beanstalk. He was dressed head to toe in bright green ballet tights and stood in a big bucket. I said, 'hey you were the beanstalk'. And this was a time when Frank had gone. This would be like 1998. I asked him what Chris was doing and he told me that he was living with him at the house in Burnage. I asked him if he felt that Frank would officially open the skate park. He said 'You'll have to pay him… say £100'. So we agreed that he would come and do a 20 minute thing for £100. Sure enough Frank turned up and just stayed all night as Frank. He was just loving it. I discouraged him from having a go on the park because it would have ended badly. But Harry, his son, is a really talented skateboarder. Frank or Chris… whoever, was totally in tune with what was going on then. That whole skateboard punk thing. He completely understood it."

DAVE ARNOLD

"FRANK IS DEAD," SAID CHRIS, "he's not coming back. He was killing me. People started to hate him. I have an idea… I have not spoken about this to a living soul. Not yet."

Hunched over iced Coke; drifting towards the softer edge of

his demeanour, apparently sober, apparently free from Frank... and reasonably happy. Chris had been working for 'Hot Animation' in Broadheath. Cathartic employment, soaking away his unsettled muse, helping him gain satisfaction from his artistic ambition. To a point. Frank had – seemingly – gone. Dead. Cast to the shadows.

But now Chris Sievey was in Liverpool. I had visited the city with him on a number of occasions. He always appeared content there. Whether this was mere Beatles affectation or not, I couldn't tell. There may have been a case for that, for I know that Chris loved the colour and brashness of Liverpool. Back in the days of The Freshies, he believed that the band had rather more in common with the Liverpool edge of the North West post-punk scene than the comparatively dour Manchester. I recall him earnestly asking me about 'Big In Japan', the delightfully visual tribe who included Jayne Casey and various future stars – Holly Johnson, Ian Brodie – in their ragged ranks. But Chris liked the joke. He may well have languished at the gigs of The Fall, Joy Division and A Certain Ration – dour Mancunians to a man – but there was a certain optimism about the Liverpool aesthetic; the notion that anything could happen. It was a more open city.

"There was a moment," he semi-correctly informed me, "when hardly any of the Liverpool bands had ever even picked up instruments. Imagine that? And yet it worked."

On this occasion, Chris had attended a cool art opening at The Tate in Liverpool's Albert Dock. He had attended alone, apparently, as had I in my capacity as *Manchester Evening News* reporter. But the event had fizzled down to little more than the usual faces, guzzling wine while staring earnestly at an uninspiring collection of artworks. It was Chris who saw me first, instantly tagging onto my lack of enthusiasm. Together we perfected our escape, sliding to the back of the crowd before hurtling down the Tate's minimalist stairs and romping into one of the bars that flanked the opposite side of the dock. It was then, amid joyful banter really, that Chris unearthed a plan that, I can confidently state, never progressed to a suitable conclusion.

"I have another character," he informed me and I instantly warmed to the oncoming plan. "He is the absolute opposite of Frank. Totally."

An antitheses?

"That's it. It might even be a 'she" (huh?)

"Little Denise?"

"Nothing like Little Denise. This is a savvy character. Streetwise and living in a flat… maybe here… maybe in Liverpool. Like Frank, he gets things wrong and everyone can see him getting it wrong. But his arrogance rides over it. He pushes ideas across and will spread in a number of different directions. Understand it."

"Not really," I replied. "But it does sound intriguing. Can I write an Evening News article on this?"

Stupid question, really. Might have known that he would instantly clam up. And clam up he did as a heavy silence prevailed.

"You have told me too much, haven't you… are you going to kill me?"

"Might have to," he laughed.

The conversation, taking place over dubious Dim Sum, veered suddenly towards football and bad Liverpudlian art. The afternoon died slowly and we made our way home, separately and, I sense, both lost in thought.

I fully expected a new Chris Sievey character to burst onto some Manchester stage during the following year. But he never arrived. By contrast, it was eventually Frank who returned with a vengeance, leaving another ghost in his wake.

With Frank – as it were – banished to the trunk, sealed and kept under the bed, Chris was determined to concentrate on a number of his passions that had been bubbling under the surface. In truth, some of this was merely a continuum, for Chris had never stopped making films, mostly and defiantly using pre-digital equipment… indeed, even using the same camera that Tosh had given him in 1982. It was something of a paradox, for Chris had always feverishly grasped technology, taken delight in it to a large extent and it seems a shame that the iPhone/Android and tablet revolution arrived slightly too late. That stated, the vast oceans of mundanity and amateur clips would probably have swamped his rather more earnest efforts. The internet had already swallowed his Rema Leema site, used to post gently surreal items, often filmed on the beaches of Formby and Southport. Chris enjoyed the surreal atmosphere of the seaside; perhaps the way it teased families out of day to day domesticity. This never more apparent than in traditional and ageing English seaside resorts. It might have been another kickback to George Formby-isms or merely another flashback to happy days of childhood spent in Anglesey, Skegness or the Isle of Man. But he also professed a love of Blackpool and Southport, the former being something else he had in common with Mark E. Smith, whose 'off-button' would so often send him scuttling to the unpretentious and bombastic South Shore at Blackpool. No edges there. No *Guardian* readers either. Chris had a similar desire... to melt. It was another antidote to the swamping power of Frank.

And then came a slice of luck. Situated in unprepossessing Broadheath, an aimless area of retail parks, decaying shop fronts and deadening pubs that borders Sale, Atrincham and Timperley, could be found one of the most innovative stop-motion animation companies in the UK - just a stride away from Chris's front door. It was as if animation had come to Chris and it would provide him with the perfect excuse to turn away from the craziness and excesses of Frank Sidebottom. Hot Animation, of course, were unaware of this.

Formed in 1998 by Jackie Cockle, Brian Little and Joe Dembinski, Hot Animation had already achieved global success with the legendary Bob the Builder, an iconic pre-school show concerning a builder and his array of talking machines. Vibrant, colourful, accessible to everyone from 1 upwards, and wily enough to gain a touch of cult status, Bob the Builder also perfectly spilled out into the world of mainstream merchandising. It reached its peak in 2000 when the Bob the Builder single, 'Can We Fix It?', aided by the Hot produced accompanying promo, became the Christmas number one, in doing so batting away Kylie Minogue's 'Please Stay', Westlife's 'What Makes a Man?' and Eminen's 'Stan'.

In its wake came 'Brambly Hedge', less successful perhaps but still a worthy series of 30 minute specials based on Jill Barklem's illustrated children's books and the bizarre 'Rubbadubbers', a series about animated bathroom toys. Hot was also responsible for the recreation of the mighty (if somewhat bewildering, to some of us) 'Pingu' in 2004. In 2007, Hot moved into a more adult arena, producing an animated sequence for an episode of the popular 'Life on Mars' retro detective programme.

BRIAN LITTLE

Originally from Middlesbrough, Brian Little attended art school in Norwich before locating to Manchester to work for Cosgrove Hall Animation in Chorlton-cum-Hardy before co-founding Hot Animation, based in unlikely Broadheath. As stated, as for Chris Sievey, actively seeking a diversion from memories and Frank's downward spiral in the late 1990s, this seemed like one gargantuan stroke of luck. Chris had never lost his passion and intrigue for the wonders of animation.

Brian was a director of Hot Animation and, although not aware of The Freshies, had learned about the existence of Frank from one of the animators at Hot, a big Frank fan, as animators tended to be. He also caught sight of Frank on the James Whale show and, while not entirely bowled over, found this appearance intriguing. There was one other connection. Hot Animation co-founder Jackie's partner, Cathy, was closely related to Marc 'Lard' Riley. Somehow a connection seemed inevitable.

Brian Little: "I was sat in the office one day and this letter plopped down with Chris' trademark scribblings all over the envelope. It was a basic letter asking for a job. Well, we didn't have a job to offer him at that point, in fact we were probably over-subscribed. A lot of people wanted to work in animation. But I was intrigued by Chris and had a word with Jackie. We decided to ask Chris to come in and we could find out what it was he wanted to do. We didn't know if we could help or not or where his interests lay. Anyway Chris duly came dawn and sat around looking a bit bored but I instantly liked him. He said he wanted to learn more about animation and I asked if he wanted to have a look around the studio. He said, 'Can the wife come and have a look too?'. So there was Chris and Paula bouncing around the props department like two excitable puppies. They were very funny and very lively. I would have loved to have offered Chris a job there and then but it was impossible.

"Basically, Chris just turned up the next day… and then the next and the next. He just wanted to learn everything and he was very funny and engaging so people just got used to having him around. He would help out in all the departments and shortly after that we managed to find him a full time job. That would be around 1998 or so. We simply became great friends. We both shared a big love of The Beatles and, well, I am not sure we had the same sense of humour but we seemed to fire off each other. Chris was a dream to have around a place like that because he was full of ideas. He fitted in really well… we had quite a vibrant little team there and we were getting lots of work."

It was still something of a wrench for Chris to pull out of the random swirl of life with Frank, to pinning himself down to the pedantic throb of a 9 to 5 existence, even within such an exciting company. Traipsing to and from work every day seemed positively alien to him. Nevertheless, fired by his passion, not just for animation but to find a viable life after Frank, he persisted.

"I was working on Brambly Hedge at Hot and Chris started to work on Bob the Builder and Bob the Builder specials. That was his main job and he was a natural. I remember him learning how to work on shots where Bob had moving backgrounds to give the impression of speed. He had a full grasp of those kinds of techniques. He had stopped doing Frank completely and seemed to relish this new adventure. I must admit, I was more a fan of Chris than Frank anyway and could see him going on to do some quality work, which he did. At one point he applied for a director's job but he just didn't quite have the experience at that point. Nevertheless, he stayed with us for about five years or so and was a major part of the team. I think that his mind started to wander a bit towards the end… he was getting a bit bored with the day to day routine of it all. Plus it wasn't great pay at Hot and he started saying that he could earn more money by getting Frank out of retirement.

"We did make the Frank's World animation. I had always had this idea that Frank would make a brilliant animation and we talked about it for a long while. Chris kept nudging and pushing me to do it, so eventually I agreed to direct it and storyboard it. Chris was living in

MICK MIDDLES

Hawthorn Road and there was a building at the back of that house that we wanted to turn into some kind of open art studio. In the end we didn't but we did film 'Frank's World' in there. Michelle Pouncey made the costumes for it. We worked on the Reema Leema stuff in there as well. We eventually showed 'Frank's World' at Tate Britain over three nights and it sold out and went down very well."

Paula Sievey: "Chris started coming round to see us a bit at Hawthorn Road. It seemed like he had straightened out a little. I mean, I missed him. I still loved him and wanted him back. Then he would move in and then go off the rails and I would chuck him out. Then he would come back… oh on and on and on. He was working at Hot Animation.

"In the end he fell in love with another woman and he left me. That was Michelle Pouncey. She was a friend of mine, only through the kids at school. Her kids were at school with Harry. I just knew her. And she met Chris one day in the park when he was working at Hot Animation. She kept telling me how great Chris was and that she was an artist and would have loved to work at Hot Animation. She would talk and talk with him about that and they just clicked and went off together. I was completely devastated. Because, no matter the things he did, I knew that he adored me and the kids. I never doubted that for a second and still don't. But then to see him go off and adore someone else was utterly devastating. I took it really badly and got quite ill. I lost loads and loads of weight. But you get over things. Soon enough, I realised that there was more of his stuff in the house than mine, so I moved out and lived around the corner. Then he started telling me that he had made a huge mistake but it was too late by then. There were some funny stories too. Funny things that happened. Bumping into each other in the street and things like that."

Michelle Pouncey. "I met Chris at an event during the 2002 World Cup. We just started talking and found that we had an awful lot in common. I was doing a Fine Arts Degree at Manchester and Chris was working at Hot Animation in Altrincham. It wasn't a sudden affair or anything like that. To be honest, I am not sure what it was. We became friends first and then started working together. I later worked at Hot Animation as well, so we had work in common too."

Paula Sievey: "She was dead arty. Chris knew I hated her at that point and he rang me up one day and told me a story about the flying train game. He sent her a copy of it and she thought it was some weird arty music. She told him it was brilliant. It wasn't even a song. It was just the funny noise it made when it was loading. He knew I would love that story."

Michelle Pouncey: "I could tell that he was troubled, but I had no idea of knowing how much. He was drinking but I didn't know it was to such excess at first. We went to a lot of parties and exhibitions together and there would always be alcohol and Chris would drink. But it soon became apparent that it was far more than just a social thing. Chris was always very good at keeping things secret. I didn't know the extent of his drinking or, indeed, if there was anything else he was taking… or doing. But he was just a lovely and very quiet guy to be with. Full of fun and mischief.

"Chris loved music in a very open way. Of course he loved The Beatles but he would listen to anything and give it a chance. He liked things like Coldplay and The Strokes, who were both big at the time. He was brilliant at absorbing information from music or whatever and using it for himself… or for us. Soon we started working on things together. We made short films. We found we could work together very well… the films were simple things. One was called 'Jesus Had a Dog.' It was basically about a dog."

All of this seemed a long way from his previous existence as Frank…

"Yes, Frank wasn't in our lives at all for a number of years. He had packed Frank away and very much wanted to get on with other things. He also helped me with my artwork. He was immensely supportive of me and took a great interest. He would also film everything. If I had an exhibition, he would film it all and later send me the completed film, which was lovely of him.

"We did do a lot together. We went away a few times… a couple of times to Wales and once to Spain. But Chris didn't really like going away much. He had all the stuff he wanted at home. There was enough going on in his head and when he was away it was like he was a bit out of context and didn't quite know what to do. He was at his happiest just messing around at home, doing all kinds of art and music. He was always writing songs and presenting them to me.

"As I said, we didn't really talk about Frank for years. But then he started to mention that he might go back to it. As soon as he made that decision, that was it. I became his driver and helper. I think his first gig back was that one at the Retro Lounge. I was surprised at the level of support for him. That said, he would do a lot of gigs when there was hardly anybody there. In the Lake District, for instance, in front of about 10 people. But he still gave a great performance… it didn't matter about the numbers. There were many odd gigs as well. Chorley Working Men's Club and places like that when nobody knew who he was and some just didn't get it. I would help him make the sets and I created all the little character costumes."

Paula: "I absolutely hated the fact that she had taken him away and it took me ages to get over it. Cos I would see her walking down the street with her kids and Chris. And it really was dead painful. But I met somebody else and we all moved on. But I still hated her. But he finished with her. I think they lasted on and off for five years. She couldn't understand why he would want to go to New York and come straight back. She wanted a holiday. Don't blame her, really. But he told her why he was doing it. She kept nagging him and he just finished with her. They had a big argument in the street. I felt vindicated."

Michelle: "There was a dark side to Chris, of course. He was naughty… very naughty. He was known for it. He could well have been seeing other people when he was seeing me… nothing would surprise me with Chris. It did get out of hand when he started drinking heavily again. It became seriously hard work and I remember pulling back and starting to question what I was doing. The performances went down in quality I think and you never quite knew what was going to happen. It all came to a head when he did that trip to New York and came back the next day. I wanted to go with him and stay longer but he wouldn't have it. That was around the point when I realised that it was over, really. I knew I had to move on… and I did. And so did Chris. I didn't really see him during the last few years. We lost contact. Well I saw him in the street a couple of times when he was with his new girlfriend, Gemma

Woods. But it was a bit painful. When we did meet it was like we didn't know each other."

Paula Sievey: "Then I saw him loads of times after that. We became quite friendly. He once told me that he had eleven girlfriends. It was great that he could tell me things like that. I told him that was rubbish and he would say, 'I really have 11 girlfriends and they are all madly in love with me' perhaps it was true. I felt a bit happier because that didn't hurt so much.

"I did see Michelle Pouncey not very long ago, actually. It was in Aldi supermarket. She clocked me and looked really worried. As if I was going to hit her, or something. It was weird. It was like Chris was telling me to make amends or something. I don't know why I did it but I just went up and tapped her on the shoulder. She was startled. But we said 'Hi'…we hugged each other and were both crying and asking how each other's kids were. I just walked away and got in the car. I felt really good then. It was a closure. We did it for Chris. I don't blame her in the end… it probably wasn't all her fault. You can't help who you fall in love with."

Michelle: "I felt really badly about the Sievey family. He loved his family that is the absolute truth. At all times. It was a huge relief when I met Paula in Aldi and she hugged me. Because I had known Paula before and didn't want any bad feeling. It was as if we had both moved on."

Dave Arnold: "Then fast forward to 2005 and we played some gigs with a band from America called Phantom Surfers. They were like a sixties surf band from LA. We were playing as The Stags and we had a beach set. We needed a host to run it and I knew there was only one guy to run this… Frank, of course. So I rang Patrick, who I had not spoken to for a long time and asked if Frank would do it. He said, 'Oh yeah… but you will have to pay him - £100?"

So Patrick brought Frank round. And he – Frank/Chris – was absolutely pissed. Like proper pissed. Paralytic. He had got the message that it was a beach thing so he had a Hawaiian shirt on. But it had no buttons and was gaffa taped up. He was great. But he did one and a half songs before falling backwards into the drums. Knocked all the drums over, which everyone thought was hilarious. He muddled through it and it was great because no one had seen him for years. And I mean, years. I wasn't shocked by him being pissed because I kind of knew about it. I had seen Chris at odd times, just enough to keep in touch. I don't think he was completely back to being Frank at that point but I do believe that 2005 gig proved the catalyst for him wanting to do it again. Not too long after that, he started getting gigs through Nigel Round, who was a showbiz agent for people like Norman Collier and Bernie Clifton. Then he did a gig in Wigan that was not very well attended but it opened doors for him. Michelle Pouncey was there. Then I got a call asking if I could come down and set his keyboards up, because they had opened the doors and Chris couldn't do it. So I did. At the end of that gig he asked if I fancied driving for him."

Brian Little: "After Hot folded I kept working with Chris. Well, we tried to make a few things happen right up until the end, really. We tried a lot of ideas on people. We went to see Steve Coogan and Henry Normal at Baby Cow and they were very keen to do something. But somehow it didn't amount to anything. Chris was back to his old ways, sending out endless postcards to animation companies. He tried all kinds of tricks to get people's attention and was very funny. With one director he took a Kit Kat in and said, 'you eat that Kit Kat and I will have finished my pitch by the time you have eaten it'. Just daft stuff but people seemed to warm to him. I am sure he would have got something off the ground in time."

Dave Arnold: "So I did five years working for Chris. After a short period of time, he started hammering it... just doing loads of gigs. Interest in him just exploded. He knew it would. He used to say that he could open the flood gates at any time. Hot Animation had gone by then, so it just exploded. At that point, I wasn't booking the gigs. I was road managing him. So I would go and knock on his door and pick him up. Sort all the gear out. Plug everything in when we got there. Take the money, because he would just lose it otherwise. I did it all and it made financial sense. We gigged all over. We went to Germany. We played at a garage punk festival, Bachfest in Liepzig. The Stags, who I played with, performed and the guy who ran it wanted Frank on in the afternoon. We did a lot of gigs where the Stags would play with Frank, this was before we put the northern version of the Oh Blimeys together. The Stags did a couple of pantomimes with Frank at Timperley Labour Club. The Stags could have been the Oh Blimeys but there were a couple of members of the band who just didn't get Frank at all. It wasn't their bag, which was fine. It is so polarising, Frank Sidebottom. You love it or hate it. But you couldn't really do it if you hated it. I wasn't going to force it. So when Chris said he wanted to do it with a band again, I just picked some guys that I knew. Jamie Owen, a guitarist and a guy called Roachie (Ian Roche, from Birkenhead) that became the northern 'Oh Blimeys'. Chris also had a guy in London who put a band together. It just made it cheap for Frank to turn up.

"We played at the Dodo Cafe in Liverpool and the band had rehearsed like crazy. We did the sound check and everything was fine. Except Chris went missing... not for long. Less than an hour. Then he turns up and we started playing and there was something obviously not right. We were brilliant that night. But he was leathered. He had just gone off and got leathered, somehow. He took his trousers off to reveal his big shorts but got them caught up and just fell backwards, really heavily. We thought he had broken his neck. His Frank head cracked open like an Easter egg. I think people thought it was part of the act. Other times he would be firing on all cylinders. Our version of the Oh Blimeys was very self indulgent. He would do like Sparks covers, Billy Childish covers. The Saints. He did The Beatles, 'Why Don't We Do It In The Road?' He was becoming increasingly eclectic, broadening out. He was moving away from that expectancy of him doing Queen covers and all those things you think of regarding Frank. Our 'Oh Blimeys' was a really stripped down punk band. Very raw. We could have become a bona fide punk band with Frank. Because Gemma was a big ELO fan, he always wanted to do a punky ELO thing, which would have been a bit odd. ELO songs in the style of The Ramones, which might seem weird but he tried it and it worked. The melodies were still there but they hammered along. That is the test of a truly great song. Strip everything off it and see if it still sounds good.

"But he could do absolutely anything. There would be no limitations at all with Frank. He could have done absolutely anything. It wasn't twee… – The Oh Blimeys could do twee if we wanted but when we did something like, say 'This Perfect Day' by The Saints, with Frank singing, it was seriously good. It was just full on with Frank at the helm. It wasn't dumbed down. This is the thing. Frank could pull it off."

This is an intriguing notion and not one that anyone has previously suggested. That Frank could have possibly mutated into a serious chameleon artist, capable of flitting from genre to genre. A gift, one senses, for a creative agent capable of filtering Frank out onto the festival circuit. His success at Rebellion certainly suggested that he could fold effortlessly into the latter-day punk scene. Perhaps his cartoonesque appearance finding easy acceptance with that arena. So why not Download? Why not Chropredy? I would have loved to see the folk version of The Oh Blimeys. And how about the large circuits of electronics that stretch through gallery and venue festivals across Europe. As a true outsider artist, would he have been comfortably place within the pages of *Wire* magazine? I like to think so. These are strange days when dance music appears to have been generally whitened, much of it seeping into galleries and performance art. Frank could have lampooned that so beautifully. I have an image of him wandering onstage with a copy of *The Guardian*, bald headed and wearing thick set glasses. Camden Frank!

All boundaries could have been crossed.

Dave Arnold: "Whatever Chris did he took to another level. That whole DIY ethos, with people like early Scritti Polliti or Desperate Bicycles or Swell Maps, that kind thing. Chris did it better and before them. Often because of Frank, he is hugely undervalued as an artist. This is one thing that might be put right this year."

Paula Sievey: "We were living in Hawthorn Road but I eventually had to move out. Then he met Gemma… this young girl. She was a big Frank fan and he ended up with her. She is an odd little thing. Quite sweet and I got on with her alright. I used to call her 'Little Denise'. She seemed like a little puppet."

Gemma Woods: "I met Chris at his film night at TV21, Manchester in 2007. I went with friends and met him afterwards. We had a few drinks at the bar, and then he moved in with me the next day. We were friends for a while, and things just progressed. We used to spend a lot of time listening to Coco Rosie and playing guitar. We basically just sat around in my flat for weeks falling in love. I asked him to marry me, he said yes. After that, throughout our relationship he would ask me at least weekly… 'marry me?' We were really happy."

# ART AS TV

AS MANAGER OF THE EXCELLENT Marple band, Dutch Uncles and head honcho for music and media company, 'Love and Disaster', Dan Parrott has emerged as one of the leading protagonists of Manchester music.

No mean feat. Manchester has been woefully short of erstwhile protagonists for many years… at least those blessed with genuine vision. It seems odd too to note that, as I write, Dutch Uncles are only just edging past their mid-twenties. They do seem to have been around a while, providing three excellent albums and slowly climbing to prominence. Most importantly, their jagged, angular and ever improving music owes absolutely nothing to the overstated and obvious 'godfathers' of Manchester music. We all know who they are. Tellingly, when asked if he listened to new band demos, Parrott suggested that new music would stand a better chance of gaining a foothold if it didn't sound like Oasis, Stone Roses or Happy Mondays. One can only applaud such Maverick vision. Significantly it may have been a similar force which lay behind Parrott's successful campaign to get Frank back on the telly. He was a senior producer at the time and pretty much given free reign. One doubts, within the conservative framework of 2006 national television media, that any kind of exposure would be granted to an artist as idiosyncratic as Frank Sidebottom.

As such, it was Parrott who was chiefly responsible for bringing Frank Sidebottom out of his lengthy retirement period and presenting him with the gloriously anarchic and flexible 'Frank's Proper Telly Show', for Channel M Music television stations, courageously based within the foyer of the Urbis building, in its previous incarnation as a museum of the city. (It is now the National Football Museum which, I guess, would also have been a suitable venue for Frank's special brand of shenanigans).

I met Dan, where one always seems to meet media executives these days, in a coffee bar in Manchester's postulating and funky Northern Quarter.

FRANK'S PROPER TELLY SHOW

April 2006 – April 2009

Daniel Parrott: "It was my brother, who is just a few years older than me, who first got into Frank Sidebottom. He became a fan after seeing the 'Shed' show. In fact he was a huge fan. He even won a mosaic of Frank, which is now in his kitchen. It's kind of funny because I had started to listen to the kind of music we listened to in the eighties. Frank was kind of wrapped up in that. I had done a lot of television jobs and started doing the music for Channel M after it moved into Urbis. It was 2006, and there was a slightly confused security guard there. He said 'I have got this package and I don't know what to do with it', it was a time when Chris and Frank had long disappeared... so he wasn't in people's heads at that point. I looked at this package and I just knew what it was. It was one of those moments that changed everything.

"Inside was a DVD in a package with lots of scrawl on it. There was a little funny note and a phone number. I watched it. It was that thing done from Andy Crane's bedroom. I phoned him up. I had this conversation with Frank and all the office was quite excited. So we got him in to have a chat at first and to meet Jerry, the presenter. Ultimately we did two series, this pilot idea and the Test Cards. Of course, Chris being Chris, he came along with his own ideas, some excellent and workable and some that would have been completely impossible. My job really was to sort out which was which. But I instantly knew that we could create something special here. We started 'Frank's Proper Telly Show' and Chris insisted it was in black and white, although it wasn't really. He was a dream to work with. I pretty much let him do what he wanted. It was the only way to be with Chris. And most of his ideas were fantastic. He did three shows a week. Great memories. We would get bands in… artists who would be playing Manchester that week so, in a way, it was a plug show for their gigs. It was the only way we could do it because we couldn't pay them. We had no money for celebrities."

'Frank's Proper Telly Show' quickly gained a cult status that, due to exposure on YouTube, continues to expand today. It was a show that faintly reflected the golden mid-seventies days of 'Tiswas'. But while such rampant anarchy seemed acceptable in those days, within the carefully controlled and patrolled arena of television today, one struggles to see it breaking through.

"There were many highlights. Andy Rourke was one of the classics. And David Soul. He was completely bemused by the whole thing. Obviously he had absolutely no idea who Frank was but how do you warn someone about something like that? How can you *explain* Frank? You can't. So you just have to throw someone in and make the best of it. You could see that David was a bit uncomfortable at first. We always had it planned out completely and there would be a crowd in the studio. We do something then stop. Then start again. And every time we stopped you could see David Soul start to think 'what the hell'. Then it would start again and he would snap back into it. It made for a great dynamic and he started to warm to it. In the end I think he enjoyed it. My favourite bit was at the end when Frank was there with Little Frank and Little Mark E Smith and right at the end, David picked up this mask and put it to his head. Frank just went, 'Fantastic'. I think David did think it was a little bit beneath him. His stock was down a bit. But he went with it."

Indeed, the David Soul episode – fully available on YouTube, as are many of the shows although so much of Frank's work on Channel M now seems lost… or sold, so might languish in some distant bedroom – is the one that remains so firmly lodged in the memory. It begs closer scrutiny. One can fully understand why David Soul, stock down or not, seemed initially reticent, for he will never have tasted such sweet anarchy in his life. And to be hurtled into what might have seemed little more than low brow student telly, a space given over to Fresher inebriation and out and out daftness. Why should he play ball? Rewatching that particular episode hints that everyone, even die-hard Frank-o-philes, might have underestimated its true aesthetic power. For this, like this entire story, is far more than episodic daftness. It is a work of art in itself. A glorious and ironic reflection of the true and tepid state of commercial television on a global scale. All the more poignant as it hailed from the city where groundbreaking Granada TV once held the ball so astutely. Of course that mighty 'dynasty' long since splintered into the kind of collective mundanity one encounters when the money runs dry and the bean counters move in. Only a completely off the wall company *not* geared to mainstream profiteering could possibly host such a show and how fitting to see a star from one of the golden eras of mainstream television skulking to the centre of Frank's set.

And what a set. Frank's World, indeed, where the main protagonist is pretty much allowed carte-blanche to offer a glimpse of the artistic possibilities that exist on a televisual shoestrong... perhaps *because* of that shoestring. There is a moment, mid interview, where Frank – for no obvious reason – stretches out to a state of semi – yawn, leaving Soul looking incredulous. The interview is patchy and genuinely bizarre. Although one might have encountered one off ventures of equal merit during the embryonic days of BBC 2 and, later, in the first six months of Channel Four at the start of the eighties, such things have long since vanished from our screens.

Also on the show was Happy Mondays' founder Paul Ryder, obviously in the know and more than happy to go with the flow (even if this meant colouring in a cartoon). You can see Soul desperately gazing at Ryder, hoping to be guided through the murk. This chaotic mix, as Dan stated, finished with an unholy run through of The Fall's 'Hit The North', (one can't imagine Soul being aware of the Prestwich despot) with Ryder pumping away furiously on bass. As the titles roll you can hear Soul gleefully claiming, "That is the stupidest thing I have ever done in my life."

And so it was. (Well, apart from 'Let's Spend a Quiet Night In').

However, and despite the enormous amount of time that Chris would put in, he would not be, in any way, financially compensated.

Dan Parrott: "We never really paid Frank much. It was terrible, really. He would get something like £50. The same really as the normal presenters and there is no way that Frank is a normal presenter. He had so many ideas going on all the time and he soon started appearing on

MICK MIDDLES

the breakfast show as well. He would have stayed there all day, doing stuff. He once had an idea that would have meant us being with him live all day long, every day. It was completely unfeasible."

Frank's Proper Telly Show stretched across two series. One senses that, given full endorsement from the channel's bosses, the entire output could have started to bulge with myriad ideas and actions from Frank. In fact, it could have been better. It could have extended to Chris and afforded him time to concentrate on animation or, better still, his non-Frank film work. The second series did see the show gaining in kudos, as word of mouth drew people to the possibilities of local TV.

Dan Parrott: "When we did the second series, there were many more highlights. We tried to get the highest grade celebrities and bands that we could. There was a great one with Andy Rourke of The Smiths, where Frank had made 3D glasses and great shots of Andy wearing them at the end. We would plonk bands in right in the middle of the show. I always regarded this as a kind of retro show, like an eighties thing and, I guess, that is where Frank really belonged. It was a bit like 'The Young Ones', when bands would just come on for no apparent reason and a lot of the stuff was written on the hoof. Very anarchic and it was a pity it didn't get a bigger audience. But we were always on the edge. To be perfectly honest, I was never sure if the people in charge of the station really got Frank. Not everyone did, of course, and there would always be detractors. But generally everyone loved it... the camera crew, sound guys – everyone just loved going with the flow. It created an atmosphere in the studio that was pretty unique. I can't think of anything comparable. Not in recent years."

It does stand, arguably, as the prime example of Frank at his most ludicrously inventive. At least on the current YouTube selection and Parrott deserves credit for allowing the performer to follow his unique comedic muse without having to succumb to the kind of director intervention that had so often seen him struggle with compromise. Parrott's gentle guiding was, I suggest, exactly what Frank always craved.

"There were some wonderfully surreal moments. The Magic Numbers wouldn't come on because they didn't understand it, but they loved it in the end. It was always that twist where they would suddenly 'get it'. Some bands would come on and worship him and love him.

Some of the American ones would struggle. There was Bradford Cox from Deerhunter. He was slightly awkward as he suffers from a genetic disorder – Marfan Syndrome – which meant that he was very tall, spindly and rather childlike. But, again we just let the cameras roll and catch that weird collision take place. You never quite knew where it was going."

Anarchy in Urbis, perhaps? And even when Frank was playing a supporting role, the level of chaos could slide towards the danger level.

"One show we did was called 'Saturday Social', which was on for four hours. I think we had Turin Brakes on the first one. It was supposed to be a Letterman style show. So you had the crowd there and half of them were there to see the headline band. But we had a green room which was onstage, which was a bar. Frank was behind the bar, getting progressively more pissed as time went on. There was a bit of conflict because some of the girls on the first row were just there for the band. And this mad Frank would wind everyone up. There was this one wide shot which saw a security guard physically carrying Frank out of the studio. Of course, Frank would be back five minutes later.

"I know everyone says this but Chris and Frank were so different. Chris the introvert and Frank the extrovert. When you worked closely with these two extremes it could be very difficult. Sometimes you wanted to converse with Chris but Frank would be there and you just couldn't. Frank had a dark side, of course. He was a child, simple as that. And as with all children, he could be incredibly self-centred and difficult, sometimes for no apparent reason. Especially if he was a bit pissed. It could be infuriating and if it was just Chris, it wouldn't have worked. But Frank would get away with things that Chris couldn't. People would just laugh because that was what Frank did. To some extent, perhaps Chris used Frank that way…but I tend to think that they thought about things differently.

"Chris had some great ideas that we never got round to doing. One of these, which I thought was utterly brilliant, was something called 'What's On The Other Side', where Frank would be watching TV with a channel changer but the viewers could only see the back of the television. So Frank would flip around and comment on each channel as it was happening. The idea was that the viewers would flip around as well, then flip back to Frank and he would talk about it and flip somewhere else. Back and forth. You know, he would say, "oooh what's on the shopping channel…" It could have been complete chaos but I think that Frank could have carried that off. That would have been genuinely inventive television and there is so little of that about these days. There were no copyright issues because no one would see it… a bit like they do with the football coverage on Sky Sports."

Despite that continuing YouTube coverage, many of the Channel M shows appear to have been lost.

"I don't know where a lot of the tapes of those shows have gone and that is a tragedy, it really is. Thankfully, a lot of it is on YouTube but the tapes would be so valuable, so incredibly special. Maybe we will find the true answer to that, one day."

Phil Jones: "By 2004 I was working on Manchester Food and Drink Festival and we put on 'Summer in the Park'. We were involved with a radio station and Chris was, too, as Frank Sidebottom. Chris was there as Frank and he saw me and went 'Fucking hell mate…' and we had an exchange. I think Paula was there and we all went for a pint after Frank's set. It felt like a real success to be friends with Chris again. It really had troubled me, that £60. Not the money but the principal, really. It was the long period of time."

Dan Parrott: "I think that Chris' life and all that was in it will eventually become a work of art in itself. Well, that process has already begun with the Jon Ronson film, and the DVD and things like this book. I know with the Ronson film that Chris was attached to it and thought it might be the way he could become a millionaire. I know he had a five-year plan in action and maybe that is still going on. I actually don't think Chris ever had any doubt that he would make it. That is the reason he was always quite happy to work right through the night… doing things like that, working for days on end would never be a problem to him. In retrospect I do wish we had done an all-nighter, which Chris always wanted to do. That would have been a bit of television history. I look back more and more, as time goes on and realise what a wonderful experience it all was. Because you never knew what was going to happen."

Gemma Woods: "Being Frank was just Chris's job. I loved the fact that he could make a career out of (in his words) 'just messing about'. He had a lovely playful side to his personality, which was so much fun. He was always fun to be around. When we got together, he said to me that life with him would always be a rollercoaster, and it was. He was an absolute workaholic. He would spend all of his time thinking about work. He had too many ideas to do them all if he had lived to be 100, because he was constantly thinking of new ones before he could complete most things. It was like his mind never ever stopped working. Sometimes I wished that he had more time for me, but I knew it was important to him. He is the most creative and productive person I have ever met. He was a great inspiration to me in that way."

With Chris, and at any given time from 1971 onwards, there would always be several layers of artistic and promotional activity. Sometimes perhaps seven layers deep and maybe more – who knows? – where he secretly worked up some wild or not-so-wild endeavour or activity. There have been many albums, for instance, each with its own distinctive twist. More often than not, an element of the whole concept would be sliced away and emerge as a vague notion into a new direction and occasionally, just occasionally, a song, a painting, a chunk of classical music, a comic book or character or radio or TV show… aspects from many of these, would slowly begin to realise. There was always that level of depth to Chris and those close to him were not always able to tap into it. It wasn't an impossible task, however and often involved the purchasing and drinking of several pints of bitter. Once this was achieved, and only if he had a mind to it, he might carry you through a number of these levels. One recalls a double album of 'western themed music'; a number of characters never to appear as Frank sidekicks – including an American GI with a Yorkshire accent and a talking rabbit – and a wide array of computer gaming ideas and scams. Occasionally this aesthetic ambition was more earnest.

John Barratt recalls: "There was always… *always* something going on and Chris would go on and on about it. While I really liked his company, there did come a time when you simply had to stop listening. It often seemed completely unrealistic. I remember an album he was working on for ages but it then became replaced by something else. Hardly anything would surface. Another one, which might surprise some people, was the time when he was learning the cello. This wasn't something he would do on the quiet. He wouldn't just say 'Oh I am trying to learn the cello,' It would be completely a whole new direction for music. I think he was serious for a while about that cello though. Then it fell away and he would enthusiastically go on and on about something entirely different. The sad thing is that it wasn't shallow, really. He wasn't just some gobshite. He really went deeply into things but his mind would simply race on to something else."

MANCHESTER TOWN HALL

JUNE 2010

SUNDAY EVENING; STRANGE GATHERING. Ageing Bohemians drifting through Albert Square, lured into Alfred Waterhouse's glorious Town Hall, unquestionably the grandest and most imposing building in the city centre. Gothic and ageing, perhaps fittingly, for this occasion saw a rather bizarre twist in terms of political acceptance and honour.

The gathering, which consisted of a fair selection of Manchester's musical luminaries dating back to – and before – Merseybeat. Silver ponytails in abundance; dusty suits, heady quips. Once these people were seen as the scourge of the establishment, now they were welcomed to the political heart of the city and honoured as high achievers. Well, two of them were. It was the 70th birthday celebration of Durutti Column and Alberto Y Los Trios Paranoias drummer Bruce Mitchell. A besuited behemoth blessed with ready wit and an ever amiable manner. Tagged on to this landmark and also duly honoured was Tosh Ryan, lynchpin of this heady story, supreme saxophonist and latent punk of a lost generation. The gathering entered the Town Hall and trudged upstairs to two waiting rooms where presentations would take place alongside much imbibing, munching and two live acts, bought to add spice to the occasion.

That's where I first saw him. Skulking sullenly in the corner. He seemed unusually grey, almost invisible by the pillar. Most did not notice him, just occasional nods of the head. Many, I thought, might not have recognised him. For he seemed devoid of the ferocious energy of old. But he was there to see his old mentor receive his honour – whatever it was – following an extraordinary speech by a mayoral figure who clearly had never heard of either Bruce Mitchell or Tosh Ryan. Many of

Frank's first regular TV gig was on Saturday morning kids TV show No. 73.

Frank made his mark with chaotic shows designed to appeal to inebriated students.

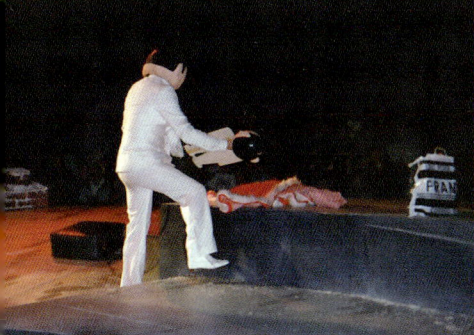

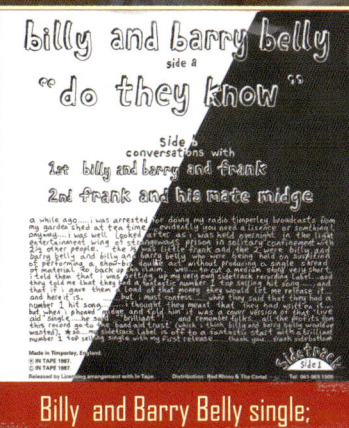

Billy and Barry Belly single; Chris Sievey and Mark Radcliffe cut loose

Frank and Jon Ronson rock o[ut]

A rare shot of Frank and Chris together.

Frank and Harry in the she[d]

Frank at Oldham's Boundary Park representing Timperley Big Shorts.

Frank at Altrincham FC - where his theme tune 'The Robins are not bobbins' became a pre-match favourite.

Stirling and Harry celebrate.

Chris enjoys a day out watching City.

Frank and John Cooper-Clarke, the northern dream...

Frank and the Magic Numbers on his chaotic Channel M show

Frank with 'The Man from The Council', Neil Taylor.

'Being Frank' Director Steve Sullivan.

The Freshies on the sofa: Mike, Barry and Rick.

Stirling, Harry and Asher conduct the statue unveiling on Sunday, 20th October 2013 at 11.37 am.

A still from from the Jon Ronson movie 'Frank' that opened to critical acclaim in May 2014.

OTHER FRANK TRIBUTES

Mural at Seven Miles Out, Stockport.

Graffiti on Oldham St., Manchester

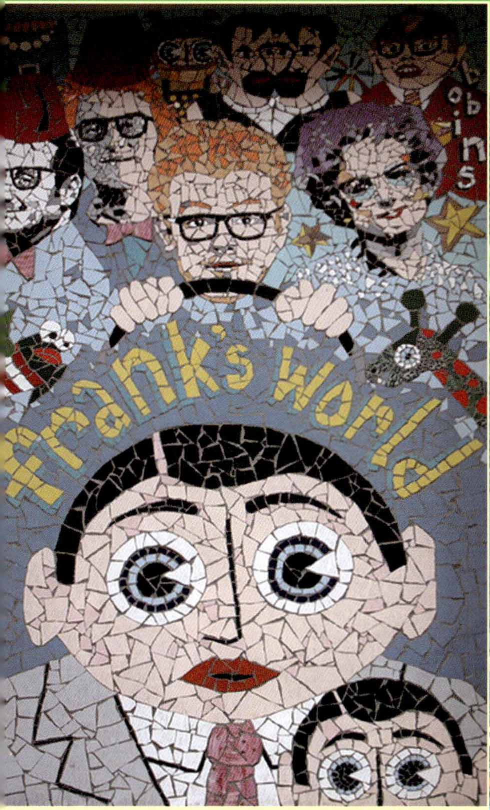

Mosaic, once at Affleck's Palace, now removed to Timperley.

Selfridge's Christmas window display, Oxford St., London, Christmas 2010

The Sievey family, 2013

CHRIS SIEVEY
1955 - 2010

these people, I mused, would once have embraced punkish persuasion. Chris too in a manner of speaking.

I looked again and he was gone. In a flash. Later Frank would bound into the rooms, as bombastic as ever and wholly incongruous within the stony ostentation. He was funny too, ad-libbing furiously and taking every available opportunity to, in true Frank fashion, 'take the piss'... Royally so.

Three months down the line, it dawned on me that this brief appearance would have been the last time most of these people would see Frank Sidebottom. It was a swansong of sorts and, in some way, I like to think of it as an unofficial honouring of Frank, alongside those two greying reprobates.

An unholy occasion, maybe? But one that gained in poignancy long after the throng had departed.

"I was driving through Altrincham shortly before he died and I saw him walking down the road. I wanted to say 'hi' but he went down some footpath where I couldn't go. He looked terribly thin and not well."

MICHELLE POUNCEY

APRIL 17TH 2013.

Tram from Sale to Altrincham. Three stops. Straight line. Punching out to gentle climes. Found myself sitting in the Costa Coffee situated within Sainsbury's... down in the corner, feeling strangely reflective.

Then it dawned on me. In the same coffee bar – although not then Costa - could have been the same chair. I was sitting there, awaiting the arrival of Chris Sievey. Must have been 1996. I had Lou Reed's 'New York' album running around my head and, amazingly, so had Chris. He wandered in with a tentative grace, sitting rather silently opposite me and ordering tea. The afternoon's work revolved around an interview on which I would base the sleevenotes for what would become 'The Very Best of The Freshies - Some long and short song titles'. Chris's call had come in two days earlier. Could I help him out... Cherry Red wanted to shunt this extensive collection out within a few weeks and were desperate for sleeve notes to map out the band's history and influence.

"They will pay… something," he nervously offered.

"Is it one of those situations where they pay from exhaustive funds or does it directly relate to any money you get, Chris?"

"Err… it directly relates."

"So I will keep the invoice low."

"Err… yes."

"If anything at all?"

"Er… nothing would be good."

As you can see, I have always been the worst negotiator in the world. I can't recall whether any money actually exchanged hands on this occasion or, indeed, 90 days later, but it didn't really matter. It was a change to mull over a lost career with a lost soul. To – at last – kick about a few memories that would not involve Frank Sidebottom. I could tell that Chris was truly enjoying this chance to ramble on. And so he did, warming to the theme once we had adjourned to a local hostelry, pints of bitter replacing the tea… mulling late into the long afternoon.

It was a lovely memory even if the sleeve notes, I always felt, lacked a certain panache.

I could still sense his presence in 2013. Distant, perhaps ghostly, but not unwelcoming. I was still thinking of him as I wandered out of the coffee shop and made my way along Park Road, turning idly left into Stamford Park. I was a little early for my appointment and, casting a nod to the leaden skies, hoping the rain would stay off, I sat on the bench overlooking the bowling green. I wondered, a little obviously perhaps, given that Chris's last address, Hawthorn Road, sat adjacent to the park entrance, if Chris ever idled similarly in the park. I would find an answer to this, almost instantly, after entering the home of Ken Nolan, almost directly opposite the ex-Sievey abode. Ken's son, noted documentary filmmaker and author David Nolan, was also in attendance. During Chris's time spent at the Hawthorn Road address, initially back with Paula and then, later, with Gemma Woods, Ken had become a treasured neighbour, often helping to ease a post-pub Sievey back into a position of domestic normality.

Ken Nolan: "I remember his agent, or someone – Dave Arnold – used to come with a van and all sorts. It had Stock Car Racing written on it. Always turning up and loading stuff. He would have the shed in it and all sorts. It confused me for a long time. I couldn't understand what he could be doing. Felt that he was a landscape gardener or something like that. I never really enquired although I got to know him well. The only odd thing was that, when I went into his house, it was full of CDs and all sorts. I couldn't believe it when he died and I realised how famous he was. It was dead scruffy that house. The stuff in there was piled high. You had to step over it. Stuff everywhere; toys, CDs. I didn't have a clue what he did, then one day he gave me a CD of a show he did on a canal boat in Timperley. It surprised me an awful lot. However, I still thought it was very local… small-scale, really because people who were successful in show business didn't tend to rent scruffy houses in Hale."

"It depends on how you define success, I guess," I ventured, while cradling a cup of tea. "Chris had his moments. Frank was quite big at various points… as he is now, sadly."

Ken Nolan: "I remember when they first moved in. Well, Paula, his wife, first moved in because Chris was still living in Timperley. Then he moved in with her. He was an 'alcofrolic' then, no doubt about that. He was always turning up late at night unable to get in the house because he never knew where he had put his keys. He used to come over here, ask me to help and I would get him a ladder and give him a lift up. He would climb in the old outside toilet. There were times when he tried to climb up the downspout, onto the roof and into his bedroom. But that was when he was a serious alcofrolic. He would be hanging onto the downspout. Well, it were plastic and it all bent. He went a bit queer when he was on the ale. He didn't see anybody for a long time. Paula had moved out and you just wouldn't see him."

CHRIS WAS REALLY FANTASTIC

I loved the simplicity and emotive ties to this poem. Paul Cookson is a performance poet working from his base in the Midlands. He is also, obviously, a huge fan of Frank. I thought the poem captured the essence of that passionate yet respectfully distant fandom.

As Paul states: "Frank – well, I have loved his stuff for over 25 years now – I remember getting the 'Space is Ace' and 'Frank Sings Freddie' EPs and then pretty much everything since. Annuals, comics etc. I have seen him perform many times, both solo and with the Oh Blimey Big Band. I even took my in-laws to see him years ago. In fact there are photos in my wedding album of me, best man and two ushers all with a Frank head on a ruler in front of our faces. I think Frank even showed it on his Shed Show, once.

As a performer I always loved the fact that he wasn't rude or offensive in any way, just silliness and child-like (not childish) enthusiasm and detail. Fantastic. Genius. Also, as a performer, I have been inspired by that and have, no doubt, taken bits here and there along the way.

I only met him once without his head. On tour with John Cooper Clarke, just before his diagnosis. It was lovely to meet him. I did once ring up about gigs years ago and got to speak to him on the phone. He was in character and asked where I lived. I said, Retford. He said, "Oh, like Robert Retford." I was genuinely saddened and touched by his death, hence the poem.

Frank Sidebottom is dead.
I know he is.
He really is.

It's just that I can't believe it.
I can't.
I really can't.

Larger than life – especially his head.

MICK MIDDLES

Blimey...

But the man behind the mask
The man underneath the papier-mâché
The man behind the voice
The master of puppets

Chris,
Has gone.

Comic genius, musician, artist
Creator of cardboard chaos,

One hit wonder of Freshies fame, but so much more,
Animator, ventriloquist and true original

And while I only ever really met Chris once,
And a true gentleman you were, too

You and Frank (And Little Frank, of course)
Have been part of my life for over 20 years,

On my wedding day four Frank heads
Posed in morning suits alongside my wife to bemused guests

Soundtracks to holidays, in-jokes and innocence
Nonsense and nonsensability

You created a world – and let us in
And we joined in with your uniqueness

The warmth, the innocence, the silliness
And, of course, the fantastic pop star show business

Little Frank and Little Denise (With no head)
Will miss you

But not as much as us (because they are only cardboard)

Freddie Mer – Cue – Ree and Queen, Elvis, Kylie and
Paul McCartney
Will never sound the same or as good without you

Space will always be ace
And Christmas and football will always be fantastic

We will never hear the word Timperley without
Thinking of you
On Match of the Day – in your big shorts

While your mum thought you were out shopping
For some of those fantastic chops

There was nothing not to like about Frank
And everything to love
Thanks Chris. You will live on,
We know you will, you really will

PAUL COOKSON.

"In a lot of ways I wish he had never dreamt up Frank. It ruined him in a way. He was actually a lot funnier than Frank. He was the funniest man I have ever met. Nobody since has made me laugh like he did. He was brilliant. I didn't really think that Frank was that funny. I liked him at first because it was spontaneous and he was living that person. But then it became an act. He started telling the same jokes all the time, like some old comedian. I must admit, I often sat there and cringed thinking 'this is not good'. A lot of that was the drinking and, more and more, he would be going through the motions. I used to think, 'oh no… you gotta get some new material.'"

PAULA SIEVEY

FINAL REEL

"Then you would see him in the park with his little dog and he would be as friendly as anything. We had lots of good talks cos he were a dead nice lad and that. He loved that little dog and just ambling around the (Stamford) Park. We talked about all sorts. I remember him telling me about that Tony Wilson chap... you know, the music chap. Chris said he 'wouldn't piss on him if he was on fire.' At one time the whole family lived there. Asher, Stirling and Harry... he were just a lad then. About 15. He would talk to me as well... well they all did. Real nice bunch really. I was sad when they moved out, really. I don't know what really happened."

KEN NOLAN

FRANK MAINTAINED A GHOSTLY PRESENCE with the neighbours in Hale. Hardly anyone, it seemed, knowing that the rather polite chap who walked his little dog, daily, was the legendary Frank Sidebottom. This might have changed if Chris had managed to perfect his Frank Head helmet, an idea that would allow Frank, rather than Chris, to ride around the vicinity on his little scooter.

Ken Nolan: "But I knew him for years and didn't know who he was. People along this road had no idea who he was. He was just such a quiet fellow who would take his little dog a walk down the road.

"Years went by and I would talk to him a lot. I was often out in the front garden and he would amble across with his dog. We would talk about all sorts. Altrincham FC sometimes... anything really. Then one day, after years and years, someone said to me 'Oh that's Frank Sidebottom. He is a comedian he is, from Timperley. Quite famous.' Well, blow me I never knew that. I must admit, I had never heard of Frank Sidebottom and no one around here seems to have known him either.

"Often I would be on the green in the park, bowling. I would be bowling a lot and Chris would deliberately come over talking to me. It was general chit-chat really.

"I remember Gemma coming to live here. She turned up with Chris's daughter… Gemma, yes I don't know where he picked her up from. But, again, dead friendly. They had so many cats there were no birds flying over there, they frightened them all away. When Gemma left and took the cats, all the little birds came back again. Eight cats and a dog. You would be in the house and cats would walk all over you. They were nice and that. But it was a bit overwhelming.

"Chris never really changed when he drank. He was always a quiet lad and still was when he was drunk. He wasn't one of those people who completely changed character. Well I didn't see any other side to him. I remember when he got his little scooter, he would be bombing around on that."

Phil Jones: "I took over managing John Cooper Clarke in about 2008. And Alan Wise, who was sort of involved with JCC had started to hang around with Chris, had already booked a few gigs with John Cooper Clarke and Frank Sidebottom. They seemed to work well together. I kind of took over John and inherited a few gigs. So I got to really know Chris again. He was a lot calmer by this time. A bit thoughtful and he had debts all over him. The first time I saw him again was at The Lowry. Me and CP Lee had invented some mad festival. CP played, JCC played and Frank did his own show. Chris and I got together and decided to do some gigs in the autumn with both of them, then John got ill so we did them in the New Year. Frank went down a storm and it seemed natural to book more and more gigs with the pair of them. The only problem was that Chris had signed this really weird deal with this London management company… they seemed to have all his money for some reason and when they did release him some, he had to give it all away to service various debts. He was obviously in trouble but the thing is that the John Cooper Clarke and Frank Sidebottom pairing was a really hot ticket. People travelled for miles. That stated, I did noticed that there were certain places where he was practically unknown. It was very strange… perhaps I should have organised more local press or telly for him. It was odd because he would be really popular in Manchester but in, say, Derby, I remember someone asking how this 'puppet thing' worked. Is there somebody in the head?"

Gemma Woods: "Chris started to get ill at around Christmas time 2009. We were having Christmas dinner at my mum and dads, and he struggled to eat. We didn't think that much of it at the time, but it got worse over the months. He kept going back to the doctor, who said it was indigestion. He knew it wasn't. Eventually the tests showed he had a tumour in his chest, against his oesophagus. He was always really positive about beating it. He would say 'I'm going to fuck this off'. I think he really believed that."

Phil Jones: "We put a gig on for John Cooper Clarke and Frank at Leeds Irish Centre. He took his shirt off when he came offstage and I told him that he was looking really trim… cos he had been a bit porky with the drink in the past. I asked him if he was ok and he told us that he had cancer. John was absolutely stunned. Chris said, 'but I'm alright. I'm having treatment.' That was the end of a run of gigs. Then we had this one off gig in Derby. Chris had been pestering John to do a song together – '36 Hours' at the end but it didn't happen. They rehearsed in the dressing room and it sounded great. It was going to be the encore. But we ran out of time. They did play it the next night at The Leadmill and we have it on film. But that was the last time I worked with him. It was about a month before he died."

This performance features as an extra on the Evidently John Cooper Clarke live DVD.

Ken Nolan: "That house. I don't know how he kept it going. He rented it and they must cost 'undred quid a week. Chris would go off and you wouldn't see him for days and days… weeks sometimes. His landlord would often be banging on the door, demanding the rent which, I think, he was often behind with. I would feel real sorry for him because I could see how much of a struggle it was. He only seemed to relax when he was with his little dog, a Heinz 57 thing, it were."

Phil Jones: "The night before the Derby gig, Chris had had a minor operation on his throat so he could actually eat, because he had been unable to eat for a while. So we went to this horrible Chinese place in Derby... the only place open and kind of 24 hour all you can eat place. He ate quite a lot that night and told me that it was the first time he had eaten for two of three weeks. He rang me a couple of days later and told me that the problem with not eating for a while is that it goes straight through you. He spent all the next day on the toilet. But he was laughing about it although he was clearly gravely ill. You could tell that. But he was asking me about what gigs we had coming up."

Ken Nolan: "In fact, I saw Chris and was chatting to him, I think, the day before he died. And he had seemed really happy on that day. Just very, very chatty. He came over and sat on my wall, chatting away."

Paul Ripley: "Chris and Gemma had been coming over to the radio station – Manchester Online – and doing a lot of stuff for us. They were due to come in that day. But I got a text saying that he was ok but had been coughing up blood. Then the next day I heard that he had died. I didn't know whether to keep that text or not.

Ken Nolan: "It was all so normal. And he had that haemorrhage... and Gemma was screaming, wondering what to do. She was knocking on my neighbour's door, Kevin. He went across and helped clean things up for her. It must have been really terrible for her."

Brian Little: "I worked with him right up until the end. We didn't know how ill he was but we all noticed him getting thinner and thinner. I remember meeting him in Altrincham and he was smoking. He just said, 'I love smoking'. Then I think I went on holiday and later got a call from Asher saying he had died. It was difficult to believe."

Ken Nolan: "After he died they all came round. Harry and Asher came. There was just so much to take. They day after he died, there were cars and vans turning up. Stuff piled high. In fact I couldn't believe how much gear he had in that house. Or indeed where he had kept it all. And there was a lad, Malcolm Kettle and Gemma came here to borrow screwdrivers so they could take some of the gear out. The house just lay empty for a bit. As soon as the pictures went... pictures that he had created, you could see all the nicotine on the walls because he used to smoke like a trooper, Chris. You could see from outside where the pictures had been. It was a terribly sad time, really. I miss him. I miss Gemma and Paula too. Gemma then got a job in Tesco's and I asked her where she was going to live. She said she got a place in Chorlton. I thought, well she wont be able to keep that job in Altrincham Tesco's if she was moving to Chorlton."

STARS LEAD TRIBUTES AS FRANK SIDEBOTTOM COMIC DIES AT 54

Chris Sievey, famous as his alter ego Frank Sidebottom, was found collapsed at his home in Hale early yesterday. It is understood that his girlfriend called an ambulance and he was taken to Wythenshawe Hospital where his death was confirmed.
MANCHESTER EVENING NEWS JUNE 22 2010.

FRANK SIDEBOTTOM COMIC FACES A PAUPER'S FUNERAL

The comic genius behind Mancunian legend Frank Sidebottom is facing a pauper's funeral after dying virtually penniless. Chris Sievey had no assets and little money in the bank, his family have revealed.
MANCHESTER EVENING NEWS JUNE 23 2010.

Rick Sarko: "I saw Chris, that week. June 10th? Not quite sure. And I saw him as Frank, dressed in his football gear with his shorts on. He was sat in the beer garden later and I couldn't believe how thin he was. He had lost about three stone. He said, 'I've got some sweets upstairs'. We went up and it was like the worst food you have ever bought in Blackpool. It was like a sit-com. Steptoe and Son, or something like that. We talked for about two hours. He did his Tony Hancock. He did a great impression of Tony Hancock. Saw him go home that night. He had his leather jacket on and jeans and it was like, 'Ok see you mate.' Then I was in Benidorm the next week and someone messaged me on my Facebook page and told me what had happened. It was a shock because I didn't realise that things were that bad."

Barry Spencer: I was going to go and see Chris. I had been putting off going to see him for a couple of weeks, on that day. I was in work I thought, I've got to delegate and get over and spend a couple of hours with him. But I never managed to get there and the next thing I knew he had gone."

Phil Jones: "Then one sunny day, I was out in the field with my daughter. She was on the swings. And Marc Riley phoned me up and told me that he had some bad news. He said 'Chris is dead!' I said, 'Chris who?'. He said 'Chris Sievey.' I thought, 'fucking hell'. It was unreal. It really was. I couldn't have been sadder. I have seen a lot of deaths, but Chris, really... but he spent his whole life smoking fags. Smoking nub ends. I never saw him smoke dope, but he smoked horrible cheap fags, like you used to smoke at school; He was chronically addicted."

Mark Alston, 34, a close friend for many years who helped organise Sievey's appearances as Frank Sidebottom, said: "He was a big comedy name in Greater Manchester, one of the biggest. He was also a musical genius and a good friend to many. He was a legend in the region and will be missed. He was saying that he was going to get shut of the cancer and not to cancel any more bookings."

Tributes immediately flooded the media. Obituaries fluttering in in every format... Heartfelt and honest. Pointed and, of course, desperately sad. Sad too, in its own way, was the flood of press that continued during the following week. Press that Chris had dreamed off all his life, local and national. Websites and radio. Stunted tabloid journalese and broadsheet theorising. There seemed no boundaries. In my immediate vicinity, I noted that the *Sale and Altrincham Messenger* provided a typically evocative front-page proclaiming, 'It's Bobbins, as our Frank Dies.' Succinct and neatly done, I admit. However, I couldn't help noting that, mere months prior to this, the editor of the same organ had professed to 'never having heard of Frank Sidebottom'. And now an 'old friend' had departed.

This was the mere tip of the iceberg. The *Manchester Evening News* provided a further splash, complete with a hastily compiled overview of Frank's life. More incredibly perhaps, a full page appeared in *The Mirror*, heartily championing 'A King of Comedy'. I might be wrong as I have never subscribed to said organ, but I wondered if the so called 'King of Comedy' had ever graced those pages before. Nevertheless, it was helpful hype. It had been Stirling Sievey who had initially broken the not-altogether-unexpected news that Chris might suffer the indignity of having a pauper's funeral; such were the sorry state of his finances.

The rallying was immediate.

Jon Ronson: "We had to do something. I would have been much more surprised if Chris had actually saved any money at all or made any provision for his funeral. It was just the way he was. It was expected, really. It reminded me of Ken Dodd after he had been done for tax evasion. His response was to say that he was an artist and was responsible for being funny and making jokes. That had been his whole world. That was the same thing with Chris. He had been so busy doing what he did, he was so full of ideas that he never really had time to think about things like money. I wasn't surprised at all. I would have been far more surprised had he died with any kind of nest egg. But I knew that something had to be done. It was important to give him the right kind of send off."

As was the immediacy of the collective. Ronson was joined by names who included Mark Radcliffe, Phil Jupitus, Jason Manford, Chris Evans and Guy Lovelady and many more.

The bereavement officer at Wythenshawe Hospital had informed Stirling that the notion of a 'pauper's funeral' wasn't actually that bad although there would be no service and the coffin would be more like a rectangular box. No gravestone either... Relaying this information to Jon Ronson proved pivotal and Ronson's subsequent rallying 'tweet' saw 554 people pledge £6,950.90. Ronson states that one hour later this had swelled to 1,108 donors pledging £14,018.90 and, by the close of the day, £21,631.55 had been raised. The money would have continued to rise had Ronson not started to plead with people to stop pledging.

What was obvious was the huge swell of love that was held for Frank Sidebottom. Clearly he had touched so many lives… clearly he had enriched our vision and, perhaps, altered our perspective on life. Surely the mark of a true artist. How the astonishing speed and weight of this support can be squared with the fading sight of late eighties Frank Sidebottom, performing to a tiny knot of inebriated students in – take your pick – Warwick University is a little more difficult to assimilate. The amount raised and continuing keenness signifies that Frank – and Chris – had enjoyed an impressive level of success. The paradox being, I suggest, that Chris's and Frank's relative failure proved vital towards that success. People recognised something… they saw and felt… heart!

Ken Nolan: "When I saw all the write ups about Frank in the papers, I thought, 'I don't believe this lot'. In fact, I know that his landlord didn't even know who he was. People said he was really funny but I don't know about that. I never saw Frank. I don't anybody in this road had a clue who he was."

The response proved beyond staggering and brought with it another problem; the prospect of this twisting naturally into some kind of celebrity funeral. Unfortunately, Manchester music had seen a number of such events, during the past few years. The Factory trio of Tony Wilson, Martin Hannett and Rob Gretton and Sad Café's Paul Young among them. It was decided this time that a public event at Castlefield Arena would offset the well-meaning public presence at the official funeral, which attracted a relatively modest two hundred people to Altrincham Crematorium. A flickering of celebrity naturally filtered into family and friends, with members of The Freshies standing alongside such eclectic faces as Badly Drawn Boy, Charlie Chuck and Mark Radcliffe.

Harry, 18 at the time, delivered a heart-felt eulogy described by Guy Lovelady, who worked as Frank's manager in the latter days, as "… beautiful and moving, exactly what Chris would have wanted."

Dave Arnold: "I initially met Steve Sullivan when he did the bus tour. The Magical Timperley Tour. I then met him at the funeral. Chris had plans to work with Steve. They were planning to go to America. The

Happy Mondays were going to go as well. Steve was going to document it. It never happened. That is partly why Steve felt compelled to make a film. This was some time after the funeral. In fact it took a while for the penny to drop that there was real interest in Frank. And then it became obvious that there was actually massive interest. For me, that is the test of a true artist. The fact that there wouldn't be noticeable interest until after they die than it explodes. I think it took 10 years to get a statue of Eric Morecambe. But with Frank, it was in place in three years. That is pretty good going. Pretty good for everyone involved."

BEING CHRIS

BOTH CHRIS AND FRANK were highly filmic; Chris mainly, though by no means completely, preferring to remain on the other side of the camera while Frank, from day one it seems, revelled in being the main subject matter. More than that, often physically wrestling the spotlight away from Little Frank, Little Denise or any passing hapless popstar who agreed to appear alongside Frank on TV.

As such, myriad images and films scatter the open universe of the YouTube generation. 30 seconds scanning on an iPhone while standing at a Hartlepool bus stop is all it takes to open up this scattered and disparate world. I do sense that Chris would approve of this eternally expanding outlet even if it now bulges with items of overtly personal, pointless amateurism.

One item seems more relevant here. This being Frank's brazen 'Magical Timperley Tour', the YouTube product of film maker Steve Sullivan, capturing the surreal taste of a walk and bus trip through the gentile and rather dull climes of Frank's favoured locale. For the moment, I choose to look beyond the all-conquering hype of the excellent 'Frank'.

OUT OF HIS HEAD

Timperley Village. 1pm Friday April 18 2013

You might be forgiven for thinking that there is little of notable comedic value in or around Timperley village. While it spreads through the dizzying mundanity of, it seems, endless areas of leafy suburbia, the village centre is little more than a crossroads flanked by a pub, three small rows of shops, sullen restaurants, a fish'n'chip shop and the ubiquitous Iceland. For Chris to prise comedy value from this overbearing normality must remain one of his most outstanding achievements.

There didn't seem to be an obvious aura of magic on this mild Friday which, at last… at last, would see shards of spring sunlight breaking through three trees. Welcome, indeed, as I sit on a pavement coffee bar watching the scurrying of mild Friday shoppers. Nothing particularly special or, indeed, particularly bad could ever happen in this pleasant and somnolent atmosphere.

However, I wandered from the village and, taking the direction of the tram station, head with unlikely purpose down Park Road. After two hundred yards I am beckoned by a garish green sign which offers the dubious delights of 'Timperley Community Centre', a faintly gothic and curiously foreboding building which offers various rooms for hire. I felt a slight sting of nerves as I pushed through the doors and immediately encounter the familiar figure of Dave. I didn't realise, though I had met him before, indeed within the opening section of this book.

"Mick?" he offers a hand, "I met you before. You told me to 'fuck off' as you pushed past me to get backstage at that Warrington gig."

"Well…"

"It was OK. I didn't know who you were and was being a bit overprotective of Chris. It was a poignant scene, wasn't it, as you wandered backstage?"

Emerging behind him came the figure of Steve Sullivan; amiable and lost to the immense task of creating and editing 'Being Frank', a documentary that, I like to think, sits side by side with this book.

Dave seemed friendly enough and immediately told me the story of how, after Frank had emerged from retirement, he had put him on at a gig in Wigan only for Sievey to turn up, in Dave's words, "So drunk he staggered in the room with his flies undone… I have never seen anyone so inebriated."

He continued to tell me how Frank slowly pulled Chris back from the brink, openly stating, "Dave, I am either a workaholic or an alcoholic. I can't do anything in-between. I can't relax. Have to be working or drinking."

I thought about this a great deal and wondered about that curious twist in the tale. That the diminishing side to Chris Sievey was the actual Sievey character himself… perhaps the man who I had found so charming and inspiring back in 1978. Time and time again through the writing of this book it appeared that there were – at least – three entities involved. Chris, the real Chris, the charming, thrillingly intelligent Chris. Again I remembered that day at The Pelican Inn… with the sand and the donkeys. It was rather like those distant Bank Holiday pictures of Mancunians enjoying the attractions of Belle Vue, an embryonic theme park and zoo set deep within the black climes of Gorton. On this Sale occasion, we had to stretch our collective imaginations to the limit in order to ignore the endless swish of cars hurtling down Washway Road. Chris had no problems, drinking about three pints and throwing himself into the somewhat vacuous event. He told me later that his dream job would be designing rides at a major theme park. The Chris Sievey theme park, I mused, would have been a truly wonderful and bizarre place and a million miles away from the sub-Disney atmosphere and greasy chip ambience of the large British parks today. 'Frank's World', perhaps, complete with giant 'Thunderbirds' rides and a 'Stingray' log-flume… the possibilities were endless and, until someone builds such a place, 'Frank's World' and perhaps this entire tale, must remain a theme park of the mind.

The second character would, obviously, be Frank himself and one could easily see him and a trail of Little Franks and Denises patrolling the imaginary park.

And then, alas, the third character; lost and forlorn, lapsing into alcoholic mist and battling with no small number of demons. The latter Chris should not be denied, for he certainly existed and was, just like Frank, a release mechanism of sorts, for a rush of genuine emotion. I remain happy to have known all three.

The filmmaker Steve Sullivan soon joined us. I immediately warmed to his drive and enthusiasm. So obvious, it seemed, as he drove me into the tiny heart of Timperley in search of lunchtime sustenance for the small film crew.

On our return, the dismay of Dave Arnold was obvious.

"No vegetarian food," he gasped, "Well, I guess that says a lot about Timperley."

"You should have filmed it in Chorlton," I joked although, on reflection, it seems difficult to imagine Chorlton's Bohemian populace fully embracing the Frank persona. Better we were here, in the simplicity of a dull suburb.

The scene inside Timperley Community Centre was suitably bizarre. Frank's full stage set to the left, spot-lit and gleaming, life-size Frank to the right and various Little Frank bodies to the rear while the shed and palm trees completed the scene. A succession of interviewees had and would stand on this hallowed set, with yours truly proud to be followed by Mark Radcliffe, en route home following his BBC 6 music afternoon show.

Making a documentary about Chris and Frank is an expensive and somewhat time-consuming business. I managed to sense the earnest diligence of Steve and, indeed, the ability to spend – literally – years in painstaking toil with little hope of true financial gain. There is a balance here, too, between the truly objective filmmaker and someone wholly immersed in the blanket of fandom. Much as one has enjoyed the company of so many Frank fans, they are not the right people to make films or, indeed, write books about the object of their obsession. Steve, I noticed, took great pains to distance himself from this problem. You could sense it in his voice, in his actions, in the programmed and logical way he went about his business, forcing it into an identifiable state of professionalism. This is particularly important in the case of Frank, whose followers share a unique approach to everyday life. The simple fact is that they are part and parcel of the story – particularly within the context of a film made after the death of its main character – and should remain firmly in front of and not behind the camera. The exception to this, I strongly sensed, was the case of Dave Arnold who was already fully built into Frank's unique touring circus.

Something else was happening. As the film ever-so-slowly progressed, shunting to a halt and re-starting when funds and time allowed, it became abundantly clear just how much love existed for both Chris and Frank… it had been out there for years. Shame on the media, perhaps, for not fully understanding the spreading concept of 'cult' in an era of short-fire, shallow celebrity.

Two weeks after the filming at Timperley Community Centre, Sullivan returned to Manchester from his base in Cardiff, in an attempt to pull media attention to his 'Kickstarter' campaign, aimed at raising the initial £20,000 necessary to take the film to the next level. One day after this launch – and with the help of local radio stations, the *MEN* and *Messenger* papers, £13,000 had been achieved and Sullivan's quest gained the support of such 'notables' as Chris Moyles and Johnny Vegas.

Yet nine months in and there is still no end in sight…

"It will probably take a further year," Sullivan explained, "It is looking like we will hit the minimum target of £20,000 and the film will happen on some level. But I would really love to have clips of Frank on TV in there and for that we would have to at least get to £40k to option stuff properly. The film shouldn't be missing such important moments as Frank's Fantastic Shed Show, Number 73, Remote Control, Match of the Day, his appearances with Stanley Unwin on TX, Ready for Transmission etc. there is so much stuff that should be in there."

MONDAY MAY 13 2013

FAINT ANXIETY, LIKE AMPHETAMINE, makes my heart shudder. It was mid-day and I was in the distantly familiar art deco surroundings of Stockport's stunningly re-born Plaza Cinema on Mersey Square. Ghosts seemed to haunt every corner. Ghosts and echoes. We sat sipping tea in a café of overwhelming quaintness, full of Lloyd loom furniture and potted palms. It was difficult not to imagine a string quartet in the corner, drifting through essential Mozart. Outside, fittingly, a hoarding boasts the arrival of the rather unconvincing remake, 'The Great Gatsby'. That alone seemed strange, when the 1974, superior version of F. Scott Fitzgerald's tale of vacuous excess was out, I would sit in this same room every Sunday evening. Back then it was 'Samantha's Disco'. A black'n'naff den of iniquity.

I was nervous, having been cajoled into taking part in a talk in the main cinema at 12.15 revolving around the myriad qualities of The Smiths, whose first single, 'Hand In Glove' was recorded in this town, at the legendary Strawberry Studios, back in 1983. The anniversary would see, following our rather frenetic chat, various Smiths orientated filmic excursions topped by Shelagh Delaney's 'Taste of Honey', from which Morrissey's muse prodigiously dipped.

But what has this got to do with Chris Sievey or Frank, you might be forgiven for enquiring? Good question. And, I had hoped the answer might be nothing. For this was to be a day excursion away from the energy of Chris and Frank. If only briefly, I had attempted to escape, if only for a short while. But Chris and Frank's presence has been curiously omnipresent for the past year or so. Randomly, I found myself moving to Ashton-on-Mersey in 2011, before I realised it to be the village of Chris's formative years. Even getting married in the village proved eerily poignant. For our wedding photographer, Martin O'Neill, was once employed as working 'smudger' for the local free sheet, *Sale and Altrincham Messenger* and in that capacity, took memorable shots of The Freshies back in 1979, famously capturing them running down the corkscrew ramp at Sale Tesco. He recreated the ramp shot for myself and wife Vicky, hurtling down between the Mercs and Range Rovers. That might have seemed coincidence enough. But we found ourselves – again unknowingly, lest this seems a somewhat geekish tale of nuptials – getting wed in the same room as Paula and Chris, all those years ago. It also dawned on us, that day, that (again randomly) Chris had been a one time partner of our guest and witness – Tosh Ryan. The coincidences were beginning to stack up.

But surely not in Stockport Plaza.

Then it dawned on me that Frank and Salfordian bard, John Cooper Clarke had performed together at the venue in 2010. An extraordinary, most welcome and unlikely bill for a Sunday evening in Mersey Square. In two minutes time, I realised, I would be treading the same boards. Ok, not quite so bizarre. However, one of the chief protagonists of The Smiths event would be the aforementioned John Barratt, the chief culprit of Frank's mercenary 'Stockport is Really Fantastic'. Furthermore, his son, Joe Barratt, our onstage interviewer, had the pleasure of Frank's company on the occasion of his 19th birthday.

He told me, "Frank just blew my birthday party apart. He was utterly brilliant and made it the most memorable party ever. Not that I regarded him as a party entertainer… but he could do anything and it would be funny."

Mulling this, I turned to mention this book to the other writer who had been chain-ganged into talking onstage at The Plazas, ex-*NME* production editor and erstwhile filmmaker, Len Brown. Given this information he almost exploded with an unbridled enthusiasm I had not previously noticed within him. It turned out he was an avid Frank aficionado and – I had forgotten this, I really had – the writer of one of my favourite reviews of Frank's work of all time.

"You can steal it if you want… put it in the book," he smiled.

I wasn't about to steal anything. I will reproduce it here in a few lines time, however. Love the way Len, and despite the overtly earnest nature of much late period *NME*, abandons his critical distance and climbs right into the Frank story, even name-checking the headless Little Denise along the way.

"They loved Frank at the *NME*," he told me.

"They did?" I replied, somewhat amazed.

"Yeah, Frank even appeared at Alan Jackson's leaving do. It was an amazing night."

It seemed fully appropriate to track down the erstwhile Mr Jackson, one of the stalwart writers of late-ish period *NME* and, apparently, a die-hard fan of all things Frank. I thought, for sure, he would have stories to impart. It did indeed seem that Frank culture had permeated that influential office; the same office that, and understandably so given the prevailing air of post-punk, so studiously ignored the pop thrashings of The Freshies. A significant point, especially if we focus on the fact that Chris's message within the framework of The Freshies was not at all dissimilar to the childlike visions of Frank. The relationship remains obvious although, as half hits and tours, solo ventures and filmic ventures passed by without generating a true level of success, Chris had to somehow discover a striking new format. Frank!

OUT OF HIS HEAD

Alan Jackson: "I don't know about 'stories' but Chris/Frank did indeed perform at my *NME* leaving do and it was an absolute thrill for me. The sheer benign ridiculousness of Frank had always struck a chord with me and I remember that whenever I was getting over-stressed or grumpy at my desk, I variously commissioned the 'Thrills' section, live reviews and was chief feature writer, news editor Terry Staunton at the next desk would talk to me in Little Frank's voice and it never failed to dissolve my mood and make me laugh. Knowing that I loved him, they asked (hopefully paid) Chris to come down and make an appearance on the night. I remember he sang a reworked version of Kylie's hit of the time, "I should be so lucky, lucky, lucky, lucky, I should be so lucky... to leave the *NME*." The sad and ridiculous thing is that when, post-performance, he was at the bar as himself I felt strangely disabled from having a proper conversation with him. Something about the magic of Frank, I guess. He gave me a Sidie which I treasured for its short lifetime, but being made of plaster of Paris or something equally crumbly its lifetime was indeed very short. But somewhere in storage I do have the other bits and pieces he gave me. I recall a guide to Timperley, and one of those funny promo mugshot pics of a variety artiste, Tony Something or Other, with a Frank-forged signature wishing me all the best. So very sad that he died so young. Frank and Little Frank still make me smile whenever I think of them."

Within the space of two minutes, I had chanced upon two tales of Frank's extra- curricular activities. Intriguing indeed.

Here is the review of the 5/9/88! Double LP (cassette only) released by Marc Riley's In Tape Records).

FRANK SIDEBOTTOM - 5/9/88!

The very existence of '5/9/88!' is a triumph of art over antagonism. Like The Smiths at 'Strangeways...' and The Beatles during 'Let It Be', Sidebottom's Oh Blimey Band (incorporating the legendary Demon Ax Warriors From Hell and Beastie Puppets) was pushed by personal and production problems to the verge of disintegration on this LP.

Not only has Little Denise lost her head and Little Frank disastrously agreed to look after Mrs Merton's wayward baby Reginald, but also the complex relationship between Little Buzz Aldrin and Little Frank – developed during the colonization of the moon for Timperley – has driven Big Frank to violence in the shed studio.

It's a desperately sad affair; and yet amidst such rancour, tension and chaos, masterpieces are invariably conceived. Führer Frank has dispensed with the tried and tested formula of cover versions, opting instead for bitter political anthems like 'Mr Custard' and 'Hey You Riot Policeman' (hard rap with a Lydonesque snarl!).

There are star interviews – Ian McAskill, Patrick Moore, Nicholas Parsons… – and fanatical football anthems such as 'The Robins Aren't Bobbins' for Altrincham FC, coupled with hostile taunts at opposition supporters ("you're going home in an organized football coach"). More important, there are classically-catchy pop songs, contagious and contemporary, eclectic and electric, with 'Me Great Big Zoo Scrapbook' and 'Airplay' ("I'm washing your brain") brilliant attacks of '80s producer-pop both.

Comparisons with 'The Double White Album' are inevitable; some will say that fierce editing would have eliminated 'The Squid Is Correct' or 'The Monopoly Game', but they are vital to this social document of the band's implosion. 'Monopoly', in particular, reveals Sidebottom as a power-crazed puppeteer: "Oh hotel on Mayfair/And I've got a hotel on Park Lane/The blue one/And Little Frank hasn't even got/A house on Old Kent Road…"

If this is really the end of Sidebottom's association with the Beastie Puppets – Goldman's soon-to-come tome implying Big Frank's a schizophrenic Northwich Victoria fan who rarely leaves his bedroom and snorts Ovaltine suggests this – we must treasure '5/9/88' for what it is. An accomplished double debut album of hit singles, bobbins, bitter disagreements and fantastic flashbacks. More Frank than 'Rank', Sidebottom is truly a head of his time.

LITTLE LEN BROWN

EPITAPH

SUDDENLY THERE WAS NOTHING. A void. A silence. Chris had left a huge hole. Frank had left a huge hole. A hollow shell of silence. The reality of what happened settled fast, leaving some dream state, some raft of loss. Altrincham, such a warm and welcoming town, seemed strangely cold. I wondered how those people far closer to Chris than I, must have been feeling. But then something happened. The sense of loss seemed to spread further than the norm. More than that, it seemed to gain energy, like some fireball or meteorite, gathering pace. From the depths came an energy. A collective energy flash. Nobody, back then, could have predicted the astonishing events of the four years that would follow Chris's death. The momentum would prove dizzying, twisting - powering this story onto new and extraordinary levels. Had this energy flash not ignited then Chris and Frank would have settled gently into the greyness of collective memory, relative obscurity perhaps. But something would have remained unresolved. Something would have been wrong. A small number of people would work tirelessly to help maintain this momentum... however I suggest and like the idea that the true power would lie in the silent masses, those Frank fans in the mists, in the distance. Something happened.

Phil Jones: "After the funeral, Jon Ronson asked me if we could hold some kind of memorial event in Castlefield basin, Manchester. Bands could play and Jon Ronson started that trust fund thing with Guy Lovelady. Ronson presented me with the idea of some kind of event and we talked about it a lot. I went to the council and asked if they could put on the Castlefield event. In the end it worked superbly... it was the greatest send off. I was sat next to Paula and we were watching Harry and we were in bits because Harry was so much like his dad."

Phil Jones and a number other other people – Nick Fraser, Guy

MICK MIDDLES

Lovelady, Jon Ronson, Neil Taylor, Dave Arnold – mentioned to me that they felt 'surprised' by the speed in which these events unfolded, as if guided? Well, perhaps although I am still fond of the notion of a collected energy.

A Frank Facebook Group had been the idea of Sale based promoter, Nick Fraser. A Facebook group for Frank: for a *statue* of Frank. It was merely a notion... at first. But surely it would prove a fitting, solid and tactile close to this story. Nick Fraser – promoter without the feisty and arrogant air one normally associates with such a beast ...sometime stand-up comedian, partner to Tim Burgess on the lively O Genesis label. And there he was. Nick Fraser, striding the stage at the Frank memorial at Castlefield. Waves of goodwill rippling out across the swelling crowd. Blink twice and wonder where these people were, back in the days of Freshies aloofness; back in the obscure corners of Frank, when the random nature of his status within rock's dark hierarchy seemed to provide him with a sadly existential air. Not here. Not in postulating Castlefield. A crowd that filtered colourfully along the bars and cafés of Deansgate and deep into the city centre. Frank T-shirts clasping bulging stomachs. Cheery, beery faces. The lovely oddballs of Frank's Manchester, sifting down and gathering before the Arena stage. And at this moment, a stage Fraser shared with a gleeful Jon Ronson, who dispelled a raft of anecdotal warmth for Frank and, beyond that, a glimpse of Chris. The departed Chris. Still here, somewhere, undoubtedly casting a smile over the proceedings.

It was, as stated, Nick Fraser's idea to erect the statue in Timperley. It might have been a half formed notion at that point. Just a whim. Just the very first step on the long and winding road that leads to the casting of bronze and eventual unveiling on the Timperley pavement. The first mention of a notion that would take £20,000 and huge blows of energy from no small number of enthusiasts. An idea that would flitter around the globe, bringing in furrowed brows of talented artists in, of all places, the Czech Republic.

But would it go down well, this initial step? It was difficult to tell. Until, of course, the voices of Fraser and Ronson were drowned by the gathering chants from across Casltlefield... chants that gained in momentum and power. Gloriously simple, effective and wonderful chants... chants unaware of the necessary political and controversial burring that goes hand in hand with such a notion.

"STATUE... STATUE... STATUE" came the cries. Inspiring cries. Cries bereft of dour complications. It was one of the most effective and warming moments in Manchester's musical history... indeed, one struggles to unearth a comparative power. It would echo into the future, too, and resonate in similar notions for a statue of Ian Curtis in Macclesfield and, slightly more controversially, Tony Wilson Street in Manchester city centre. Not since the frock coated gents of the Victorian age had such honours been bestowed. Far better, perhaps, than the plethora of blue plaques that gather little interest as they sat like full stops on houses stretching out into the suburbs.

The seed had been sown.

Mark Radcliffe: "I remember at Chris's wake in Castlefield that night. There were loads of people there. I did a bit of talking but I felt just a bit distant from it because there were lots of people there and I didn't really remember them from my time with Chris. I saw this big crowd of people and thought that there was never an event that big that Chris performed to in his lifetime. So I found it a bit strange. In a funny sort of way I felt I wanted to say a private goodbye. I stood on the steps and looked at all the people... I was pleased about that... but I looked up at the sky and just said 'See you Chris'.

"I went to the funeral at Altrincham Crem and a bit of a do, afterwards. I hadn't seen Mike Doherty for ages but he was still hilarious."

Phil Jones: "We had spoken about going to the States with the pair of them. John Cooper Clarke and Frank. John has never done the States... Chris had told me that he wanted away from the management company in London even though he owed them money. But Chris and I agreed that I would take over managing him. I decided to do it when he asked me. I didn't bite his hand off but I wanted to do it. But I did wonder about his illness"

Mark Radcliffe: "The time I spent with Chris had a profound effect on my life. Sometimes you look back and wonder who the people have been who made a difference to the way your mind has been shaped. I think that Chris was definitely one of the few I could put into that category. On his death and the press he received afterwards; it is a bit like Wilko Johnson and Doctor Feelgood, who were one of the seminal British bands. Wilko is getting loads of attention now because he is dying. And it's great that people know about him even though for many years he never got any attention. Same with Chris, although Chris never made it easy because he couldn't be relied upon. He never even did a proper tour. He was always so disorganised. I don't think Chris could conform to the rigours of a tour. A tour is a job and that is just not Chris.

OLDHAM STREET, MANCHESTER.
DECEMBER 2012.

HISTORIC STREET OF RAUCOUS HEDONISM. A legacy that casts an unholy nod back to the soot-lined days of pulsating industry, perhaps the very root of Manchester music. I've always loved the street, the echoes and ghosts that creep out each evening, be they from the punkish trash of '77, or Merseybeat or beyond. Somehow the street still holds that vibe and long may it linger in the historic glory of pubs like The Castle and Gulliver's. Halfway down the street, on the right hand side as you walk away from Piccadilly, a Banksy-esque stencil of Frank Sidebottom will greet you. Many times I have seen this life-size graffito used as a photo opportunity. The same was true of the Frank mosaic that adorned the wall of Affleck's Palace - two precursors to the statue. People desired a Frank, somewhere, to stand next to. To languish, for a while, in a lovely memory.

If, one evening on 15th December 2012, you wandered along Oldham Street and entered the lively venue, Night and Day – a café bar that doubles as perfect low level music venue – you would have encountered another musical ghost. A rare event indeed. The band known as The Freshies, complete with Harry Sievey on guitar and vocals, performing before an audience of family, friends, fans and more casual imbibers. At the time it seemed like a mere dip in nostalgia although it would prove it to be more than that. More than a mere fundraiser. It was a flash of future events. Of a future for Frank.

Barry Spencer: "The gig at Night and Day was really weird, actually. We were onstage, standing in front of Paula and the kids and Chris's brother, Martin. Harry was singing. I have got to say it was a really strange atmosphere. Harry did a great job but there were moments, mid-song, when you would look across and it was almost like a young Chris singing again. He does look a bit like him and, well, in just a split second it was like going back in time. Just flashbacks. It was good though and we enjoyed the whole experience. We rehearsed at Dave Arnold's studio in Wigan. We rehearsed more than we used to, actually.

"I am the kind of person who moves on in life. I don't own any Freshies records or anything like that. Which is one reason why I am not always sure about Frank fans... they tend to collect everything they can and hoard it. It is funny, all this stuff about Frank and The Freshies coming back because I haven't really thought about it since leaving. I have just got on with whatever is in front of me. And it has been quite nice having it all brought back to life. If I am honest, until recently, I wouldn't have done that interview on the radio – on Stephen Doyle's punk show with Steve Sullivan – but I really enjoyed it. It was good fun."

The Night and Day gig encouraged momentum. Flashes of the set on YouTube certainly helped prove something that shocked even Barry and Rick. That out there, somewhere, wasn't merely a great deal of fondness for Frank, but for The Freshies too.

Stephen Doyle: "I always knew that The Freshies were a bigger band than they were ever given credit for. It could be that they were underrated for years after they folded because they never really looked like a Manchester band. Or sounded like one."

On an artistic level, one man more than most, I suggest, is responsible for the continuing legacy of both Frank and The Freshies. Dave Arnold seems to breath the breath of the Oh Blimeys... tirelessly injecting energy and freshness. Even within the context of his own band - or *one* of his own bands, The Stags, you can sense a spirit of Chris. It is just... *there*!

Barry: "I think Dave Arnold is a professional geek. In a really nice way. But he is typical at the moment. I can't believe how interested people have been. If I am honest, if it had stopped at The Freshies and there hadn't been a Frank, nobody would have been interested. But that was Chris, he just carried on. Chris, like a lot of people, decided to live his life trying to achieve his dream. All his stuff: animation, puppets, that childlike artistic stuff… everything he did was part of him. I noticed this from very early on in The Freshies. His obsessional enthusiasm. When he was doing all the mail outs and poster designing in Tosh's place, I didn't have anything to do with it and didn't want to have anything to do with it. It is not me. The effort and time he put in to do that is just geeky. In that respect, Dave certainly reminds me of Chris."

Phil Jones: "Then came the Selfridges story. We had heard that Selfridges, in London, had put all these images of Frank in the window of the Oxford Street shop. This was part of their Christmas display from mid-November. They had used the images of Frank Sidebottom as their Christmas image. It was all over the shop as well as in the window. There were 28 images of Frank Sidebottom. Real papier-mâché heads. Frank as Santa Claus. One of the family rang me, Asher perhaps, and asked if I could sort this out for them. So I did. I ended up getting the family a large sum of money. To allow Selfridges to keep them there, I got the family a five figure sum. I was quite chuffed about that. It also helped pay off Gemma's problems… she was saddled with the debt on the shed. The family could pay other debts off and made a bit. This story reached North West Tonight and I went on to be interviewed… Selfridges didn't pay as much as I asked. But it was a good sum… a neat ending."

★

And so slowly came the statue, flickering temptingly through myriad local press articles that stretched through the scorching summer of 2013. It was a curious and protracted period which, although unavoidable, caused frustration to ripple throughout Chris Sievey's close circle.

The initial unveiling was due to take place during a wild and highly publicised weekend in June that started to gain the weight of an unofficial festival. Plans were made, hotels and, in some cases, plane journeys booked. At one point all appeared done and dusted. A fact yet again celebrated in tiny local press articles, more often than not referring to Frank Sidebottom as a '...Timperley funnyman'. Not a phrase that has sat easily with me, to be honest although, after spending ten years as a news-sub in the area, I had perhaps become over-sensitive to the clichés of local journalese, much as I remain fond of local papers.

To some extent, this was understandable. It is not – believe me – easy to convey just what Frank Sidebottom was within the templated bounds of a local press report. It amused me, also, to note him continually credited for writing 'Timperley Sunset' although I am not sure that Ray Davies would so heartily approve.

However by early September 2013 – a final unveiling date had yet to be settled. Nevertheless, considerable movement did appear to be taking place. A report in the *Manchester Evening News* on Friday August 30, displayed a photograph of the bronzed and yet still unpainted figure flashing his thumbs from the foundry in the Czech Republic. The cast had been directly taken from artist Colin Spofforth's model, with the head taken from a 3D scan of one of Frank's head's, to accentuate the authenticity.

One quote, more than any, made me smile. Timperley Lib Dem councillor, Neil Taylor, soon to so forcibly head up the statue campaign, stated: "We hope to bring Frank back home very soon for him to gaze at the Timperley sunset, forever."

MICK MIDDLES

JOHN OTWAY

ONE NIGHT, IN THE SUMMER OF 2013, I found myself chairing an event at Manchester's Cornerhouse Arts Centre revolving around the screening of John Otway's celebrated documentary, 'Otway; The Movie, Rock's Greatest Failure'. The itinerary for the evening was simple. Thankfully before a packed house, my task was to introduce John to his fans immediately prior to the screening. During the screening of the film, Otway and ourselves would retire for a meal upstairs only to return at the close of the movie to initiate a hearty Q and A. But, as I was sitting on that stage, gazing at the crowd gathered before us, one fact emerged in my mind. These seemed lovely people. Committed to the point of obsession; balancing on the very edge of 'geekdom' – no bad thing, really. What seemed blindingly obvious was the similarity, not just between Otway and Sievey – of which there are many – but the similarities between the aficionados of both artists. Otway's catalogue of failed singles and squandered monies paralleled the career of The Freshies. In addition, Otway's restless muse carried him away from the simplistic art of music making and into an area of blatant and hilarious self-promotion. An outsider artist indeed. Mentioning this to Otway during that dinner elicited this response: "Yes, I am very much aware of Frank Sidebottom and played with him on a number of occasions. I never thought we were similar musically and Chris seemed a much quieter character than me… I am just an idiot who likes to bang away."

Manchester promoter Chris Coupe, who spent a great deal of time with both Chris and John, noted, "They were similar in a way. Both lovely people but they always seemed to have something going on in their heads."

Oddly enough, as the event was drawing to a close, one of the questions from the audience asked of Otway: "We have clubbed together and bought a statue of Frank Sidebottom to be put in place in

Timperley. Do you think there could be a similar statue of John Otway in Aylesbury?"

Otway looked bemused... then openly started to consider the possibility. It could happen. Perhaps it should. One could sense a campaign taking root in his head. At least, in his case, the bronze edifice might emerge proudly while he was still alive and still performing?

Not so with Frank, of course. Which leads me to another question and one which might seem unpalatable to heartened devotees. Is it given that a statue of Frank Sidebottom is a positive prospect? On the face of it, it would seem so. Surely Chris would be proud? It would add a flash of genuine idiosyncrasy to a dull suburb as, indeed, Frank had done during his time. Why not, therefore, extend it to eternity. But, of course, the posthumous Frank remains an 'outsider' artist.

In Steve Sullivan's 'Magical Timperley tour DVD', a gloriously poignant moment occurs when the assembled throng of Frankophiles were confronted by a local lady who, with genuine concern, earnestly posed the question, "What are you protesting against?" Clearly neither she nor her friends had ever heard of Frank Sidebottom. I would also suggest that it is only the constant stream of local press articles that has floated him to omnipresent status during the past three years. Most people living in Timperley would not fit within the Frank Sidebottom demographic at all. If this is so, and given the paucity of the times, could there not be a better way to spend £20,000?

It is a question that might make me unpopular with the aforementioned aficionados, who remain a powerful force. Also, as they are the very people who supplied the funding, surely this is justification enough? Maybe. I still wonder, however, if this bubble of devotion actually represents any kind of wider feeling within the boundaries of Timperley?

MICK MIDDLES

THE MAN FROM THE COUNCIL

A great many people helped carry the statue from Nick Fraser's enthusiasm-fuelled notion on the stage that day, through to its eventual erection in Timperley village. However, without the political knowledge and ferociously driven nature of Timperley Liberal Democrat councillor Neil Taylor, it is safe to presume that this extremely difficult task would have crumble to the dust of good intentions. Taylor was a guiding force throughout the protracted process, flickering regularly in press interviews while feverously beavering away in the background.

I met him on a Saturday evening in November 2013 in the spacious King George pub, situated fittingly next to the Altrincham FC football ground. I realised then that the last time I had visited the home of The Robins, it had been in the company of Frank Sidebottom. On that occasion, Frank had cheerfully endured a good deal of taunting from the opposing fans, although I do not recall who they were. At one point, and displaying an unlikely degree of personal courage, Frank strode across the pitch and, hands on hips in true Frank style, proceeded to administer a good telling off. Not surprisingly, this was met with a hail of unwelcoming projectiles, causing him to retreat readily to the friendlier confines of The Robins end. Later, Frank would tell me, "Wasn't that brilliant?" He was, I believe, genuinely pleased to have stirred a reaction. Nothing worse, for Frank, than a blanket of apathy. Not that that was something Frank often encountered.

I was mulling this over as I strode across The King George car park and then, in a flash of déjà vu, I envisaged Chris sitting in the corner. I simply have no idea if I ever met Chris in that pub. It is quite possible, for the pubs of Altrincham, Bowdon and Hale, were often used for his impromptu meetings.

Garbed in bright yellow trousers, "I used to wear black all the time but I have brightened up and it makes me feel better" Neil Taylor arrived with his wife, Sandra. Both of them held an amiable and helpful air as, over pints of bitter, he guided me through the roller-coaster background that preceded Paulina's enigmatic statue. As stated, Taylor's importance in the conclusion of this tale can't be overstated. Like Chris, he was a local lad who seems to have been defined by the brusk leafiness of the area.

Neil Taylor: "I had a business in Timperley and lived there for 25 years. Going back to those 70s days, the thing that was big around here was CB radio. I ran three or four clubs at the time. I never got round to seeing The Freshies or much around here. There was that famous occasion when they played at Bowdon Vale Youth Club during the same series of gigs that featured Joy Division. Although I was a big music fan, I somehow didn't attend. My association with Chris didn't start until around 2006 when I was elected as councillor in Timperley. I am very proud of this and very proud of Timperley. Chris wasn't particularly recognised at that point. Or if he was, he was seen as some kind of a crackpot. It wasn't generally understood how clever the concept of Frank Sidebottom was. So I made an effort to get in touch with Chris. I told him, 'Look, you and Frank are very much associated with Timperley. Let's try and biff it up a level… you are not just a comic.' So we did an afternoon when we went round Timperley with a camera… it was a lot of politics… what Frank would do if he was given the keys to Timperley. He was absolutely hilarious. I couldn't believe how brilliant he was. The humour was just cracking me up all afternoon."

Taylor's next stage was taking Frank to the Timperley Country Fair, which attracts around 15,000 people and then the Altrincham Festival. Almost immediately Frank gifted him the character name, 'The man from the council'.

Neil Taylor: "Yes Frank, slightly tongue-in-cheek, started referring to me as 'The Man from the Council' and I kind of became a Frank character. But Chris, in real life, kept a lot of his acquaintances to himself, so you would rarely meet his other friends. I got Frank to be the judge at the fairs, which is something he absolutely loved doing. It gave him a whole new angle, I think. Frank being Frank was absolutely manic with it all. Slightly dangerous, of course, but brilliant as well. It seemed perfect for him."

It also provided Frank with contact with an audience that lay beyond the norm, providing him with a local omnipresence; something that had previously eluded him. This worked on several levels. Talking face to face with steely elements of the Mother's Union over a raft of cakes and jams was a perfect platform for Frank. It also helped to ease his distinctive head back into the local papers, providing essential coverage that hadn't previously been forthcoming. It is a debatable point, but it could be argued that it was Taylor who pulled Frank from comparative obscurity and helped to guide him towards his more hallowed latter status.

"I was also a local press photographer for a spell. I was working mainly for the *Timperley Independent* and it was a paper that really did operate from a shed. It was fortnightly, I think, and Frank Sidebottom had his own column in it. I remember photographing him a few times… doing things like pushing a pile of coins over in The Stonemason's Arms. I also photographed him with Miss Timperley when they both turned on the Timperley Christmas lights. So I kind of had a long association, but more with Frank than Chris.

"We built up a bit of a friendship because of this. Then Chris came to me and requested that we try to find a home for the Frank Sidebottom mosaic. It used to be on the side of Affleck's Palace in Manchester. But when the changes happened, all those mosaics got pulled down. So I was frantically trying to find somewhere where the mosaic could go. I discovered that this wasn't an easy task… to find somewhere where it would be safe and there would be a long term home for it. We were going to put it outside The Stonemason's pub. But you can't just put something like that on any wall. We spent a lot of time talking about this. The only place that I kept coming up with on a regular basis was at the Community Centre on Park Road in Timperley. Ironically enough this the place where Chris Sievey and The Freshies initially recorded, down in the basement there. There was a studio. Not many people actually realised that. I had been involved with the community centre and there had been a few changes. This was around 2008. There was a cellar full of junk… 30 years of junk down there. So much stuff and a load of old recording stuff. All the old fashioned tapes and recording devices. I told Chris that everything had to go to a skip but I would put money on it that some of the stuff that would go in the skip would belong to him. He told me that he would go and have a look. Whether he actually did or not, I have absolutely no idea. But we eventually managed to get the mosaic in there."

The tragic aspect of Neil's association and friendship with Chris was, of course, the timing. While it provided a new angle for Frank and chance to work beyond the deadening circuits of music and comedy, it came late in his life.

"When Chris was diagnosed with cancer, everyone was quite shocked about it. I don't think anyone quite realised how serious it was. I spent some time with Chris a week before he died. I asked him if he would be a judge at the Altrincham Festival. He said 'Yes, don't worry I will be there. Everything will be fine,' that was on the Friday. I think the following Monday, he died.

"It was very awkward for a while in regard to the mosaic. Because I knew Chris but I didn't know anybody else. But I managed to track down a few people. I found a guy called Mark Kennedy. I got in touch with Gemma and Paula. We managed to get the mosaic. It was situated in an old mill on the other side of Stockport. It was on display at the community centre until summer of 2013. But Mark Kennedy has found a new home for it at a hotel in Manchester."

As hinted, the mosaic could be seen as a precursor for the statue; offering a permanence that would have previously be seen as absurd. This only really became apparent at Castlefield.

"Yes, it was after the event at Castlefield that the notion of a statue started being bandied around. It is a bit fuzzy how it gained momentum. I think the original idea probably did come from Nick Fraser and Jon Ronson. But it just took off. Jon was exceedingly supportive throughout. Nick Fraser did come to one or two of the early meetings."

Not that the initially flurry of excitement could stand the laborious process of gaining permission.

Brian Little: "I became the treasurer for the statue. It was a difficult situation at one point. Nick Fraser and Gemma had helped get the thing rolling and raised a lot of money at the beginning. But after a few meetings people tailed off and it started to look very unlikely. We really thought that, if it happened at all, it would take about six years. But when we found the new sculptor, the whole thing just took off again."

Neil Taylor: "Unfortunately, trying to get a statue in place is a very tedious and boring process. A lot of the early excitement went as we had to have meeting after meeting. You have to have a constitution. You have to write minutes and there are certain procedures that you have to follow. If you put a statue on public land it has to be covered by the local authority. There are all kinds of legal loopholes. Who owns it? Who insures it? Would it cause danger on the roads? All kinds of stuff and, even for a councillor like me, it was a hugely tedious process.

"We knew we had to raise a lot of money but we didn't know how much it would cost. One person gave us a quote and said he could produce it for about £2,000. But we weren't confident about this at all. So we contacted another guy called Colin Spofforth – a really nice guy – and we worked out it would cost about £60,000 to cover all our costs and get the statue cast. So we thought 'ok', we will raise £60,000 in a year. So a number of events were put on. Bits of merchandise were produced and we raised the first £10,000 very quickly. But once we got to the £15,000 mark it started to slow down. Obviously you can only ask people to give a fiver once and the real Frank fanatics all gave money early on. So how do you continue? Although people were very supportive, it proved difficult as the meetings started to pile up. It is understandable. People get bored and simply don't have the time to go to endless committee meetings. You know spending two or three hours is a dull thing to do.

"So it soon boiled down to a handful of people. The key players were Gemma Woods and Brian Little, who worked with Chris at Hot Animation. In about 2012, soon after Christmas, we had a meeting with Gemma and Brian. But Brian was going to London and Gemma, understandably, wanted to move on. So it was left to me to work out a way of doing this. What should we do? We had got £15,000… should we admit defeat and give it to charity? It was definitely an option at one point. Then Martin Sievey said it would be possible to get this cast at a DIY job. We started looking at figures. But it was Colin who came up with another idea and that was to get the statue cast in the Czech Republic. Colin had an association over there. But he made it quite clear that, if we did that, he did not want his name attached to that statue in any way shape or form. It would not be his creation. So Colin put us in touch with Paulina Skakova in the Czech Republic.

"This was becoming nerve-wracking now. We kind of lost control…

here we were, a long way away and I had my neck on the line over this. If this didn't work out it would be letting the family down. So we tried to gather some troops to bring it forward. Dave Arnold came in to help. We realised that, in the Czech Republic, the statue could be achieved for around £25,000 which we knew was doable. We did a few fundraisers, one at Christmas 2012. With a few final pushes, we managed to get the money by February 2013. So then there was a mad scramble and lots of paperwork. We had to get planning permission. We had to find a designated area of public land. So we came up with four or five places of where to put this. Fortunately, the leader of the council, Matthew Colledge was a big Frank Sidebottom fan. He understood the humour. He understood what Frank was trying to do. He was incredibly supportive. And we eventually got the site sorted. But there were things going on in the background. Who should take ownership of this? Is it street furniture or street art? Who will insure it? More and more meetings… boring, boring. But I had to keep the momentum going while, under the water, I was paddling away like a swan. The original date we had was April 1, which was Frank Sidebottom's birthday. We had indications that that would be possible, so we approached the press. Unfortunately this stalled and couldn't happen. We kept on calling the press. Dave Arnold had produced an exact reproduction of the Frank head. There was some unseen footage of the work that was being done but we were still a bit nervous because we had not actually seen it.

"There were also issues with the pavement. After a terrible June and July we were going for the end of August, to coincide with Chris Sievey's birthday. But everyone was away on holiday and we were having the hottest summer in years. Everyone was out enjoying it. So we eventually went for Sunday.

"We installed it on the Saturday. There are pictures of it wrapped in bubble wrap. It looked like a dog cocking its leg. Really surreal. When we picked the statue up in Chester and put it in the back of Dave Arnold's van to drive it over, it was really eerie. We would tease people by releasing a few photographs… one of a hand. One of an eye. I got a lot of press interest. I managed to get Granada Reports to do a pre-story on the Wednesday, which is very rare. We wouldn't let them see anything other than an eye. It actually took four hours to film. But it you watch that footage very closely, you can see me revealing the eye, then I shut it down.

"We put the shed over it and, at about five o clock, I was knackered and went home to have a power nap before returning later. But the moment I put my head down there was this gigantic clap of thunder and a huge storm. I'd never seen a storm like this in Timperley. We feared the worst. The forecast was not good for the Sunday at all. But somehow the sun shone… miraculously, really. It was just an amazing day."

How late it was, how late. At this point, with the statue in place, nobody could tell just how sizeable this event would be. It was simply impossible to judge. Nobody had sold tickets… there was simply no way of knowing.

"It started to dawn on me on the Friday when I received a phone call from the council saying that we would have to close the roads just how successful this had become. By this stage it had been on TV, all the local papers, Radios One, Two, Three and Four. Radio Manchester. The penny was dropping that this was going to be really big.

"By ten on the Sunday morning, it wasn't busy but there was people about. By 11 o'clock the numbers were really building. I had no idea where all the people came from but by ten past 11 it was obvious that there were going to be issues. The police were on the perimeters. But at 11.35, two minutes before, two police cars screamed in and the road was blocked. If Chris was watching this he would have been in pieces. The whole village ground to a halt. At 11.37 the proceedings started and people have been taking photographs ever since. Just incredible."

TIMPERLEY VILLAGE

Sunday October 20th 2013

MERCIFULLY AND MIRACULOUSLY, the blanket storms of Saturday evening had receded and a window of sunshine embraced Timperley village… at least until the events of the day had collapsed to an unusually lively Sunday evening in the Stonemasons Arms, where exhausted bar staff rediscovered their smiles and their busiest day of all time emerged from a state of blind panic.

It is not often that a village plays host to 1,300 visitors, firmly wiping away the standard Sunday somnolence.

We arrived at 10.30, parking neatly behind a Timperley Library that, within the foyer at least, boasted a preview of an exhibition of Martin O'Neill photographs of The Freshies of Dixon/Maunder vintage. These included the aforementioned scramble down the circular ramp at Sale Tesco. For some reason, seeing them hoisted into exhibition position, seemed to gain them extra kudos. A Granada television crew had already cast its roving lens among them before the crew sauntered the 100 yards to discover the sight of a shed situated directly outside Johnson's the Cleaners, across the roundabout from the Stonemasons.

Still, nobody really knew what size of crowd would assemble, come the unveiling at 11.37 precisely By 10.45 it seemed little more than the casual milling of, perhaps, two or three hundred. people Certainly the police, who were not in noticeable attendance at this point and hadn't taken the sensible procedure to close the road, clearly underestimated the full level of the appeal of this unique and bizarre event. This fact became dangerously evident as the numbers swelled on both sides of the busy road, causing a degree of friction between the Frank fans and the testy batch of locals ploughing their 'Chelsea tractors' through the thickening crowd. This seemed indicative of some greater local tension.

MICK MIDDLES

By this time we had stumbled among the greetings of several dozen long lost friends before gratefully landing at a café that was clearly stretched to capacity. Although the Hilal Indian Restaurant remained bizarrely closed throughout the proceedings. Opposite, on expansive football fields framed by Turner-esqe skies, the Timperley Big Shorts prepared for a timely kick off. The vibe was good despite the fractious nature of the traffic. Thankfully, the situation was relieved just as the bulging numbers started to edge towards the deeply concerning. A single squad car screamed to a halt in a hail of blue lights, finally shutting Stockport Road and allowing the numbers to flood evenly across the village. On the pavements opposite, bewildered octogenarians attempted to rationalise the strange event that was unfolding before their eyes. It was difficult, impossible, not to be moved. The Sievey family gathering shed side, encircled by Steve Sullivan's two-pronged camera crew and a plethora of hastily scribbling journalists, both national and local. Faces in the crowd. The unmistakable hat of Badly Drawn Boy, ex-Smiths stickman and BBC 6 Music DJ Mike Joyce, Edweena Bangor, Barry Spencer, Rick Sarko and, disappearing along the pavement, Mike Doherty, having been picked up by Barry earlier.

Soon, many of the people in this book would be kerbside – John and Ro Barratt, Gemma Woods, Bob Dickinson, Patrick Gallagher and so many more… a kerb full of back pages, later to slide purposefully towards the Stonemasons.

Tension mounted noticeably as the selected time, 11.37, grew closer. Dave Arnold wore the jacket of officialdom and attempted to keep the PA running from a car battery. Something which tended to falter during speeches from Neil Taylor and Timperley Mayor Cllr Dylan Butt.

And soon Barry and Rick would be looning as a Timperley Big Short and milkman respectively alongside family members Asher, Stirling, Harry and, garbed as Sgt Pepper era John Lennon, Paul Molyneux. As the shed's roof became dismantled, allowing the four balloons that spelled 11.37 to become caught – literally so – on the television camera before sailing beyond Sainsbury's and into the clouds. No doubt to cause considerable bewilderment in some pensioner's garden in Brooklands.

And there it was. Life-size and curiously understated. A statue you could hug. During the coming months - years, one senses – it became impossible to drive through Timperley village without encountering the sight of the statue being used as a photo opportunity for some stray Frank aficionado. This fact itself helping to add continuum to the story. Eternity, perhaps, or as near as it is possible to get. The statue has also given something else to Timperley aside from adding considerably to the local economy. It has given the village an iconic centrepiece. The only one that I can think of, between Manchester city centre, which contains many, and the bridges that span the Manchester Ship Canal at Latchford, Warrington. What is an iconic centrepiece doing, slap bang in the centre of such a pleasantly dull suburb? I am sure, even given the lavish scattering of publicity the story of the statue has provided, that many will continue to cast bewildered eyes towards the precocious edifice, especially from the caravanning fraternity who languish in beige within the locality. The 2014 Greater Manchester run would have its route bent to allow the runners to thunder by, with television cameras spinning down from above, hovering briefly over Frank and his cheery thumbs.

As the scramble for on-the-day photos continued, we wisely chose to depart the scene for the lively throb of The Stonemasons Arms where, at that moment, a tribute act was punching solidly through the songs of – among others – The Stone Roses and Buzzcocks. Later they would be replaced by an utterly off-the-wall performance by Harry Sievey, all electronic pumping and guitar slashing, topped by vocals that eventually spilled into hilarious vulgarity… and all before the eyes of his family. Paula, casting motherly looks of warning from the front of the stage.

"I don't know how my dad used to perform with his head on," he mused. "I am so fucking hot." There is a lovely edge to a Harry Sievey performance that could be found within the more extravagant outings of Frank – the Chelsea arts space incident, for example – but rarely surfaced within the more controlled unit of The Freshies. Perhaps that really was the spur for Chris to break free and live a more unpredictable life within the persona of Frank. And it is true that Harry seems to relate more firmly to Frank, even if his music spits and snaps from a completely different heart. Surely such individualism is the mark of a natural artist? Whether this, in such days of template music, is enough to gain any degree of success in a commercial sense, remains to be seen.

But Harry is, as I write, ploughing a unique furrow and can only be commended for that.

"He is so like his dad," sighed Paula... and later, it was my wife Vicky who herded Barry, Rick and Harry onstage, the afternoon fizzing into an impromptu glimpse of The Freshies.

★

"You know that 11.37 thing? His number. It was his record label. I remember we all sat round that day, trying to think of a name for the label. It was just the time. But me and the kids have always kept that as a significant number. And anything that ever happens always seems to happen around that time. But there are all sorts of crazy things that he does. Even now that he is no longer with us."

PAULA SIEVEY

★

Friday June 21st 2013

It was three years to the day since Chris died. A day of surreal calm and blinding sunshine. Knots of youth huddled on Ashton-on-Mersey's soft corners, breaking the somnolence of the day with raucous guffaws. Irritating perhaps, though hardly threatening. By chance I walked past the end of Cedar Road. It was still lost to profound mundanity. No small children played on the pavements anymore, such had become the times. Parents living in endless cycles of mild paranoia. Even on sunny days, children were kept indoors.

Many people, I knew, would be thinking of Chris on this day. A fact confirmed by Facebook's wide and disparate community. On my 'newsfeed', a string of Chris and Frank photos. Short messages of latent condolence. Family messages flickered too. Back and forth. They would all go out tonight.

And tomorrow would be Harry's 21st. Harry, now firmly locked in place as a songwriter, reachable by the Facebook medium. I had started to listen to his songs a couple of weeks back. Enjoyed them. Had, naturally enough, searched for echoes of Chris. They were there, perhaps, albeit in a tenuous manner. Harry had inherited his father's gift of melody, of phrasing even, although it wasn't so obviously in place. Mercifully. But even from my distance at the other end of emails, or Facebook scanning, I could sense a difference. I thought Harry might tread in hallowed areas that had always eluded Chris. I hoped so. Chris would have liked that.

I sent Harry a 'happy 21st' message and he responded in an instant. The celebrations would begin that night, one day earlier, no doubt tinged by the poignancy of his father's anniversary.

The unusual suspects appeared on that newsfeed. Well meant, A 'Timperley Sunset' video, complete with Little Denise. I smiled and share it with my FB friends who, I hoped, smiled levelly and shared it on… ad infinitum. A Frank moment zipping through the ether, firing into areas previously untouched. Many photographs of Chris slipped into view. Mainly a young, suave Chris, that warming half-smile, dark features. Dave Arnold posted an older version. Shirtless on a beach. This seemed almost shocking, at first. But even the older Chris seemed lost to the moment. Lost in the magic of a trip to the seaside. A very Chris thing.

Other Facebook notices seemed more random. My recent friend, Heath Common, writer and band leader from Yorkshire way, surprised me by stating that his Halifax home was called 'Timperley'. He had, he stated, performed after Frank in Liverpool, back in the day.

"Frank played 'Born in Timperley' that night", he stated. "I mean, how do you follow that? I still shudder at the thought."

Ha. I like to think of excellent musicians struggling to follow the cultural destruction of a Frank Sidebottom show. For, after all, how does one reconstruct a concert in wake of such anarchy? I think I remember that once happening to The Membranes too. Frank could be a difficult old bugger, really.

Two days later came a void. It would have been the unveiling of the statue in Timperley but, alas, a further delay had shunted this back a further two months. A pity but it mattered not. I smiled again and though, perhaps, I would watch a Frank DVD for the umpteenth time, that night, cradling a glass of red. Cradling many memories. As I sat there, many of the faces I re-met during the past few months drifted through my thoughts. I didn't know the family and they were out there, in a bubble somewhere.

A 6pm that evening, something unusual happened at our home in Ashton-on-Mersey. There was a sudden blast of music, ringing out from the conservatory. Bit random, those DAB radios. It has happened before. We were sitting in the lounge watching the murders and drive by shootings that comprised the local news. That is when the music started. I went to the conservatory and noticed that the radio was not plugged in. Couldn't figure that one out. Where was the music coming from? The answer was simple enough. The iPad, also turned off, had triggered into action, bringing up the iTunes app and, selecting from that, Chris Sievey's song 'Riding Out to Devils Ridge'.

From two thousand possible tunes… why that one? Even within the scope of The Freshies and Chris Sievey, that would be an oddity. It was one of Chris's attempts to break from the pop norm and create something truly different. Recorded at Mars Studio, Altrincham in 1980, it was a beautiful faux – Western soundtrack. Several fused layers of desert orchestration, swirling and building melodies and dynamics. I imagined Chris would have been so excited in the studio, that day, as a music that completely defied a logical progression would be slowly unearthed. Of course, and despite gaining a Razz release, it was barely anything more than a demo. However, in the best tradition of demos, it distinctly pointed to a different reality. I wondered what it could all mean? Probably nothing. I noticed too, that the track featured none of the classic Freshies line up although, on the day of the recording, Chris had been aided and abetted by Rick Sutton, who also featured on the obscure track, 'Hey'. As I was mulling this, another track cranked into action. Not at all the next track on this Freshies iTunes collection. You could probably guess which song it was. Indeed, it was 'Hey'.

Stunned I sat on the conservatory sofa and glanced at the photograph on my wall. It depicted 'The Freshies' bumbling and tumbling down the circular driveway of Tesco in Sale. A mischievous smirk crossing the familiar facial feature of Chris Sievey. Mischievous old bugger.

FRIENDSHIP PUB

Fallowfield, Manchester.
August 27th 2013
6pm.

GARBED IN THE TUBULAR TIGHTNESS that defines the era – pin-tight jeans, spectacular flecked black and white jacket, gloriously sculpted hair – Harry Sievey caught my eye as he skirted around the pub's sun scorched veranda. It was my first face-to-face meeting with him even though we had been conversing via social media for a large part of the summer. He seemed immersed in the excitable chatter of possibility, immersed in his work, in his ideas and songs. And his songs seemed beautifully jagged and ill-fitting plus points, in an era so tediously awash with band and artists of a template nature. Grasping a half of Stella, we moved to the decking and, ignoring the girls and cragged men wafting plumes of smoke and talking of football, I searched for recognition of his father. It wasn't immediately apparent. Harry was intelligent – obviously so – alert, witty… sharp as a button, really; and endearing to boot. But his natural approach, his attack perhaps, seemed almost the antithesis of Chris; like two inter-locking jigsaw pieces. There was closeness and distance. I mentioned his father twice, but only in passing. It wasn't a place I felt that Harry wished to linger.

He was a mite over-tired, having just worked the bar at that weekend's Leeds Festival. Hard work and a tremendous way, apparently, of catching the best of the music action. I didn't ask who his favourite bands were.

Harry had taken every opportunity to perform low key gigs in Manchester all summer. His attempts to form a band had kind of fallen by, as fellow musicians often failed to match his steely determination or, indeed, share his exact vision. He still performed, under the moniker MASK, occasionally with the aid of friends on bass and drums, but he felt more at home performing alone. Electronic drums, guitar – be it electric or acoustic – sharp jagged vocals. Some of these occasions would be little more than open mic nights where he would fall in line with a plethora of dour folksy strummers. At one point he causes heads in the pub to turn in alarm as he mimicked their relentless drone.

"Woooaaaaaarrrrrrrrr… just vocals going nowhere," he almost screamed. "I like to throw things in… mix things up a bit. Mostly I am playing to people who have absolutely no idea what I am doing."

Such was the case at the recent outing at The Salford Arms.

"I am not playing *there* again!" he stated. "Just a couple of elderly couples eating their dinner. They *hated* me. Oh and one guy who kept saying how brilliant I was."

Harry shrugged.

"That must be a bit dispiriting," I ventured.

Nevertheless, it is all experience. Earning the chops. At 21 years old, Harry appeared to be punching away on his own. With a small batch of inventive, lively, effervescent and infectious songs, his small body of work seemed packed with aesthetic aspiration. That said, he didn't quite know which way to turn.

"I call myself MASK and promoters always expect a band… I sense their disappointment as I walk in alone. But it is so difficult to explain to people what I do. I make a big noise… I think I have the noise just about right now. I work so hard at it. I know a lot of people don't get it but I know exactly what I am doing."

And what Harry is doing owes little, beyond its sheer prodigious nature, to the work of his dad. And then he told me: "I make up CDs individually. Send them out. I put my music on the net. I would rather 50 people heard it for free than three people bought it."

That reminded me of someone.

And then there is another vision of Harry. Armed with no traditional mode of transport. There he is, post-gig, on a late-night bus. Grasping his growing array of musical equipment and, at times, a tent. Shuffling on and off the bus. A vulnerable but determined figure.

As I leave him, on the streets of Fallowfield, he asked me about the book… *this* book.

"It won't be a standard rock biography," I told him. He seemed assured and sauntered off into the steamy evening. Was that, I mused, reminiscent of a meeting with Chris. Yes and no. The music has changed. The haircut has changed. But something remains the same.

EPILOGUE

I

BEAUTIFUL WEEKEND, SOFT HAZE diluted by a weak vanilla sun and the first traces of springtime warmth. It had been a big weekend for the newly established Frank Sidebottom industry, with Steve Sullivan delivering a talk about the documentary at the Manchester Histories Festival. On the Sunday evening, a small part of Manchester's Oxford Road seemed awash with Frank devotees of a certain again, tumbling down from Cornerhouse to Dancehouse where Jon Ronson was about to deliver a pre-publicity talk for the 'Frank' film, concentrating on his time with the Oh Blimeys and the lead in to this extraordinary cinematic fictionalisation. The Dancehouse was a cauldron that night; bulging crowd, familiar faces flicking past in the half light. Dave Arnold, naturally. Neil Taylor and Sandra. Paula Sievey, Harry Sievey. CP Lee and wife Pam… beyond them several hundred faces that carried vaguely familiar echoes of the past. Students from the 80s heyday, thickened, darkened, lugging beer bottles into the hall. The general atmosphere one of suppressed excitability. Very few people – six perhaps – in the audience had actually seen the film and its very concept had yet to settle. In a sense, a difficult sell.

    The next morning, resplendent in the BBC's studio at Salford Quays, Ronson struggled to condense the fictionalisation of Frank within an eight minute interview which began with Bill Turnbill stating that Jon Ronson had made a film about Frank and had written a book about Frank. Neither statement strictly true. Ronson speedily back-pedalled, explaining to blank stares that it was a fictionalisation that was more about outsider artists than Frank Sidebottom. But in making the film, hopefully he had brought one outsider artist a little closer to the mainstream. Blank stares. The interview concluded with Bill Turnbill stating, "and Jon Ronson's film about Frank Sidebottom will open in May." This little problem was going to run and run.

In a sense, the kernel of misunderstanding began with Chris Sievey's unease with the idea of exposing Chris, in any context, as the creator of Frank. Particularly in the context of a blockbuster Hollywood production. When Jon and Chris initially spoke about the possibility of Ronson writing such a beast – at the time, George Clooney was just grasping hold of Ronson's 'Men Who Stare at Goats', thereby propelling the self-effacing Ronson into a new life that fizzed with the dizzy highs of Stateside success – the initially question seemed unanswerable. 'Would Chris be in it?'. A simple enough question. Though it deeply troubled Chris who hated the idea that it would be a biopic (which is why this book is not a biography). If it was to stay true to Chris's loose outsider ethos, it would simply have to twist into something very different. As, indeed, it did and while Chris would be excited by the very idea of completely fictionalising Frank and spinning it as a dark, gargantuan tale, obviously he never saw the final result. The danger, of course, would be that the real Frank would be swamped by the sheer gargantuan scale of this new image. It was a concern that many Frank fans shared. In America, where Frank had hardly any presence, it would prove particularly worrying as this new, dark and, frankly, rather unsettling Frank would essentially be the 'only' Frank.

Ronson alluded to this during his excellent Dancehouse talk and concluded that, if you wished to discover more about the 'real' Frank, you could watch Steve's DVD or, indeed, read the book you are currently digesting. Fair enough. The Dancehouse talk revolved mainly around Ronson's time with The Oh Blimeys and his further adventures within the worlds of weirdness and, while he spoke eloquently about the lead up to the film, no actual clips were shown, thereby intensifying the intrigue. Nice trick. We would wait and see. Some Frank fans, I am sure, might not wish to see it although, surely, their sheer sense of intrigue would take hold. Much as I admire Jon Ronson, I wasn't fully sure what to do. On one aspect I was certain. Shrouded in a certain irony, Frank

Sidebottom's posthumous star was set to rise to unheralded heights.

I noticed Joe Barratt, son of John, in dutiful attendance at Ronson's talk. As mentioned, Frank had performed at Joe's 18th birthday party and, of course, had interviewed Steve Sullivan at the Plaza talk. Two days before the talk, flushed by a grant from Mary Portas, Joe had opened an 'artistic hub' on Stockport Market, using the name 'Seven Miles Out', which had been the title of a Bohemian head shop on Stockport's Wellington Road in the late sixties, early seventies. It was an incredible emporium, a virtual cornucopia of all things alternative, bewildering indeed to a 14 year-old, immersed in strange new sounds and sensations. It sold everything from clothes, jewellery, bootleg albums, incense, the *Oz International Times* and myriad items of underground press. It provided an entrance into a land of unparalleled exotica. The owner used to park his Harley Davidson and basset hound on the outside pavement. The shop, named because it was seven miles out of Manchester city centre, attracted customers from across the city. Including a 14 year-old Chris Sievey, who purchased a black and white Beatles 'Hey Jude' poster from the shop. Unfortunately, he squandered his bus fare on said item and had to walk the considerable distance back to Sale… in the rain.

Joe Barratt wouldn't have known this tenuous connection, however, as he opened his hub on Friday March 28, 2014. Adorning the inside wall, a mural created by artist Bob Oxley 'all things Stockport', from according to the *Manchester Evening News* – 'The iconic Strawberry Studios' to cult comic hero (yawn) Frank Sidebottom.' Frank and Little Frank are depicted with speech bubbles displaying the lyric, 'Stockport is really fantastic'. Quite what close links Frank Sidebottom had with Stockport, apart from recording 'Stockport is Really Fantastic' for Joe's Dad, John and occasional gigs at The Plaza and The Brookfield, remains problematic. But it was a lovely artefact and Stockport Market's continued used of the phrase, 'Frank says, Stockport is really fantastic' remains somewhat endearing.

But I thought of that young Chris, trudging through the Levenshulme rain, poster in hand, his obsessions already defeating any trace of pragmatism. I though of him holding Subbuteo tournaments with Paul Molyneux and friends in that Ashton garage. I thought of Chris, back in 1980, resplendent in Hawaiian shirt and red corduroys, beaming smile, heart of energy and hope, mind pulsating with schemes, scams, notes and notions. I thought of Chris politely introducing songs at Oldham's Boundary pub. I though more of Chris than Frank. I thought of how Chris was an artist estranged even from his own comic creation. Now how 'outsider' can you get? Now there is existentialism, for you.

There is a dream that continues to live, somewhere in the shadowlands.

★

II

A CURIOUS BUBBLE of Frank-related activity enlivened the scorching July of 2014. In my mind, this book had reached a conclusion, of sorts. I had made the decision not to watch the 'Frank' film after all. It might be fun, I thought, if readers and Frank fans knew more about the film than I. Somewhat stubbornly, I decided that Michael Fassbender's semi-Frank portrayal should remain a mystery to me... forevermore, perhaps?

A number of tiny incidents served to change my mind.

One Sunday evening, just as I was slipping into 'Countryfile' with a bottle of Mythos, a shrill of the phone revealed the voices of Dennis and Lois, direct from New York. They had apparently been on one of their infamous toy purchasing expeditions and noticed Jon Ronson's 'Frank' hardback beaming from the shelves. One could understand their anguish. For Jon's fine little book was only ever intended to be an explanatory essay aimed to add a little background to the film. This would be particularly useful in America, where Sidebottom's standing was largely unknown. The book was also initially intended to be in eBook format; a post-film download, perhaps, to be hastily perused in some bar, be it in Manhattan or Manchester. Obviously, Ronson's high profile caused the publishing powers-that-be to clasp it in an instantly recognisable hardback format. I knew that Jon was uneasy about this and conveyed this reality to Dennis and Lois, who accepted it in good faith while expressing ongoing reservations about the nature of the film. I thought, at that moment, that I had better watch 'Frank' after all. On a lighter note, they displayed a desire to visit Frank's Timperley statue when they arrived in the UK in the Autumn of 2014 to catch shows from the remarkable John Grant. I knew that we could help in this respect and wondered how surreal it might seem to them to gaze at Frank's statue from within the Hilal Indian restaurant, where they had previously enjoyed the company of Chris Sievey. I hoped that this would happen.

It had been an odd kind of week. A call to Steve Sullivan had proved oddly fruitless and I sensed a slight edge, of sorts, as the editing process of his documentary slowed to a definite close. A full stop. I had no doubt that all would be well in the end and thought no more of it.

Then, in the same morning, came two completely unexpected breakthroughs. As Lenny Abrahamson's 'Frank' film steadied itself for a US release – with a grand opening in New York – I received an invite to speak with the director himself. This came from the unlikely source at the *Warrington Guardian* – thank you David Morgan – and I realised that the film would have to be devoured within a couple of days. Ten minutes later, Marc Spitz of the *New York Times* contacted me requesting an interview regarding 'the real' Frank Sidebottom. The eventual article proved a lovely half page affair.

Things were now rolling. I took a few moments to ponder just what Chris would make of all this. A chance meeting with Paula Sievey in the Altrincham Waitrose eased my fears.

"Oh he would have absolutely loved it," she exclaimed, between the pasta and the rocket salad sandwiches. Yet again, this brief meeting seemed unlikely. I had never set foot in the shop before.

With all this stuff fizzing about, I allowed my distant stance to cave in and, from the safety of my front room, watched 'Frank' twice in succession, firstly alone and secondly with Vicky. To our astonishment, we both adored it.

The next day, as planned, I spoke with Lenny Abrahamson. The resultant brief article, which fluttered in various north-west newspapers that weekend, is as follows. Not terribly good, I fear, but it may amuse you.

OUT OF HIS HEAD

★

There is a moment, and it is only a moment, towards the end of Lenny Abrahamson's courageously existential film, 'Frank', that takes my breath clean away. This 'flash' occurs when lead actor Michael Fassbender, having finally lost his Frank head following a collision with a speeding car, stands in a room at his parents house and twists himself gently towards the camera. Right there... right in that split second, I glimpse the sight of Frank Sidebottom's creator, Chris Sievey. It is in the light, in the face, in the hunch of the shoulders. Not sure anyone else has noticed.

"You know what... I am pretty sure I know the moment you mean," says producer Abrahamson. His disembodied Irish tones skipping through the phone from — where else? — LA, where he is currently casting for his forthcoming cinematic venture, 'Room'.

I tell him that I found the film to be compelling and, although dark clouds drift around the edges, full of shards of brilliant wit, no doubt injected by writer Jon Ronson.

"So pleased to hear that," he admits. "It is the kind of film that could so easily have been a disaster. We had no way of knowing whether having a movie where the lead character's face is hidden inside a huge head, could possibly work."

The film, released in the UK back in May, is now steadying itself for exposure to US audiences on August 22. It is, to say the least, an abstract and difficult sell. Ronson's official line, that it is "inspired by Frank but not actually about Frank," has not necessarily cleared the fog. I wonder if Abrahamson, when presented with the initial script, immediately 'got it'.

"It took me a long time to decide to do it," he admits, "but sometimes you just have to take the chance. As it turned out, the majority of people tend to understand it straight away. There was a bit of unrest from a few of the hardcore Frank Sidebottom fans in the UK, (I bet) but I think in general the reaction has been extremely positive."

Fassbender's performance is spectacular. Somehow, through the distance of that head, he conveys the twin artistic pillars of vulnerability and uniqueness. I wonder if the actor had studied the real Frank in preparation for the role.

"Michael says not," explains Abrahamson. "He wanted to use the concept of the head to create his own thing... and he is such an exceptional talent, that he succeeded and, I think, discovered something of himself. There are two ways of watching the film. Either you fall for Frank and go with his aesthetic flow or you kind of project your own emotions onto that head."

In essence, this is a tale of any outsider artist. When the film decamps for the isolation of a forest, which is Sweden masquerading as rural Ireland, the story takes on an isolationist stance reminiscent of Captain Beefheart or, indeed, Bob Dylan and the Band at Big Pink... or Led Zeppelin at Bron Aur in Wales.

"Definitely," Lenny agrees, "I love the idea of taking a band wholly out of context and forcing them to create a whole new album from scratch, absolutely fascinating. The odd thing is that that is how most films are made. A gang like mentality sets it."

A part of this, of course, is band dynamic. In 'Frank' there is certainly plenty of conflict. I ask if that conflict reflected in the relationships of the actors.

"No," he swiftly counters, "that can happen but this is one of the happiest films I have ever made. We had a great time, every moment, really. Everyone really seemed to understand what was happening."

Rather like Anton Corbijn's Ian Curtis biopic, 'Control' there seems to be a freshness to the actual musical performances, no matter how eclectic or difficult that music may initially seem.

"It was difficult to cast because all the actors are actual musicians. That was my stipulation. We couldn't have faked it. They played every note which gave us that feeling of realness. We didn't even fake the Frank character. That is Michael in every shot. Many people have asked why we didn't just fly him in for the final shots, where the head comes off. That would never have worked."

Despite the film's oblique nature, it is possible to glimpse the true Jon Ronson story, lying firmly beneath the script. Ronson escaped from London to Manchester to join Frank's shambolic Oh Blimey Big Band in the late eighties. The fear, especially in America, is that Fassbender's creation might displace the genuine twin tales of Frank Sidebottom and Chris Sievey.

"That may happen in places... probably will," he concedes, "but I hope it also creates a desire in people to discover the real Frank Sidebottom and Chris Sievey. I hope they discover what a major artist Chris always was. For that they can reference the documentary due later in the year. Oh, yes, *and your book."*

There does seem to be momentum, here. The intelligent distance of Fassbender's 'Frank' does not really impinge on the real deal. Although Dennis and Lois remain understandably sceptical, as do those pockets of Frank aficionados across the UK, there appears the very real possibility that, at long last, the work of Chris Sievey, the artist, may be freed from the shackles of Frank's dominance. One envisages further books. A quality large-scale art tome, perhaps, containing myriad examples of his work beyond and before Frank. One sees exhibitions on a scale that Chris could only dream about... and often did.

Wouldn't that be a glorious release? Chris Sievey as a major UK outsider artist, universally celebrated and finally, gloriously and literally... out of his head!